Guerrilla War
in the Easter Rising

Guerrilla War
in the Easter Rising

Joseph McKenna

Pen & Sword
MILITARY

First published in Great Britain in 2023 by
Pen & Sword Military
An imprint of Pen & Sword Books Limited
Yorkshire – Philadelphia

Copyright © Joseph McKenna 2023

ISBN 978 1 39905 137 8

The right of Joseph McKenna to be identified as
Author of this Work has been asserted by her in accordance
with the Copyright, Designs and Patents Act 1988.

A CIP catalogue record for this book is
available from the British Library

All rights reserved. No part of this book may be reproduced or
transmitted in any form or by any means, electronic or mechanical
including photocopying, recording or by any information storage and
retrieval system, without permission from the Publisher in writing.

Typeset by Mac Style
Printed in the UK by CPI Group (UK) Ltd, Croydon, CR0 4YY.

Pen & Sword Books Limited incorporates the imprints of After the Battle, Atlas, Archaeology, Aviation, Discovery, Family History, Fiction, History, Maritime, Military, Military Classics, Politics, Select, Transport, True Crime, Air World, Frontline Publishing, Leo Cooper, Remember When, Seaforth Publishing, The Praetorian Press, Wharncliffe Local History, Wharncliffe Transport, Wharncliffe True Crime and White Owl.

For a complete list of Pen & Sword titles please contact

PEN & SWORD BOOKS LIMITED
47 Church Street, Barnsley, South Yorkshire, S70 2AS, England
E-mail: enquiries@pen-and-sword.co.uk
Website: www.pen-and-sword.co.uk
or
PEN AND SWORD BOOKS
1950 Lawrence Rd, Havertown, PA 19083, USA
E-mail: Uspen-and-sword@casematepublishers.com
Website: www.penandswordbooks.com

Contents

Preface		ix
Introduction		xii
Chapter 1	The 5th Fingal Battalion	1
Chapter 2	He Rises on Sunday, and We on Monday	22
Chapter 3	Monday: Confusion and Certainty	30
Chapter 4	Tuesday: Waiting for Orders	38
Chapter 5	Wednesday: On the Offensive	45
Chapter 6	Thursday: Controversy and Conviction	51
Chapter 7	Friday: The Attack on Ashbourne Barracks	55
Chapter 8	The Battle of Ashbourne	62
Chapter 9	After the Battle	80
Chapter 10	Prisoners	92
Chapter 11	Executions and Deportations	98
Chapter 12	Frongoch	105
Chapter 13	The Aftermath	113
Chapter 14	An Analysis of the Battle of Ashbourne	125
Appendix I: Volunteers of the Dublin 5th Battalion		132
Appendix II: RIC Men Killed and Wounded		135
Appendix III: Awards to RIC Men		136
Postscript		139
Notes		140
Bibliography		150
Index		153

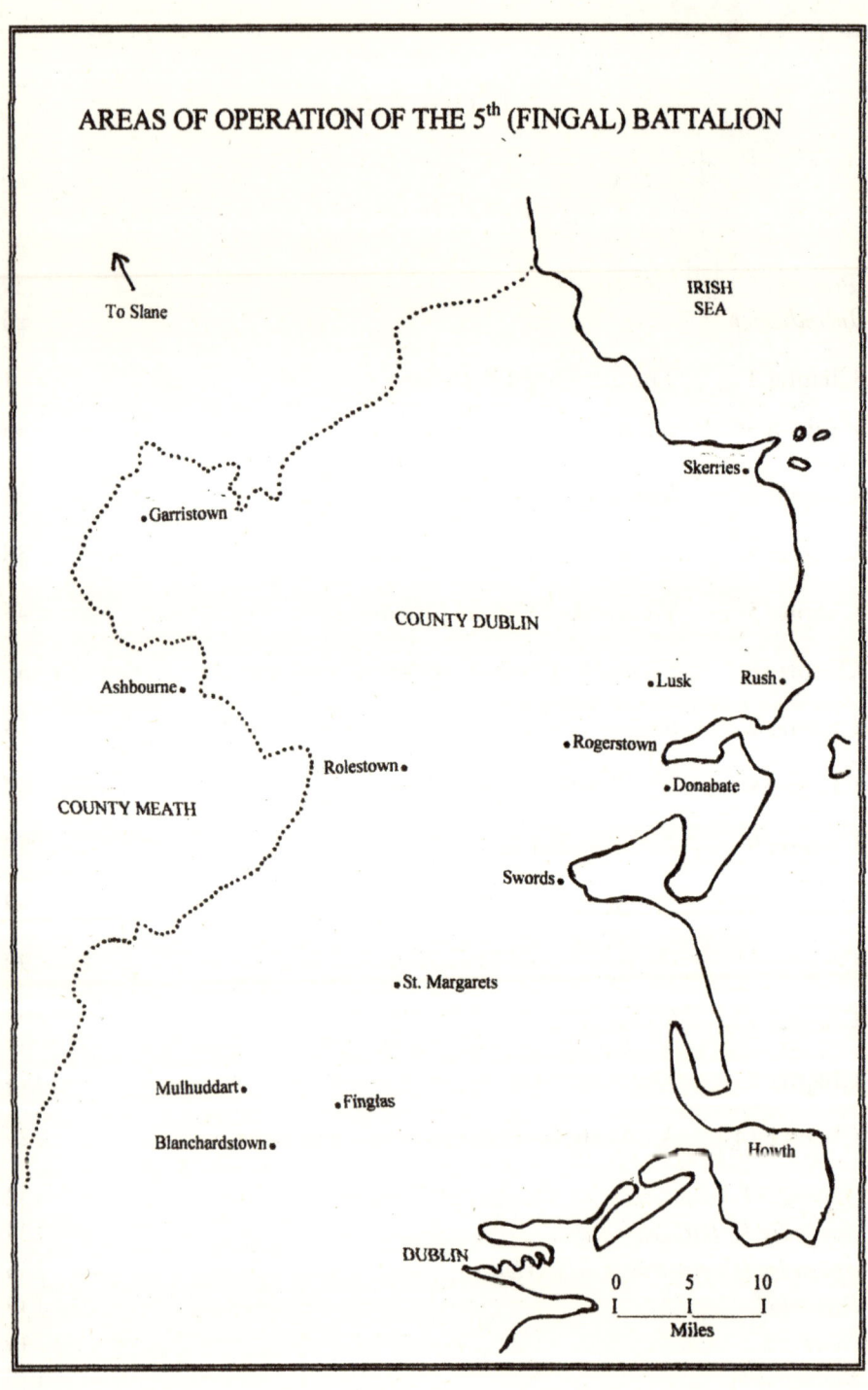

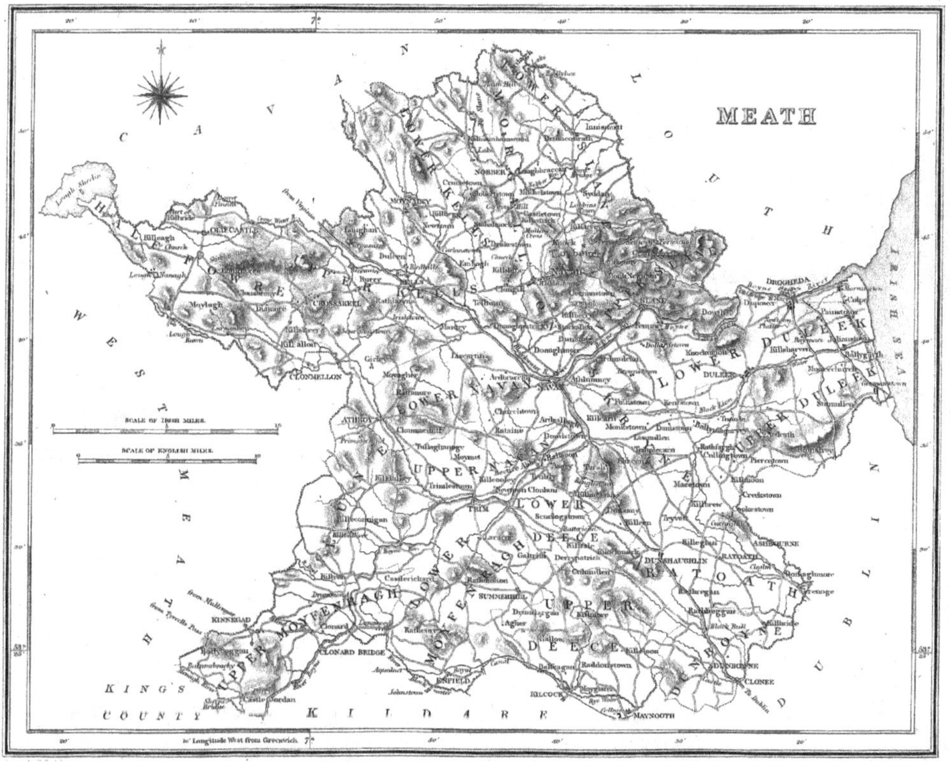

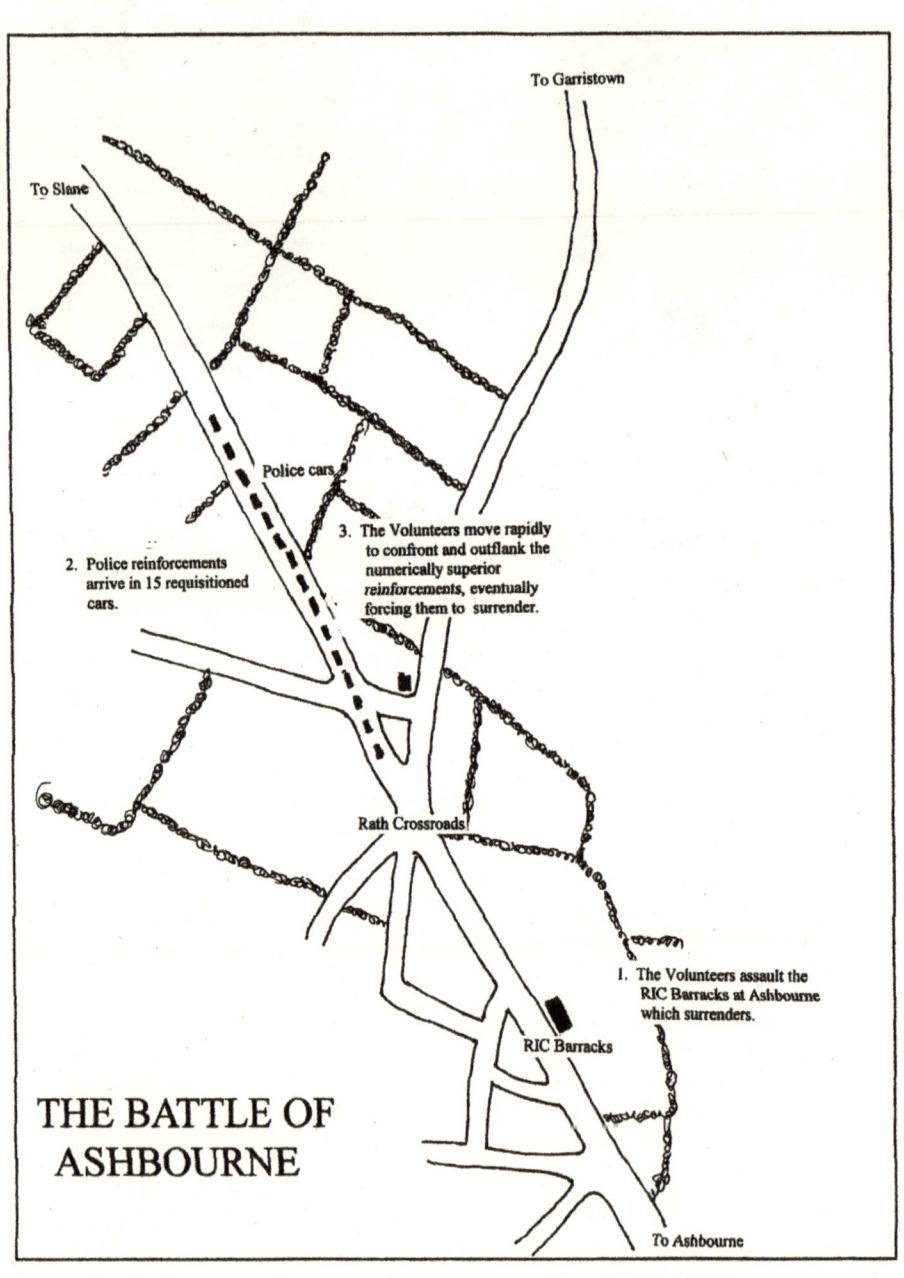

Preface

The Battle of Ashbourne was the culmination of a flying-column campaign conducted during the Easter Rising in Dublin in 1916. Ashbourne, 20km north-west of Dublin City, in County Meath, was originally known as Cill Dheaglain – Deaglan's Church. It takes its present name from Frederick Bourne, a wealthy nineteenth-century businessman, who made his money in the transport industry in Ireland. He built the village in 1820 with an inn, a hotel and shops. A police station, or barracks, was later added. Bourne named the village after his favourite tree and himself. He also named the main street, Frederick Street, after himself. Its population in the year after its construction, according to the census of 1821, was 133. Throughout the early-twentieth century, Ashbourne continued to prosper, being the focal point of the neighbouring farming community.

In this unlikely setting was fought perhaps the most significant, but neglected, conflict of the Rising.

The main protagonists in the battle were the Royal Irish Constabulary (RIC) and the Irish Volunteers of north County Dublin, alternatively known as the 5th Battalion of the Dublin Brigade. Like most volunteer units, the 5th was never anywhere near battalion strength. It was more like an infantry company at best.[1] Due to the cancellation order on Easter Sunday, just 65 members mobilized on Easter Monday. Twenty of these were sent under order from James Connolly to aid the beleaguered garrison at the General Post Office, and others, within the city. Where the remaining forty-five volunteers differed from other units of the volunteers, was their mobility. They travelled on bicycles, rather than on foot. This was an innovation recently adopted by the British Army. Travelling by bicycle enabled them, during the Rising, to engage in a series of lightning raids upon RIC barracks and damage railway and telegraphic communications in the area just north of Dublin.

Their initial orders, issued by James Connolly, were to take the form of diverting British troops from entering Dublin. Without further orders, when Dublin was sealed off, the volunteer commander Thomas Ashe took the initiative and went on the offensive culminating in the Battle of Ashbourne. Here the volunteers confronted, and defeated, a force of perhaps twice their size.

This account of the Battle of Ashbourne is drawn, in the main, from nine separate Witness Statements collected by the Irish Bureau of Military History in the early 1950s. Eight of these accounts are by Irish Volunteers who took part in the battle. The other two accounts are by members of the Royal Irish Constabulary, who took part in the battle. Also included is the Witness Statement of a bystander who watched the battle unfold.

By far the most detailed account of the battle is a Witness Statement given to the Bureau of Military History by Joseph V. Lawless, who was a colonel in the Irish Army by 1954. Other statements are by Dr Richard Hayes, commandant and later adjutant and medical officer of the Fingal Battalion. Jerry Golden, a member of B Company, 1st Battalion, provided two statements, 521 and 177. Other statements are by Bernard McAllister, a member of the 5th Battalion (Fingal), Michael McAllister, a volunteer in the Swords Company, James O'Connor, of the St Margaret's Company, Thomas Peppard, Intelligence Officer of the Fingal Brigade and Charles Weston, Lieutenant of the 5th (Fingal) Battalion.

The RIC account is by Constable Eugene Bratton, who served as a policeman in County Meath. He was later presented to King George V at Buckingham Palace, where he received a medal for gallantry. Later, faced with the brutalities of the Auxiliaries and Black and Tans, he changed sides and passed on information on these para-military forces to Irish Intelligence. The witness was John Austin, who lived in Ashbourne. His is a fairly impartial account, valuable for its description of the terrain in and about Ashbourne. In addition, there are two partial accounts not listed in the Witness Statements. They are by Tommy McArdle and Paddy Doyle. They appear in Sean O'Luing's 1970 book, *I Die in a Good Cause*, a biography of Thomas Ashe, a leading player in the Battle of Ashbourne. Paddy Doyle is listed as partaking in the Battle of Ashbourne (see Appendix I) but not Tommy McArdle. His may possibly be a second-hand account. Either that or the list of participants is incomplete.

It should be noted that the Witness Statements are occasionally at variance. Names, and sometimes sequences, do not always coincide. It should be remembered that these accounts were taken thirty to forty years after the event, and some errors have understandably occurred. Only one of the volunteer accounts I have discovered has been distorted to show that participant in the battle in a better light.

In addition, there is a largely forgotten account of the battle written by a participant, William O'Connell, an RIC officer. It was published in *The Constabulary Gazette* of June 1916. He was riding in the car with District Inspector Harry Smyth and Constable Eugene Bratton.

The main published sources relating to the battle, and in no particular order, are, Sean O'Luing, *I Die in a Good Cause*, the biography of Thomas Ash; Paul O'Brien, *Field of Fire*; J.V. Lawless's account in *Dublin's Fighting Story*; *The Capuchin Annual 1966*; Peter Whearity's *The Easter Rising of 1916 in North County Dublin: A Skerries Perspective*; F.X. Martin's *The Irish Volunteers 1913–1915*; White and O'Shea's *Irish Volunteer Soldier 1913–23*; Michael McNalley's *Easter Rising, 1916*; Joseph McKenna's *Voices from the Easter Rising*; and the *1916 Rebellion Handbook* published by the *Weekly Irish Times*.

British accounts of the battle in the various record offices and archives in Britain are scant, concerning themselves mainly with the rebellion in central Dublin and, in particular, the GPO. In some respects, this was to be to the British detriment. An analysis of the campaign by Ashe and the men of the Fingal Brigade might have led the British to better counter the IRA's later guerrilla campaign. British accounts and, indeed, some contemporary Irish accounts refer to the events at Ashbourne as an ambush. It was far from that. The volunteers, having captured the RIC barracks at Ashbourne then had to rush to confront the arrival of between fifty and seventy armed policemen, who had taken them by surprise. By their training, using British Army manuals, the volunteers were able to adapt to the situation, to manoeuvre and outflank the policemen and finally defeat them in a five-hour battle.

Introduction

Late on the evening of 10 August 1911, the two Houses of Parliament, Lords and Commons, waited for the clerk to announce the result of the vote on the Parliament Bill. It was a pivotal moment in British democracy. The clerk announced, 'Contents 131, not contents, 114'. The government's threat to create as many peers as was necessary to pass the bill had done its work. The bill was through, ending the upper house's absolute power of veto over legislation. Under the terms of the Act, bills would become law without the consent of the Lords if passed in three successive sessions by the Commons. The passing of the Parliament Act made some measure of Home Rule for Ireland inevitable. The Liberal government had become dependent upon the Irish Nationalists to remain in power. The price of that support was a new Home Rule Bill.

Prime Minister Herbert Asquith introduced the Home Rule Bill to the Commons in April 1912. It proposed the transferring to an Irish Parliament matters relating to Ireland. Asquith reserved to the Imperial Parliament all matters relating to the crown, foreign policy, army and navy, the making of peace and war and customs duties. To the Protestants of Northern Ireland, even this modest concession was an anathema. For four centuries, four counties of north-east Ulster had been settled by Scottish Presbyterians. Their religion, politics, economic and social life were profoundly different from the rest of Roman Catholic Ireland. For them, Home Rule would be Rome rule. In the British Parliament, the Ulster Protestants had their champions who voiced their anti-Home Rule view. Conservative Party leader Andrew Bonar Law declared that if any attempt were made by a Dublin Parliament to impose its will upon Ulster, 'I can imagine no length of resistance to which Ulster can go in which I should not be prepared to support them, and in which, in my belief, they would not be supported by the overwhelming majority of the British people.' Sir Edward Carson, a Protestant and Unionist from Dublin, and a leading barrister of his day (who prosecuted Oscar Wilde) added his eloquent voice in opposition to Home Rule. In Ulster itself, Captain James Craig led the Protestant and pro-Unionist population in opposition to the proposed Bill. Asquith acknowledged this opposition in a letter to Winston Churchill in September 1913: 'I always thought (and said) that, in the end, we should probably have to make some sort of bargain about Ulster as the price of Home Rule.' In that statement the partition of Ireland was being privately considered.

The fiery speeches of Carson and Craig led to the formation of a physical force of resistance movement. By the summer of 1912, the members of Orange Lodges throughout Protestant Ulster had begun to drill and take instruction in military tactics and techniques. In the autumn of that year, more than half a million men and women signed a covenant (some unbelievably in their own blood) that pledged loyalty to King George V and the continuation of their part within the United Kingdom of Great Britain and Ireland. They proclaimed that they would use 'all means which may be found necessary to defeat the present conspiracy to set up a Home Rule Parliament in Ireland...and to refuse to recognize its authority'. In January 1913, the Ulster Unionist Council, an alternative Ulster government in all but name, formally established the Ulster Volunteer Force (UVF). It became an army of 100,000 men organized along regular military lines. Senior British Army officer, Lieutenant-General Sir George Richardson, was appointed commander-in-chief. Their actions were treasonable, but Carson declared, 'I am told that it will be illegal. Of course it will. Drilling is illegal...the Volunteers are illegal and the government know they are illegal, and the government dare not interfere with them...Don't be afraid of illegalities.' Carson and the UVF need not have worried, for what they were doing was not strictly illegal. Colonel R.H. Wallace, the Grand Master of the Belfast Orangemen discovered that, by some legal anomaly, any two Justices of the Peace could authorize such drilling within their area, provided – and in this case it was the supreme irony – that the object was to render citizens more efficient 'for the purpose of maintaining the constitution of the United Kingdom as now established and protecting their rights and liberties there under'.

It was beginning to look like the ominous prophesy that Member of Parliament F.E. Smith had made in the Commons on the night of 16 January 1913: 'The Home Rule Bill will not be determined in this House of Commons. It will be decided in the streets of Belfast.'

At Corduff, north of Dublin, the local schoolmaster Thomas Ashe, wrote in a letter to his American cousin Gregory:

> They all say here that Home Rule is as dead as a door-nail. Carson has frightened the Government. He's getting fellows to join his army every other day, and we have it on best authority (our own) that they are continually drilling. If he only gives them the guns some good may come out of it, and good that neither he nor England expects.[1]

In his naivety perhaps, Ashe firmly believed that the British government would act against Carson and the UVF. Meanwhile, the Home Rule Bill was passing through its various stages in the House of Commons. As was expected, it was rejected by the House of Lords and, under the terms of the Parliament Act, it was therefore necessary for the government to obtain the approval of the Commons in two subsequent sessions. As long as the Liberals were in power, the bill would become law in 1914. In the rest of Ireland, the Catholic population had become concerned over the opposition to Home Rule and the formation of a Protestant army to prevent it. Here was a curious anomaly. The Protestants, while opposing the will of Parliament, also professed their loyalty towards the king and the union with Britain. Nevertheless, the UVF was an illegal army, and moves had to be made to suppress it. To counter any military repression of the Protestant army, pro-Unionist Bonar Law sought to amend the forthcoming Annual Army Act in the House of Lords to exclude the use of the army in Ulster. Matters overtook Bonar Law's proposal when, in March 1914, the senior army officers in Ireland agreed in private to refuse to coerce Ulster. The episode, and what was to follow later, became known as the Curragh Mutiny. The senior army officers in Ireland were overwhelmingly Protestant and Unionist, and many were Ulstermen. They refused to march against Ulster. If so ordered, they announced that they would sooner give up their commissions and resign from the army. Asquith, aware of the rumblings, sought to diffuse the situation. He announced what he thought would be a major concession to Ulster. The Home Rule Bill, he announced, would be amended so that any county in Ireland might vote itself out of Home Rule for six years. Uncompromising as ever, Carson rejected the proposal. 'We do not want sentence of death with a stay of execution for six years.' Churchill, whose father, Lord Randolph Churchill, had opposed the two previous Home Rule Bills, sided with the Liberal government. At Bradford on 14 March 1914, he described the Ulster Provisional government as 'engaged in a treasonable conspiracy,' adding, 'force would be met by force'.

Sir Arthur Paget, the British Army's Commander-in-Chief in Ireland, was ordered to take steps to secure the safety of the depots of arms and ammunition in Ulster. Paget was then summoned to London on 18 March to receive orders to move two battalions of infantry close to the border of Ulster. He was promised further reinforcements from England 'that might be required to maintain law and order'. The Third Battle Squadron of battleships of the Royal Navy, with a destroyer escort, was moved up to the Firth of Clyde in support and was made ready to sail to Belfast. In London, Paget raised the question with the government over those senior officers whose sympathies were with Ulster. He was told that they might be allowed to 'disappear' for a time. Others would be dismissed. Returning to the Curragh, Paget briefed his senior officers. Brigadier-General Gough, commanding the Third Cavalry Brigade, and 57 of his officers stated that they preferred to accept dismissal. Gough and two of his colonels were summoned to London to explain. In the face of their intransigence, Asquith remarked, '...there is no doubt if we were to order a march on Ulster that about half of the officers in the Army... would strike'. Such an action might bring down the government. After further talks, the government caved in. It announced that the government would 'have no intention whatsoever of taking advantage of this right to crush political opposition to the policy or principles of the Home Rule Bill'. Colonel Seely, Minister of War, gave written reassurances to Gough that the forces of the Crown would not be used against the provisional government of Ulster, or their military arm, the Ulster Volunteers. The whole affair was rightly seen in Nationalist Ireland as a case of betrayal, mismanagement, indecision and even cowardice on behalf of the British government.

In the face of a successful military mutiny supported, perhaps not openly, by the Conservative Party opposition, a weakened Liberal government, led by Prime Minister Asquith, sought a compromise. John Redmond, leader of the Irish National Party at Westminster (a man and his party now losing touch with the reality of what was happening in Ireland), was persuaded to accept Home Rule by stages as the price for peace. In further discussions, the Unionists conceded the principle of Home Rule for the rest of Ireland if they themselves were excluded. The Ulster Unionists held out for the exclusion of all nine counties of Ulster. Redmond conceded the principle of exclusion for a limited time of those Ulster counties with Protestant majorities, but he would only accept the exclusion of the four majority Protestant counties of Derry, Antrim, Down and Armagh, and only on a temporary basis. Asquith convinced Redmond that the Unionists would bring about their own downfall by seeking inclusion of all nine counties, some of which had Catholic majorities, and others had sizeable Catholic communities, which would make them ungovernable. Home Rule for all Ireland would be achieved and sooner than later. Redmond for the moment saw the sense in that.

In Dublin, the subtlety of Parliamentary shenanigans was viewed with frustration. The UVF was a force under arms, determined to prevent Home Rule being successfully carried out throughout all of Ireland. In response to the formation of the UVF and the British Army's unwillingness to move against them, the Irish Nationalists decided to form their own volunteer army to force through the democratic process of Home Rule. It was pointed out that since the British government had not interfered in the establishment of the UVF, it could hardly prohibit Nationalist Ireland from doing the same. In

Dublin, schoolteacher Patrick Pearse began publishing a new newspaper, *An Barr Buadh* (The Trumpet of Victory). Its line was Republican. The theme of the paper was the procrastination of the politicians. It was time to stop talking and do something concrete, Pearse advocated. If they (the Irish National Party) would not lead a rebellion, then he would. He spoke of the sacred use of force. Some viewed him as a fanatic; others, such as the Irish Republican Brotherhood (IRB), as a potential leader. They could make use of him.

Professor Eoin MacNeill, a leading light in national and literary life in Ireland, believed that it was now necessary to raise an army in defence of the cherished dream of Home Rule. He wrote an article in the Gaelic League's newspaper, *An Claidheamh Soluis* (The Sword of Life) under the headline, 'If the North, why not the South?' The shadowy Irish Republican Brotherhood, dedicated to the physical overthrow of British power in Ireland, saw this as a great opportunity. Here was a known pacifist urging the formation of a defensive army to protect Home Rule. Such an army, infiltrated and controlled by them, could be turned in the fullness of time from a defensive to an offensive army. Bulmer Hobson, then head of the Dublin section of the Irish Republican Brotherhood, sent a non-IRB member, The O'Rahilly (Michael Joseph O'Rahilly), to sound out the professor and ascertain whether he was prepared to implement his ideas of forming a new volunteer organization in the south. MacNeill was only too willing, and O'Rahilly agreed to work with him. The two men drew up a list of prominent Nationalists and invited them to Wynn's Hotel at 35–37 Lower Abbey Street, to form a provisional committee. Among those chosen were prominent members of the cultural association, the Gaelic League. They included Thomas MacDonagh, a tutor of English literature in University College, Dublin; Patrick Pearse (or Padraig Pearse as he was now known, the son of an Englishman), founder of St Enda's Irish School; and Eamon Ceannt, a fellow founding member of the Gaelic League. They praised MacNeill for his courage and gave him their full support for the formation of a national militia to defend Home Rule. In November 1913, *An Claidheamh Soluis* published an article calling for the setting up of this armed force of volunteers in defence of Home Rule.

As far as respectable Ireland was concerned, and no doubt in liberal England too, MacNeill was the perfect man to lead this movement. He was a professor of Irish, a respected scholar and a founder of the Gaelic League. Nobody in Ireland, it was believed, had worked and devoted themselves so arduously to all aspects of the struggle for nationhood. He was a known pacifist and was held in high esteem throughout the entire country. Nobody would associate his name with any fierce militarism. As such, the image of a political moderate, calling for the foundation of a volunteer army, downplayed the fact that the men he had consulted with, and was encouraged by, were members of the IRB. These men, MacDonagh, Pearse and Ceannt were content for the moment for MacNeill to be head of what was being portrayed as a defensive force. It was their intention, though, to take control of the volunteers in the fullness of time, to bring about Irish independence by force. Following MacNeill's call for the establishment of an Irish volunteer army, the IRB started to make plans to take over the nascent volunteer movement. At the next meeting of his branch IRB Circle, Sean McDermott announced that, in view of the setting up of the volunteers, every member would have to do a certain amount of preliminary drill, and arrangements were then made to make drill compulsory for all younger members. The idea was that once the new movement was established, those with knowledge of drilling would automatically come to the fore.

A date was set for the founding of the Irish National Volunteers. It was to be held at the Rotunda Rink in central Dublin on 25 November 1913. Present upon the stage was Eoin MacNeill, Pearse, Sir Roger Casement and the old Fenian, Tom Clarke. MacNeill put the objectives of the proposed volunteers before the huge crowd that had gathered. The new organization was not designed to oppose the Ulster Volunteers, but rather to co-operate if the occasion demanded in the defence of their common country. It was to be non-sectarian and open to all who wished to join. Its aims were purely defensive, and it was not contemplating aggression or domination. Amongst the crowd, one of the spectators, Michael Walker, wrote that the meeting 'pulsated with an intensity of national feeling'. Pearse addressed the thronged hall and declared that citizenship involved the enjoyment of certain rights and the acceptance of certain duties; the most essential being the bearing of arms. He reiterated MacNeill's sentiment that the new organization did not wish to appear to be an answer to the Ulster Volunteers, but rather as a complementary body. Many felt that Ireland could only achieve freedom outside of the British Empire, whereas others felt that they could achieve all the freedom they wanted within the Empire. Opinions might differ, Pearse suggested, but an unarmed Ireland could never achieve or demand as much as one that could stand up and defend itself. To the casual listener it all sounded so reasonable.

Amongst the crowd in the Rotunda was a young man from Swords, a parish just north of Dublin. For Joseph Lawless that day, and forever more, proved to be a momentous occasion:

> The meeting at the Rotunda Rink in November 1913 was a memorable one. The building was at the time the largest in Dublin, in point of open floor space, and was packed to capacity. A succession of prominent Nationalists of whom I can remember Arthur Griffith, Alderman Tom

Kelly, Sean McDermott and Tom Kettle, addressed the people explaining the purpose of the meeting and the political situation which called for the formation of the Irish Volunteers. The constitution of this new organization was announced, and received tumultuous approval, and then the enrolment for the various city battalions began.[2]

During the course of the meeting, enrolment forms were handed out amongst the crowd, and to those outside who could not get in. In patriotic passion, they signed the forms and enrolled themselves into the volunteer army. It was a declaration that they would fight for the freedom of Ireland. Time would tell how many of them actually would.

Upon signing, they were given a green-coloured membership card on which was printed the aims and objects of the Irish Volunteers:

1. To secure and maintain the rights and liberties common to the people of Ireland.
2. To train, discipline and equip for this purpose an Irish Volunteer Force.
3. To unite, in the service of Ireland, Irishmen of every creed, and every party and class.

It was a very egalitarian army that was formed. Irish Volunteers were grouped according to locality, irrespective of class or creed. Any competent volunteer might be elected as an officer, though in practice many turned out to be educated IRB men. Colonel Maurice Moore of the Connaught Rangers became Inspector-General of the Volunteers, giving the embryonic army a degree of respectability. Bulmer Hobson was appointed secretary to the volunteers, and the humanitarian but flawed Sir Roger Casement, who had exposed Belgian atrocities in the Congo, became its treasurer.

As the volunteers increased in numbers, drilling and marching, the RIC County Inspectors sent in reports of their concerns. Their concerns were not shared by Augustine Birrell, the Chief Secretary for Ireland, however. Was not Ireland about to get Home Rule? Soon, the whole machinery of government was going to be dismantled. Why bother about slight irregularities like drilling and cause unnecessary problems? The Dublin Castle officials had learnt that it did not pay to act. Any attempt to disarm the volunteers would have been a major exercise, possibly leading to loss of life. Best let sleeping dogs lie.

Chapter 1

The 5th Fingal Battalion

Up at Fingal in north County Dublin, the establishment of the Irish Volunteers was initially met with great enthusiasm. When it came to commitment, however, with the prospect of giving up time for drilling and long route marches, particularly at sowing or harvest time, lethargy crept in. Gradually though, recruitment improved when the volunteer leadership made themselves known as they toured the country and gave rousing speeches. Likewise, the IRB were also recruiting and ensuring that their men attained influential positions within the new formed companies.

Companies were started up at Swords and Lusk. At Skerries, two local men, Patrick Matthews and Patrick O'Donnell discussed establishing a company at their little seaside resort. They held an initial meeting on 10 May and followed this up with an open-air public meeting in the square on Sunday, 24 May. It attracted a crowd of about 300 people. Laurence J. Kettle, a founding member of the volunteers in Dublin, was invited to speak. He told those gathered about him that the volunteer movement was essentially a movement not of oratory but of action: 'The voice of this movement was the tramp of marching men and the crack of rifles…Yet the Volunteers were not formed in any aggressive spirit, they were essentially an army of national defence.'[1] Following the meeting, some 200 men enrolled in the newly established Skerries Company. In Fingal. some seven companies were eventually formed:

1. Swords, established on 6 April with fifty to fifty-five men enrolling. Richard Coleman was elected captain.
2. Balbriggan, formed on Sunday, 4 May with just five men.
3. Lusk, established on 19 May 1914. It had a company of 40 volunteers led by Edward Rooney. The company trained at Donabate, at the home of the MacAllister family, where they also stored their weapons.
4. Skerries, formed on 24 May 1914. Joseph McGuinness was appointed its first captain. He was later succeeded by Joseph Thornton.
5. St Margaret's, formed in early 1914. James Vincent Lawless was appointed its captain.

Two other companies, Garristown and Santry, were later formed in the first weeks of June 1914. Following some amalgamation, the seven companies became four.

Doctor Richard Hayes[2] was appointed commanding officer of the Fingal Battalion, Thomas Ashe[3] became battalion adjutant and Frank Lawless[4] was appointed quartermaster. By the early summer, the structure of the Fingal Volunteers was as follows:

Commandant: Dr Richard Hayes
Adjutant: Thomas Ashe
Quartermaster: Frank Lawless

The Company Captains were:

Swords – Richard Coleman
Lusk – Edward Rooney
Skerries – Joseph Thornton
St Margaret's – James V. Lawless

The men who joined the rank and file of the volunteers were just ordinary men but with one exception; they would have been brought up with stories of the United Irishmen of 1798 and with the more recent Fenian Rising of 1867. The stories were very vivid still and, of course, there were family members and family friends, among the older generation, who had taken part in the Fenian Rising. This latent nationalism was channelled physically in enrolment into the Irish Volunteers. Thomas Peppard was just such a recruit, as the introduction to his Witness Statement reveals:

> I was born in the year 1894 at Brunswick St., now Pearse St., Dublin, but was reared at Lusk in north County Dublin. I attended the local national school at Lusk. Our teacher there – a man called Fenton – was very keen on teaching us Irish history and the Irish language. The Irish language was not one of the subjects catered for by the commissioners for education at that time and for this reason he had to teach us Irish after normal school hours. There was a hurling and football club in Lusk at this time and I was soon a member. The brothers John and Edward Rooney were the principals in the organising and running of the club. In July 1914 companies of the Irish Volunteers were started in Lusk…One company was started by the Rooneys and had its origins in the hurling and football clubs.[5]

Michael MacAllister joined the Swords Company at its inauguration in April 1914. Some 40 years later, he recalled in his Witness Statement:

> When the Irish Volunteers were started in Swords in 1914, I joined that organization. I think it was Frank Lawless who took me in. There was no Oath to take, not even a declaration of any sort. We were issued with membership cards and we paid a small weekly subscription towards the funds of the unit. There was a big number of men of all types in the Volunteers then and very different ages. I think that Dick Coleman, who later died in Usk Prison [from the flu pandemic], was in charge of the Company. Parades were held every other evening and nearly every Sunday. Parades were held every other evening and nearly every Sunday. A man named Eimar O'Duffy[6] used to come down from the city and put us through drill and other exercises, and also to give lectures. We had no arms except a few .22 Sporting Rifles with which we had target practice. Most of the men were good natural shots, which is usual with young men from the country, while some of them were exceptionally good and could be said to be marksmen with a rifle. The .22 Rifles were the property of individual members of the Company and some few of the men also had revolvers. I had a small Calibre Revolver which belonged to our family.[7]

Elsewhere, James O'Connor, who was to fight in the Battle of Ashbourne, related his early experiences upon joining the volunteers:

> Thomas Duke was the Company Captain. We had parades for training twice a week and route marches on Sundays, We had no arms and did our drill with wooden guns. We had firing practices with a .22 rifle at Mr. Tyrell's place at Dunsoghly Castle. Mr Tyrell was also a member. One or two of the RIC always attended our parades and accompanied us on our route marches...Michael Masterson was the instructor. He was a British Army Reservist.[8]

Inside the nascent volunteer movement, the secretive IRB was at work. Michael McAllister of Donabate confirms the infiltration:

> The late Thomas Ashe [the local schoolmaster] was a frequent visitor to our house...On one occasion I mentioned to him that we in this country should have some kind of an intelligence organization to counteract the propaganda about this country in the English press. He said we had such an organization here and asked me if I would like to join. I said I would.

The organization that I visualized was quite different from the one which I discovered that Ashe belonged to. He took me to a meeting of this organization, which was the IRB. There were quite a number of men at this meeting whom I knew, including the Taylors of Swords and the late Frank Lawless of Saucerstown.

On 4 December 1913, just nine days after the inauguration of the volunteers, the British government prohibited the importation of military arms and ammunition into Ireland. This decision outraged the volunteer leadership. It was brought about by the Liberal government, who were only maintained in power because it had the support of the Irish Parliamentary Party at Westminster. In essence, Redmond and his fellow Irish MPs had agreed to the ban. The IRB saw the action for what it was: the attempted neutering of the Irish Volunteers. The Irish Party had opposed the formation of the volunteers from the start, who saw them as the army of the rival nationalist party, Sinn Fein. Though, in fact, it was not. Redmond saw the volunteers as a threat to his position as leader of the Irish nation. He saw himself as the 'uncrowned king'; the man who had achieved the winning of Home Rule for Ireland. Unable to prevent the growth of Sinn Fein and the volunteer movement, he now attempted to gain control over the army. In June 1914, Redmond issued an ultimatum. Either the volunteers would have to accept twenty-five nominees of his on the governing body of the volunteers (thus seemingly giving him control of policy) or he would set up a rival organization. Redmond at this stage, by June 1914, was at the height of his popularity. Rather than risk dissention, the leadership of the volunteers, notably Eoin MacNeill and Bulmer Hobson, agreed.

Meanwhile, the organization of the new army, with Redmond contending leadership, began to develop into a proper army with command and structure. Following the British model, it was divided up into battalions and sub-divided into companies. These in turn were organized into four sections, each consisting of two squads formed on a residential basis in such a way as to facilitate rapid mobilization. Each squad was in the charge of a squad commander or sergeant. Numbers one and two sections were in the charge of a first lieutenant, and numbers three and four sections were in the charge of a second lieutenant. The company staff consisted of a company captain, the two lieutenants mentioned above, a company adjutant and a company quartermaster, with the last two ranking as senior NCOs. Taking as an example A Company 3rd Battalion, which was probably typical of other companies in other battalion, it was divided into half companies; these were divided into sections and the sections were divided into squads. To facilitate the mobilization of a unit, the officers, section commanders and squad commanders were augmented by individuals who were known as mobilizers. These mobilizers usually consisted of an older member of the unit, who lived in an area where there were one or more members of his company, which did not include an officer, section commander or a squad commander. Company runners usually lived near the company commander and were employed by him for the purpose of taking mobilization orders out to members of his unit who were responsible for the mobilization. The runners subdivided the area to be mobilized, and each of them took dispatches to the mobilizers with instructions to hand the dispatches personally to the person addressed or to leave it at his home address and, upon completion, to report back to the company commanders. Test mobilizations were carried out from time to time to test the efficiency of the system.

As an army, the volunteers needed a distinctive uniform and accompanying accoutrements. A list was prepared and distributed throughout the various battalions. For several companies drawn from Dublin's poor, it remained an aspiration. On Easter Monday, some volunteers in Dublin wore nothing more than an armlet to indicate their status as soldiers. It just about complied with the Hague Convention of 1907 respecting the wearing of distinctive uniforms. Officers, though, were expected to kit themselves out in the prescribed officer's uniform with distinguishing marks of rank. Up in Fingal, at the outbreak of the Rising, it is said that about 15 to 20 of the volunteers, including most of the officers had uniforms. The remainder wore their equipment of bandolier, haversack and belt over their civilian clothes. Invariably, as a photograph of the men shows, many of them wore flat caps. Henry Murray, later appointed a lieutenant in A Company, 4th Battalion, described his initial company adjutant uniform in his Witness Statement 300 to the Bureau of Military History:

> My uniform up to December 1915 consisted of a green tunic with blue facings and brass buttons with a harp design, green breeches, green puttees and a cap with a black glazed peak. My arms consisted of a Lee-Enfield rifle, 100 rounds of .303 ammunition and a bayonet. My equipment consisted of a leather belt, leather bandolier, haversack, water bottle, trench tool, bayonet frog and whistle. In addition I carried a notebook and first aid dressing.

Later, as a second lieutenant, Murray was obliged to purchase a Sam Brown belt and a .380 revolver with 50 rounds of ammunition. Of his training, Murray recalled:

> The early training...was carried out under the supervision of a British Army reservist NCO who was paid for his services. This man was

competent to give instructions from the current British Army manuals on squad, section, company and battalion close and open order drill with and without arms, musketry, bayonet fighting, military ceremonial and elementary tactics.

Training was organized using the British Army's *Field Service Regulations* training manual, first published in 1909. It was freely available in all government book shops. This manual covered all aspects of soldiering from drilling, marching and actual fighting. Of particular interest to the Fingal Battalion, being out in the country, was the section on field craft; how to manoeuvre across land.

Musketry, or the lack of it, was a problem. The country had been largely disarmed by the British government following the Fenian Rising of 1867. In the early days, the volunteers fashioned for themselves, and trained with, rifles made from wood or even, in some cases, used broomstick handles, before the real thing filtered through. Some of these, Lee-Enfield rifles in particular, were procured from hard-up British soldiers, who smuggled them out of their barracks and sold them for a couple of pounds. Other arms came in dribs and drabs, smuggled in from abroad, by friendly sailors and other ship-board staff. Within the city of Dublin itself, some battalions joined British shooting clubs, which entitled them to legally purchase target rifles.

Things in Ireland changed dramatically on the night of 24–25 April 1914. The Ulster Volunteer Force succeeded in smuggling in almost 25,000 rifles from Germany. This rather gave the lie to John Redmond, who had assured the Nationalist population of Ireland that the UVF were engaged in a 'gigantic game of bluff and blackmail'. From the very inception of the UVF, Major Frederick Crawford had been tasked with acquiring guns. A previous attempt had been thwarted by vigilant customs officials. But Crawford now surreptitiously purchased from Benny Spiro, an arms dealer in Hamburg, 11,000 Mannlicher rifles, bought from the Steyer Works in Austria, 9,000 ex-German Army Mausers and 4,600 Italian Vetterli-Vitali rifles. These weapons were transported through the Kiel Canal to the Baltic island of Langeland and loaded aboard the *Fanny*. Here, the Danish authorities stepped in and attempted to seize the ship, believing that the cargo was destined for Iceland; a Danish colony agitating for independence. The *Fanny* managed to escape and sailed out beyond Danish territorial waters. An overseas representative of *The Times* newspaper picked up on the story of the attempted seizure of a British ship and put a new slant on the story. Perhaps the arms were intended for Ulster rather than Iceland the writer contended. In London, the authorities took notice. The Royal Navy was alerted. With the unwanted publicity, Crawford became concerned. Contacting the *Fanny*, he made arrangements for her to head for a trans-shipment at Tuskar Rock, off the coast of County Wexford. Here, she was met by the SS *Clyde Valley*, which Crawford had purchased earlier in Glasgow. The entire cargo of the *Fanny* was transferred to the *Clyde Valley*, which was renamed the *Mountjoy II* by using a six-foot long strip of canvas painted with white letters on a black background. In the early hours of the morning, the '*Mount*' docked at Larne, twenty miles away from Belfast and began discharging part of her cargo. At 5am, she left Larne for Bangor, where she discharged the remainder. On the face of it, the Larne gunrunning was a huge success. This success was tempered, however, for there were three separate types of guns, lacking in the correct ammunition. In Dublin, there was a degree of horror at the news of the gunrunning. Patrick Pearse was more philosophical. 'Personally I think the Orangeman with a rifle a much less ridiculous figure than the Nationalist without a rifle,' he observed.

From April to August 1914, the question of Ulster became pivotal. The Irish Volunteers had now outstripped the UVF in numbers, and they had every intention of arming themselves in the same way. Seemingly, the threat of civil war was close – and yet – both armies had declared that they meant to oppose the British government and not each other. It was ironic; the Orangemen who claimed to be arming in order to hold four Protestant counties 'for the Empire', were in fact intent upon establishing their own objective of self-government rather than Home Rule.

The speculation was ended in July 1914, when 900 Mausers and 29,000 rounds of the appropriate ammunition were smuggled into Ireland for the volunteers. The guns were landed at Howth, just north of Dublin. The Mausers dated from the Franco-Prussian War of 1870. Though dated, and with a terrific kick-back, they were still effective after training in their use. They were brought into Ireland aboard the yacht *Asgard*, which was owned by Erskine Childers, author of the novel *The Riddle of the Sands*. Here was a man with strong English credentials. He was a graduate of Cambridge University and a former clerk in the House of Commons. He became disillusioned with Britain though over the Boer War and left England for Ireland, where he had maternal relatives. In fact, he had been raised by his mother's family in Glendalough, near Annamore, County Wicklow. Influenced by the family, and taking a keen interest in Irish politics, Childers became an ardent Irish Home Ruler. Supported by the IRB, Childers sailed aboard the *Asgard* with his American-born wife, as well as Mary Spring Rice, Molly Osgood and three Donegal sailors from Gola Island – Patrick McGinley, Charles Duggan and a third man by the name of Cahill. There is perhaps a certain inconsistency in Childer's actions one might feel. After the gun-running for the Irish Volunteers in July 1914, Childers then returned to England to join the British forces in the war against Germany. For him, it was a case of doing the right thing on both occasions. The landing of arms was not to assist a revolt but rather to strengthen the Liberal government's Irish policy of Home Rule against the Unionist rebels in Ulster. As an Englishman, it was his duty to fight for his country against Germany.

Accompanying the *Asgard* was a second yacht, the *Kelpie*, owned and skippered by Conor O'Brien, and his crew. The two boats rendezvoused at the Ruytingen buoy, just off the Belgian coast, with a tugboat that had carried the arms from Hamburg. To confuse the British, a rumour was spread that an Irish trawler was transporting the cargo to Mexico. Nonetheless, British warships were sent out to intercept all Irish trawlers in the North Sea. The two gentry-owned yachts sailed on untroubled. As the *Asgard* proceeded on to Ireland, the *Kelpie* sailed to the Welsh coast, where 600 rifles and ammunition were transferred to another yacht, the *Chotah*, skippered by Sir Thomas Myles, a Dublin surgeon, with a crew including Tom Kettle, politician and barrister, and James Meredith, also a barrister. The arms were later landed at Kilcoole in County Wicklow.

Up until now, news of the *Asgard*'s arrival was known only to a few. Many suspected that something was up, however. Seamus Daly of F Company, 2nd Battalion, Irish Volunteers, wrote in his later Witness Statement (360):

> For some months before the gun-running at Howth we were always being cheered with the news that guns were coming but where or when we did not know. We were keenly interested because every Sunday route march we had around this time was always to the coast and rightly or wrongly each time we went on these route marches we had high hopes that we were going for the guns.

Likewise, there was a similar expectation up in Swords, north County Dublin. On a seven-mile route march to Howth on 26 July 1914, the company was halted just before it reached the town. Instead of being allowed to fall out by the roadside as normal, they were ordered to remain within their ranks and ordered to be ready to move at once. There was speculation amongst the ranks, as Lieutenant Joseph Lawless as he now was, reported. Excitement mounted. Was there going to be a landing of arms? After a short while, the company moved forward again, wheeling left on to the East Pier. Here they saw a confrontation with volunteer officers, including Sean Heuston, and one or two members of the Royal Irish Constabulary. The policemen were intimidated by the sheer weight of numbers and withdrew. Lawless noticed a Fianna boy,

Paul Marshall, standing on the wall near the lighthouse at the end of the pier. The Fianna were a Nationalistic boy scout movement whose members inevitably, when old enough, joined the volunteers. The young lad was making a rapid series of signals out to sea with two signal flags. Joseph Lawless takes up the story: 'The sea wall on our right prevented us from seeing what lay out to sea, but very soon we saw the white painted yacht *Asgard* swing around the Lighthouse and slide smoothly and silently into the wharf.' There was a fever of activity amongst the volunteer officers now, ensuring that their men remained in ranks, leaving a clear passage on one side to allow the columns to march off. Lawless described the efficiency of the operation:

> I watched with interest the activity aboard the yacht as she was being warped in to the wall by lines thrown ashore. While some of the crew remained watching carefully the movement of the ship, the remainder were engaged in a furious stripping of hatches so that there should be no delay after tying up. A group of officers of Volunteer headquarter staff waited near the edge of the wall to greet the arrival of the yacht and its cargo and, while it was yet two or three feet from the wall, Sean Heuston and a couple of others sprang aboard. Almost at once, long rifles with gleaming barrels began to appear from the hold and were passed from hand to hand to the men waiting on the pier. We began to move forward slowly, dreading lest there should be no rifles left by the time our turn came.
>
> As each company was armed it moved back towards the pier entrance and in an incredibly short time every man on parade was armed with a rifle.

In disciplined ranks, the various columns moved forward to collect their 'Howth Mausers' (as they came to be known). The Fingal Volunteers, about 40 of them, arrived by bicycle.[9] They claimed their rifles, strapped them to their bikes, then cycled off back to Swords, Lusk and other Fingal centres. The Donabate Company were not so fortunate. They had been detailed to prevent anyone except the volunteers from getting on to the pier. By the time they were relieved by the Lusk Company, now all bearing arms, there were no rifles left. A disappointed Bernard McAllister espied one rifle aboard the *Asgard* that had apparently not been claimed. 'I jumped on to the boat,' he recalled, 'and succeeded in getting one, and ten rounds of ammunition. I had the only rifle the company got. It was the type known as Howth Mauser. Subsequently, the Company purchased six or seven Italian (Garibaldi) rifles.'

Lawless and his company, now armed, marched off back to Swords. 'We forgot how tired we were as we sang lustily on the homeward march,' he recalled. On the roadside at Raheny village, they espied a group of some twenty or thirty RIC men. Considerably outnumbered by the armed volunteers, they made no attempt to stop them. However, the officer in charge telephoned Dublin Castle. As the volunteers marched onwards, they were confronted by the response to that telephone call. At the junction of the Howth Road at Clontarf, they were confronted by a strong force of the Dublin Metropolitan Police, who were lined two-deep across the road. They were supported by a company of armed soldiers from the King's Own Scottish Borderers, with bayonets fixed. The leading volunteer column halted about 100 yards from the police line. After a brief discussion, the volunteers divided into two parties. To the right, just before the police blockade, lay the Malahide Road, an alternative route into the city centre. Down this road, they marched with pace. The remainder of the column wheeled right to cross the Diamond in an attempt to outflank and get behind the blockade. Seeing this, the police made to stop them. Assistant Commissioner Harrel, who was in charge of the police, advanced to parley with the volunteer officers. He demanded the surrender of the rifles. The volunteers demanded that he clear the way. Within the volunteer ranks, some of the men demanded that their officers issue ammunition. For, in truth, the Mausers were not loaded – but the police did not know this. Bravely, with batons drawn, the police advanced on the volunteers. They, for their part, turned their rifles stocks upwards, to act as clubs. It came to blows, and the police fell back in disorder behind the military lines. The soldiers now moved forward to confront the volunteers, who also moved forward and blocked the road in large numbers. Joseph Lawless recalled, 'I could not see clearly what was happening in front as I was some twenty or thirty yards behind the front rank.' There was a confrontation; one or two volunteers received bayonet wounds but nothing lethal. The volunteers rushed the military line, which they easily outnumbered. Rifles were wrested from the hands of some of the soldiers. The outnumbered soldiers moved back, fearing that they might be rushed and overpowered. The order was given, and the soldiers fired a volley over the heads of the volunteers. This seemed to halt the volunteer advancement. Lawless climbed on top of a wall, the better to see what was going on:

> I saw the captain of our company, M.J. Judge, who had received a bayonet wound in the left side, being assisted to the rear, so I drew my revolver, holding onto my rifle and the bars of the paling with my left arm. A Fianna officer…Eamon Martin – was standing on the wall in front of me calling out to those in front to stand fast and not give way before the

charge. Seeing me with the revolver in my hand he shouted at me to 'put that away.' ...Apparently he realized the undesirability at that stage of events, of giving the British authorities an excuse for military action, by gunfire from our side.

Meanwhile, a sufficient number of volunteers and their officers still confronted the police and military. Other volunteer officers, further back from the confrontation, instructed their men to disperse individually and make their way across the fields and back into the city. As such, most of the rifles were secured. Those that were seized by the police, just nineteen in number, were eventually returned following the intervention of Colonel Maurice Moore, the volunteer's inspector general.

Later that Sunday evening, 180 soldiers of the King's Own Scottish Borderers, having failed to stop the volunteers, had withdrawn to Dublin and were marching along Sackville Street (now O'Connell Street) when they came under attack from an angry crowd of reputedly 1,000 in number, who threw stones and rotten fruit at them. Major Alfred Haig was sent for, to lead them off to their barracks. When Haig arrived, he found his men in complete disarray and surrounded. A number of his officers had serious head wounds. He organized his men and marched them off towards the River Liffey and right down Bachelor's Walk. Believing the soldiers to be on the run, the crowd followed, throwing more stones. As they approached the Liffey, another crowd appeared and cut them off from the barracks. One of Haig's men was then grabbed, and some members of the mob attempted to drag him off. His comrades, with bayonets fixed, succeeded in rescuing him. At this point, Haig turned his men to face the mob. A stone struck him on the bridge of his nose. He shouted at the top of his voice for the crowd to disperse. A second stone struck him on the chin, and a third hit his ear. Haig ordered twenty men at the rear of the column to form into a double line. The front rank kneeled, the second rank stood behind them, rifles aimed at the mob. Haig raised his hand to silence the crowd and ordered them once more to disperse. But his men, mistaking the gesture, as he lowered his arm (as a later enquiry discovered) opened fire on the crowd. When the shooting had stopped, three civilians lay dead and thirty-two were wounded. The three dead were 50-year-old Mary Duffy, 50-year-old Patrick Quinn and 18-year-old James Brennan. Another man, having been bayoneted, died some days later. Among those wounded was a boy called Luke Kelly who had no part in the riot. He was cycling over O'Connell Bridge some distance away when he was shot by a stray bullet.

Events now overtook the 'trivialities' of Home Rule. The Archduke Franz Ferdinand of Austria was assassinated, and the First World War broke out.

On 4 August 1914, the German army invaded Belgium. In response, Britain and France declared war against the German Empire. On 18 September, the Home Rule Act was passed into law but was shelved until the end of hostilities. The Ulster leaders in Parliament pledged to call off their opposition to Home Rule for the duration. The UVF showed its continued devotion to Britain and formed two divisions of soldiers to fight in France.

In the remainder of Ireland, as Volunteer Michael McAllister pointed out, 'Quite a number of young men joined the British Army or were called up to that force of which they were members of the Reserve…and there was a surge of pro-British feeling throughout the country.' Redmond, carried away in this seeming euphoria of the moment, gave a speech at Woodenbridge in County Wicklow, on 20 September. It caused a split in the ranks of the volunteers. Without reference to the Volunteer Executive Council, he called upon the volunteers to join with Britain in its war against Germany in defence of small nations. It would be to Ireland's eternal shame, he declared, if Ireland's young men did not go and fight. The speech brought to a head a situation that had been brewing for quite a while. Overnight, the volunteer population was split. The IRB Provisional Committee called a meeting to repudiate Redmond's statement, and to revert to the original concept of the formation of the volunteers. A vote at a convention of the volunteers, some 180,000 strong, gave their support to Redmond, and they became known as the National Volunteers. Some 9,000 to 11,000 of the original founding members (the figure is uncertain) reaffirmed their allegiance to Ireland and Ireland alone.

In New York, the commandant of the 5th (Fingal) Battalion, Thomas Ashe, was raising money for the volunteers, alongside Diarmuid Lynch. Redmond's speech curtailed their activities. The speech had so infuriated the Irish in America that they refused to go on donating funds. Ashe returned to Ireland. Passing through Belfast on his way south to Dublin, he called into the branch office of the Irish Transport Union to see, and confer with, James Connolly. Connolly, the Labour leader and commandant of the Irish Citizen Army, was now also a leading member of the IRB.

Up in the parishes around Fingal in north Dublin, Redmond's call split the ranks of the volunteers there too. Of those men who later took part in the Battle of Ashbourne, there was dismay, as Volunteer Michael McAllister revealed:

> In our Company in Swords, as was generally the case elsewhere, the greater portion of the Volunteers declared for John Redmond. I would say that about seventy per cent or more went on the Redmond side while about thirty per cent remained loyal to the Irish Volunteer executive. I remained with the Irish Volunteer Party.

In fact, seventy-five members went with Redmond. Bernard McAllister confirmed Michael's recollection, adding, 'The only ones who remained loyal were John and Mick McAllister, Charles and Bartle Weston and myself.' There was a strong family connection with some of the men. The McAllisters were cousins of the Westons, and they were cousins of the Kellys. There were a few more that remained loyal, not included in Michael McAllister's list. They were Richard Coleman, elected captain within the new grouping, Frank (Christy) Lawless, Edmund Colm, Joseph Lawless, Thomas Duff, Pat Early, Christopher Nugent, James Marks, Thomas, Joe and Christopher Taylor, Peter and John Kelly, Joe and William Norton, Peter and James Wilson (Peter was killed in the Mendicity Institution), and James and John Crennigan (John was killed at Ashbourne). Not all of them, however, turned out on Easter Monday.

Without direction from others, Bernard, or Bennie McAllister as he was more popularly known, seized the initiative:

The Company rifles at this time were kept by my father at our house. He had decided on the Redmond side. After the meeting at which the split took place, I went home, got a car and loaded all the rifles and equipment into it and brought them to McAllisters of Turvey. After that I had no further contact with the Donabate Volunteers and transferred to Swords.

At Swords, they also felt the pain at the split. As most of the volunteers there went with Redmond, the remainder were forced to look elsewhere for training. The young Christopher 'Kit' Moran relates:

We – the Swords Irish Volunteers – now secured a hall in Connor's Lane, and we met there openly for drill and other purposes. There was a rifle, with bayonet, left in the hall for drill purposes. I think this was an Italian rifle. It was kept in the hall continually, and neither the RIC or anyone else interfered with it. Dick Coleman now acted as our instructor. He had no previous experience in military matters but, with the aid of British Army manuals, he was able to carry on in a limited way.[10]

On 25 October 1914, five weeks after the split caused by the Woodenbridge speech, the Irish Volunteers held their first convention at the Abbey Theatre in Dublin and elected an Executive Committee. Eoin MacNeill remained chief of staff. Unknown to him, a majority on the executive committee that were also elected, were members of the IRB.

In Fingal, the Irish Volunteer deputy commandant, Thomas Ashe, collected together the remnants of his battalion; the men who had remained loyal to the original concept of the Irish Volunteers. They drilled and marched, manoeuvred and trained in the terrain which at some stage in the future they knew they must fight in. In reflection, years later, Piaras Beaslai wrote about the dedication and determination of the Fingal men in a series of articles, 'A Nation in Revolt', in the *Irish Independent* (14–15 January 1953):

> Early in November 1914, just after the Volunteer Convention in the Abbey Theatre, Tom Ashe, who was then a National Teacher at Lusk, and already the leading spirit of the Fifth, or Fingal Battalion, of the Volunteers, issued a challenge to the First and Second Battalions to march out to the Swords area and make a joint attack on a position prepared by him and occupied by his men at Broadmeadows, near Swords. The challenge was accepted and Sunday, November 8, was fixed as the day for the fight, which we came to call 'The Battle of Broadmeadows'.

For the clash, Ashe placed his men in a strong defensive position on the other side of the river at Broadmeadows. No matter how they manoeuvred, the First and Second Battalions could not overcome the Fingal men. Sean O'Luing in his biography of Ashe, *I Die in a Good Cause*, wrote that the experience of the ensuing engagement 'was a useful and instructive manoeuvre, one of many from which the Volunteers drew lessons…'. Ashe no doubt would have consulted his British Army manual for the best way of defending his position:

> When it is intended to occupy a defensive position, the chief points to be noted are:
>
> i. The best distribution of the infantry, and the means of protecting the flanks.
> ii. The positions which the enemy may endeavour to seize in order to develop an effective fire against the position.
> iii. Any points the possession of which might exert a decisive influence on the issue of the fight.
> iv. The most favourable lines of attack.
> v. The most favourable ground for the counter-attack.
> vi. Positions to be occupied in case of retreat.

Volunteer Christopher Moran of Swords appears to be referring to this exercise when he wrote:

Training went on continuously and included night exercises. On one occasion, our battalion successfully defended the Finglas area against the remainder of the Dublin Brigade. We also had exercises on the Dublin mountains with the other battalions of the brigade, and also in the Fingal brigade area.

At the beginning of 1915, a volunteer convention was called to restructure the Irish Volunteers after the Redmond split. Piaras Beaslai in his *Irish Independent* article wrote:

> On January 30 1915, a meeting of the Captains of the First Battalion elected Ned Daly, brother-in-law of Tom Clarke, as Commandant: and, at a subsequent meeting on February 10, I was elected Vice-Commandant. About the same time Thomas Aghas [Ashe] was elected Commandant of the Fifth Battalion, which at the time consisted of the Volunteer Companies in North Dublin – the bodies known in 1921 as the 'Fingal Brigade'.

Doctor Richard Hayes, the former commandant of the 5th, suggests that Ashe's appointment came much later, in April 1916, just days prior to the Rising. He relates that Ashe:

> was officially informed (verbally) by Connolly that the Rising was fixed to take place on Easter Sunday. He was permitted to impart this to Frank Lawless (Quartermaster) and myself. I immediately had a long conversation with Ashe regarding preparations &c, as he was at the time almost every day in Dublin and in close touch with things, he agreed to my suggestion that he should take over the function of Batt. Commandant while I would take on his duties of Adjutant. And in view of the nearness of the Rising we did not think it necessary to acquaint H.Q. of this. But I think (though not quite sure) that he informed Connolly.

There were three representatives from Fingal who attended the 1915 conference, held in the Abbey Theatre in Dublin, Frank Lawless, Michael McAllister and Kit Moran. Moran recalled of the meeting:

> Eoin MacNeill presided. And Bulmer Hobson, who was secretary, read a report on the organisation throughout the country. A committee of high officers, constituting an executive committee, was appointed, which included most of the men who afterward signed the 1916 proclamation

and were executed. A further committee was also appointed, and I was elected to represent the Swords area on this.

The IRB was successfully manoeuvring its men into senior positions within the executive. It was also recruiting new members. Joseph Lawless, upon reaching the age of eighteen, was sworn in as a member of the local IRB circle:

> I, ------ ------, in the presence of Almighty God, do solemnly swear allegiance to the Irish republic, now virtually established; and that I will do my very utmost, at every risk, while life lasts, to defend its independence and integrity; and finally, that I will yield implicit obedience in all things, not contrary to the laws of God, to the commands of my superior officers. So help me God! Amen.

Charles Weston from the Lusk Company also joined the secret organization, as he likewise testified in his Witness Statement (149):

> I joined the IRB about September 1915, and in being in close touch with Tom Ashe I understood there would be a rising and a fight. About a week before the rebellion Ned Daly paid us a visit. He made a speech to us and told us he expected to see us again very shortly under very different circumstances.

Intensive training continued at a pace. At Easter 1915, the Fingal Volunteers, along with the other Dublin Battalions, took part in manoeuvres which were intended to be reflected in their actions one year later. The exercise was mounted over an extensive front, from Blanchardstown to Santry, with a front launched south into County Wicklow. In September, there was another manoeuvre covering a similar wide area. This time, as before, the Fingal men were the defensive force, fending off the other companies of the Dublin Brigade. Jerry Golden of the 1st Battalion of the Dublin Brigade was in the attacking force:

> About the middle of September the entire 1st Battalion were ordered out for manoeuvres on a Saturday afternoon. The area covered was from Phibsboro to Blanchardstown and back down to upper Finglas and Glasnevin. The village of Upper Finglass was supposed to be held by two companies and the other four companies were to attempt to capture it. I had a busy time of it bringing messages from the Comdt. [Edward Daly] to the attacking Companies and bringing reports from them back to him, while at the same time avoiding capture by the scouts of the defending

Companies. However, my knowledge of the country over which the engagement took part enabled me to get through with all my messages safe. This experience of manoeuvres with the then entire battalion stood them well, for shortly afterwards the entire Dublin Brigade carried out a similar engagement.[11]

What Golden fails to record was that it was another victory for the Fingal men and their co-defenders. The war games did not go unnoticed. The police took notes of the procedure and reported accordingly to the county inspector, who included them in his report to government:

A large contingent of the city Sinn Fein section proceeded to Rush and Lusk railway station where they detrained and were met by contingents from Lusk, Donabate, Swords and Skerries in the county Dublin. 100 had bicycles and 250 were on foot. Those on bicycles went on to Skerries where they stacked their bicycles and scattered on the different roads leading out of Skerries to attack the 250 on foot who were the invading party. Subsequently the various contingents returned home.[12]

In addition to their own training amongst the local terrain, the battalion also received pep talks to increase morale and theoretical training, derived from the British Army's training manuals. Now, more frequently, they were also visited by the volunteer executive and its appointees. The Fingal men, Bernard McAllister recalled, were visited by Commandant Edward Daly, as referred to above, Con Colbert of Fianna Éireann and Bulmer Hobson, who was now a leading member of the IRB inner circle.

Charles Weston details in his Witness Statement how the Company progressed during 1915 and beyond:

We had plenty of .22 rifle practice. We bought our own ammunition; it was plentiful then. We also had a pistol about .38 calibre and we got practice with this also. We won a shooting competition for which we got a new .22 rifle. We had lectures each week by a Mr. S. O'Duffy who was an ex-British officer. These covered general field training, running of camps and field tactics. We had exercises with the rest of the Battalion at Broad Meadow and on one occasion staged an attack on the town of Skerries.

In the Swords Company, post-split, Bernard McAllister recalled the continued training for his unit, in preparation for the longed-for and inevitable day. In his Witness Statement, he recalled:

> We had field exercises for the Company and Battalion around Saucerstown and the Broad meadows. We had had Brigade exercises at Finglas and St Margaret's and on one occasion we went to Ticknock with the Brigade. We cycled to the city and marched from the city to Ticknock and back. Each section had a .22 rifle for target practice and .22 ammunition was plenty… We got plenty of practice with the .22 rifle. We were still very short of service rifles and were mostly armed with shotguns for which we made some buck shot. There was also some hand grenades which were made locally.

Lectures for the Fingal officers were organized weekly at Turvey. These lectures were given by Colonel J.J. (Ginger) O'Connell on tactics and Thomas McDonagh on supply problems, as Volunteer Lieutenant Joseph Lawless revealed in his Witness Statement. Inter-company and inter-battalion exercises now became more and more frequent:

> Sometimes we travelled towards the city or even across it to the Rathfarnham side to attack or defend against one of the city battalions, and on at least one Sunday a representative parade of all the city battalions marched out to Swords under Éamon de Valera, and engaged in an exercise at Skerries against the Fingal Battalion, marching back to the city that night. This provided great fun for the local RIC who frantically endeavoured to keep a close watch on all that went on, not knowing whether we were trying to cover a German landing at Skerries or Rush, or merely causing a diversion to cover something equally dreadful elsewhere.

On 17 March 1916, St Patrick's Day, there was a volunteer review at College Green in Dublin city centre. Eoin MacNeill, chief of staff, took the salute. The different companies of the Dublin Brigade paraded in the morning at the various churches throughout the city. Later, they assembled in College Green, where they gave a display of military manoeuvres, concluding with a march past Eoin MacNeill and the members of the volunteer executive, who had previously inspected the men in the ranks. Ashe led the Fingal Volunteers, preceded by the musicians of the Black Raven Band, of which he was a member. Brother Allen from the O'Connell Schools in North Richmond Street recalled that he stood out amongst his fellow volunteers. He created a strong presence. Allen remarked, 'You could not take your eyes off him. He had charisma.'[13] The operations lasted from 11am until 1pm, and for two hours, the trams and other vehicular traffic was peremptorily suspended by the volunteers, most of whom carried rifles and bayonets, and whose numbers were estimated at 2,000. This was an incident that should have rung alarm bells in the British administration within Dublin Castle. It was an indication of the determination now felt by pro-Republican Ireland. Some British officers in a car approached from Dublin Castle, wishing to drive through the assembled volunteers. Éamon de Valera's 3rd Battalion was lined up and blocking the way. The driver blew his horn but without effect. The senior British officer in the car insisted that they should be allowed to pass, determined not to turn aside. De Valera was equally insistent that they could not come through until the parade was over. Words were exchanged before de Valera warned them that, if necessary, he would use force if they attempted to push their way through. De Valera gave the order, 'Don't let that car through!' In the end, the British officer backed down and the car was reversed, its driver finding an alternate route. The *Irish Times* observed that, 'This demonstration in the centre of Dublin on St Patrick's Day was the first time the Irish Volunteers had taken aggressive action in daylight, but on several occasions previously they had conducted night manoeuvres and practised street fighting.'

Having been appointed commandant of the Fingal Battalion, Ashe was asked by Joseph Plunkett, Director of Military Operations, to draw up a plan of future activity in his area, which was outside the city boundary. A couple of months later, with his plan prepared, Ashe met up with Piaris Beaslai and Con Collins at what was then a regular weekly meeting place, the Tyrone Restaurant in Cathedral Street, Dublin. 'After lunch,' Beaslai recalled in his series of accounts for the *Irish Independent*:

> I brought Tomas and Con to 61, Middle Abbey Street, the office of the Irish Journalists Association, of which I was secretary, and there Tomas… submitted some plans and details. I remember that he had two or three maps of areas in Fingal, drawn by himself, with positions marked on them, and some explanatory papers. I listened attentively to his explanations and it is recorded that I submitted his plans and papers to Plunkett at the next meeting of the Volunteer Executive, four days later.

Ashe and his men were training hard now they had a clearly defined plan of operation. They awaited only the day when that plan could be put into operation.

Ashe's plan was absorbed into a greater plan. Donal O'Hannigan, a regional organizer was summoned to Dublin by Pearse. Quite unexpectedly, but perhaps because of his organizational ability, Pearse informed him that he was appointed commandant to take charge of the Louth–Meath–South Down–South Armagh and South Monaghan area. The number on the volunteers roll in that area was 1,337. The biggest unit in the area was Dundalk with about 270 men. For the moment, there were no specific instructions regarding the plan to be followed.

During Lent 1916, training was intensified, with the Fingal men engaged in long route marches and exercises in the Garristown–Naul–Swords area. On the Thursday before Easter, Charles Weston was talking to Ashe. The talk got around to when they would put their training into action. Ashe was guarded in his response. He did not confirm the date of the Rising but hinted 'that Sunday would be our last mobilisation'. From this, Weston took it that the big day had at last come. This belief seemed confirmed when Ashe later instructed Weston, a fellow IRB member:

> to go to Swords on Good Friday night to Lawless's shop and that there would be arms and ammunition coming from Dublin. He said that Frank Lawless might want some help and he did not want the Volunteers to generally know about this. I went there on Friday night. Rifles, ammunition and medical supplies had arrived from Dublin.

In the week leading up to Easter, before the arrival of any promised additional arms, Kit Moran revealed:

> By now, all our men were armed with a rifle of some sort and some ammunition, or a shotgun. A few had revolvers also. Some of the rifles were the ones that had been landed at Howth. Each Volunteer had to pay for his own rifle or other weapon which he received. He was at liberty to buy arms from any source he could, but the great bulk of ours came from Volunteer headquarters in Dublin. Our men were generally good shots as they had been used to handling and firing sporting weapons, but very few had had practice in firing service weapons.

This was soon to change when practice became reality. Joseph Lawless in an article in *The Capuchin Annual 1966*, recorded the summary of arms, ammunition and explosives held by the Fingal Battalion by Easter Monday:

> Arms:
> Modern service rifles including long and short Lee-Enfield and 9mm Mauser – 12–15
> Old-type Mauser (Howth Rifle) – 10–12
> Martini Enfield single shot carbine – 12–15
> Single-barrel 12-bore shot-guns – 20–30

Revolvers and pistols, various types and calibres (.455, .38, .32, .25) – 12–14

Ammunition (total available to all units):
.303 and 9mm – about 100 rounds per weapon
Old Mauser about 60 rounds per weapon
Shot-gun loaded with buck-shot – about 300 rounds per weapon
Pistol ammunition, various – about 30 rounds per weapon

Explosives:
Sixty pounds of gelignite and two home-made canister grenades

The arms and ammunition were loaded aboard Lawless's horse van and driven to Lawless's home in Saucerstown. Weston reported back to Ashe, who told him, 'the Rising was starting on Sunday and that everything was ready'. Earlier that Good Friday morning, on one of his almost daily trips into Dublin, Ashe got a verbal order from Connolly that operations should begin at 7pm on Easter Sunday night. In accordance, an order was sent out on Saturday morning to the four companies of the battalion to mobilize with a day's rations at 12 o'clock (midday) on Easter Sunday at Rathbeale Cross, a few miles north of Swords.

Chapter 2

He Rises on Sunday, and We on Monday

Previously in the 8 April 1916 edition of the Volunteers' own newspaper, *The Irish Volunteer*, Padraig Pearse issued the following directive:

1. Following the lines of last year, every unit of the Irish Volunteers will hold manoeuvres during the Easter Holidays. The object of the manoeuvres is to test mobilization with equipment.
2. In the Brigade Districts the manoeuvres will be carried out under the Orders of the Brigade Commandants. In the case of the Dublin Brigade, the manoeuvres will, as last year be carried out under the direction of the Headquarters General Staff.
3. Each Brigade, Battalion or Company Commander as the case may be, will on or before 1st May next, send to the Director of Organization a detailed report of the Manoeuvres carried out by the unit.

Headquarters: 2, Dawson St., Dublin 3rd April 1916
P.H. Pearse, Commandant, Director of Organization.

This was the announcement to those in the know of the date of the Rising. In the days leading up to the announcement, secret instructions were issued by Pearse to the IRB commandants of volunteers throughout Ireland. He outlined the territory each brigade was to hold in the coming insurrection, while they in the Dublin Brigade, combined with the Irish Citizen Army, would seize the capital. Before the 'manoeuvres', each commandant was to receive further specific instructions. Up in Fingal, Thomas Ashe was charged with destroying all communications north of the city and preventing British reinforcements from Athlone proceeding south into Dublin. Details of the part to be played by the Fingal Battalion are outlined in two later Witness Statements; those of Piaras Beaslai and Donal O'Hannigan.[1] O'Hannigan described his part of the plan of operation:

> On Tuesday morning I went to see P. Pearse at St Enda's at 11 a.m. Pearse went through the plans for the Rising. Sean Boylan from Dunboyne arrived also after some time and Pearse gave me instructions about my

own role in the general plan. I was to mobilise the Volunteers from the area at Tara in Meath on Sunday (Easter) at 7 p.m. …then to march via Dunshaughlion, Blanchardstown where we would contact Sean Boylan and the Dunboyne men. We were to seize the railway at Blanchardstown and cut the line there to prevent the English Artillery coming from Athlone. The Fingal Bn. (5th Bn. Dublin Brigade) were to contact us on our left flank and the Kildare men were to come in on our right flank. The Wicklow and South Co. Dublin area was to be on the right of them again. In this way we would form a ring around the city. The ring would extend from Swords via Blanchard town – Lucan – Tallaght and thence across the hills to the sea. All units forming this line except the Fingal Bn. came under my orders when established. Pearse did not inform me why the Fingal Battalion would not come under my command and I did not ask him at the time.

Pearse explained the object in taking and organizing the encirclement of the city. Firstly, to prevent an attack on the city from the rear; secondly, to prevent reinforcements reaching the city; thirdly, to maintain a supply of food for the volunteers and people of the city; and, finally, in the case of an evacuation of the city being forced on them to hold lines of retreat open towards the west. Pearse gave extra emphasis to the final point. He pointed out to Boylan, the Captain of Dunboyne Company, the importance of holding the Blanchardstown position and awaiting the arrival of Commandant O'Hannigan.

The plan in essence was that the 5th, under Ashe, was to act as the fulcrum of a huge wheel encircling Dublin, to link up with Edward Daly's 1st Battalion along the North Circular Road at Phibsboro'. As the 5th moved south, Donal O'Hannigan's 4th Battalion were to swing round in a huge arc to link up with Ashe's men, just to the west of the city. O'Hannigan was instructed like Ashe, to report to the Executive Council on the following Friday, Good Friday, for a final briefing. At this point, they were both informed that the Rising had been provisionally fixed to start at 7pm on Easter Sunday night.

Then the volunteers' plans started to unravel. MacNeill discovered that the IRB had taken over the volunteers and were going to use them in the Rising. Angrily, he confronted Pearse, who told him that there was nothing he could do about it. Plans were in motion. MacNeill was pacified a little when he discovered that a ship from Germany, loaded with arms, was about to land its cargo off the west coast of Ireland, and German soldiers would also arrive to aid the volunteers. The arrival of German troops was a fallacy, but the arms ship was very much a reality.

On 9 April, the SS *Aud* (formerly the *Libau*), an impounded Allied vessel under the command of Captain Spindler of the German Imperial Naval Reserve, with a crew of 21 officers and men, sailed out of Lubec. The ship was disguised as a Norwegian freighter. Ostensibly, she was shipping a cargo of timber. Below decks, she carried a cargo of 20,000 captured Russian rifles, 10 machine guns and a million rounds of ammunition. Spindler sailed his ship between Norway and the Shetland Islands, then south between Iceland and the Faroes, and on to Ireland. The plan was that the ship would appear off the western coast of Ireland to the north of Inishtooskert Island, at the entrance to Tralee Bay, sometime after 10pm on a date not fixed but during the period of Thursday, 20 April to Easter Saturday, 22 April. One major problem with the operation was that the *Aud* lacked a radio. So, each night during that period, a pilot boat was commissioned to sail off the coast and identify herself to the *Aud* by displaying two green lights. Evading a Royal Navy blockade off the west of Ireland, the *Aud* approached her destination on the morning of Holy Thursday.

Previously, on 12 April, Sir Roger Casement, his aide Robert Monteith and a third man, Daniel Bailey, had boarded a German submarine, *U-19*, commanded by Lieutenant Commander Raimund Weisbach with a crew of 30 officers and men. The trip from Heligoland to Tralee lasted five days; most of the journey was carried out on the surface. Unknown to the IRB Military Council, British Naval Intelligence had broken the German naval code back in February 1916. All messages between Germany, the United States and Ireland were intercepted and decoded. Alerted to the presence of the *Aud*, Admiral Sir Lewis Bayley, commander-in-chief at Queenstown, County Cork, instituted special observations along the west coast of Ireland. Some twenty-nine auxiliary ships and boats of the Royal Navy began looking for the ship. On Holy Thursday, they were joined by the cruiser HMS *Gloucester*, plus three destroyers. Then Bayley received a wire that there had been a concentration of cars near Fenit, in Tralee Bay – a possible landing site.

Approaching Tralee, the *Aud* jettisoned her false cargo overboard. Steam winches and unloading tackle were made ready. The hatches were uncovered. Everything was made ready for a swift unloading so that they could be away before the British got wind of what was going on. Spindler was in no position to defend his ship against a heavily armed Royal Navy ship, nor could he outrun one. Shortly after midday, Spindler sighted the Irish coast. Gently, he eased the *Aud* toward Inishtooskert to rendezvous with the U-boat carrying Sir Roger Casement. As she progressed along the coast, she came to the attention of the coastal watch station at Loop Head. They reported that a steamer was acting suspiciously. The *Aud* sailed on to Fenit, with its little pier and lighthouse.

Here, she remained overnight eagerly watching for the pilot boat with two green lights. On Good Friday morning, the Royal Navy armed trawler, *Setter II*, spotted the *Aud* and went to investigate. Spindler explained away the *Aud*'s presence because of engine problems. Satisfied, the *Setter* resumed its patrol. Spindler, to avoid further speculation, decided to sail his ship down to Queenstown, then return back to Fenit at dusk. About 1pm, Lieutenant W.H.A, Bee, aboard the trawler *Lord Heneage*, received a message that a suspicious vessel had been sighted in Tralee Bay. As the *Heneage* approached the *Aud*, Spindler's nerve broke, and he decided to try and outrun the armed trawler. The *Lord Heneage* opened fire at long range, but the shot fell short. Bee sent a radio message to Admiral Bayley, 'Suspicious vessel sighted south of Tearaght, steering south-west.' Orders went out, and two sloops, *Zinnia* and *Bluebell*, hastened to intercept the fleeing steamer. By 6.15pm, the naval ships approached the *Aud*. By flag message the *Zinnia*'s commander, G.F. Wilson, signalled the *Aud* to enter the port at Queenstown for inspection. With no opportunity of escaping, Spindler ordered the *Aud* to be scuttled.

Unknowing of the drama being played out at Queenstown, shortly after dark *U-19*, with Sir Roger Casement aboard, passed the mouth of the Shannon. The submarine continued on to Inishtooshert where it expected to rendezvous with the *Aud*. The *U-19* cruised off the coast for about an hour and a half, waiting for the two green lights to show. Lieutenant Commander Weisbach announced that he could not risk his boat any longer. The *U-19* headed off for Tralee Bay, where he put the three Irishmen ashore. Robert Monteith, Casement's able lieutenant went off to look for assistance. Casement, not the healthiest of men, had not slept for 24 hours. He was tired and exhausted. Bailey, the third Irishman, also went off to search for help. A little later, the boat they had come ashore in was discovered. A search was begun. Casement was discovered in a ruin known as MacKenna's Fort. He was questioned but nothing was forthcoming. In the end, he was sent to Dublin for further questioning, but his identity was still unknown. News of the *Aud*'s scuttling and the arrest of a stranger at Tralee reached Dublin. Having read the censored accounts in the Saturday morning newspaper, O'Rahilly went to see MacNeill. The newspapers reported that a man had been captured at Ardfert in Kerry after landing from, it was believed, a German submarine. Casement was not named, but both MacNeill and O'Rahilly could make a good guess as to who it was. Then came the news of the sinking of the arms ship. MacNeill rightly decided that a rising now would be suicidal. He wrote out a set of countermanding orders to be delivered to all the Battalion commanders in Dublin and all the volunteer units throughout the country, cancelling any instructions they might have received regarding a rising. Then he and O'Rahilly drove over to

St Enda's school where they confronted Pearse. The IRB leader was resolved that the Rising would go on, callously observing 'We have used your name and influence for all their worth – now we don't need you any more. It's no use you trying to stop us. Our plans are laid and they will be carried out.'[2] MacNeill warned Pearse that he intended to forbid any mobilisation. Pearse dismissed the threat, but MacNeill was in earnest. Without the arms, any rising was doomed, and the volunteers would be needlessly killed. He went to the offices of the *Irish Independent*, and had the following announcement inserted in the next day's edition:

> Owing to the very critical position, all orders given to the Irish Volunteers for tomorrow, Easter Sunday, are hereby rescinded and no parades, marches, or any other movement of Irish Volunteers will take place. Each individual Volunteer will obey this order strictly in every particular.

All over Ireland that Sunday there was confusion and disbelief. There had been high expectations all the previous week that something special was in the offing. Joseph Lawless of the Swords Company of the Volunteers summed up the expectation when he wrote:

> One might think that, at this stage, excitement would be at fever pitch, seeing that we had already been warned for a muster parade on Easter Sunday. This and the other indications seemed to place beyond doubt that a general rising was planned for that day. Strangely enough, however, I remember discussing the probabilities in this way with Joe Taylor of Swords, who was my constant companion at the time, and, while there was a certain pitch of anticipation in the air, there was a considerable confidence that victory was within our grasp.

Then it was all snatched away by MacNeill's cancellation order. No one knew what to believe. Certainly, through the newspapers was not the accepted way of receiving instructions. Bernard McAllister was up early that Sunday morning. Reading the *Irish Independent*, he saw that the parade was off. Rather than waste the day, after Mass, he went in to Dublin to play in a football match. Dublin was quiet like any normal early Sunday morning. Cancellation orders or not, and many would not have seen MacNeill's order, the Fingal men assembled as per their original orders. Lawless again:

> The town was in a buzz of discussion, everybody scanning the newspapers and then watching the Volunteers coming in from Lusk, from Skerries

and from St Margaret's,…nearly every man on the rolls in every company turned up that day, but no official orders arrived which, I think, worried the battalion staff considerably. Ashe, therefore, decided to take the men away from the town and give them something to occupy them, so they marched to Saucerstown where a tactical exercise was carried out.

Charles Weston, a lieutenant in the Lusk Company, was one of those who assembled at the Rathbeale Cross at 12 noon. He estimated the muster to be 120 men. Intelligence Officer Thomas Peppard estimated the number to be a little fewer at 100. Frank Lawless of Saucerstown, the battalion quartermaster issued a lot of single-barrel shotguns to those who had no weapons. They were new and of American manufacture. With no orders from Connolly, Ashe decided to take the men on a route march, hoping beyond hope that orders would arrive. After their route march, the volunteers reassembled at the home of Frank Lawless. There they waited until midnight, before Ashe told them that the 'big event' had been postponed, but they were to hold themselves in readiness. Then they were dismissed. Charlie Weston decided that the day was not completely wasted. There was a weekly dance at Lusk that went on until the early hours. He and a few others set off to that. Thomas Peppard the Fingal Brigade's Intelligence Officer was one of the group. He wrote: 'After the dismissal at Saucerstown on Easter Sunday night some of us went to a ceili in Lusk and turned in to our normal work on Easter Monday.'

In Dublin, there was furious activity, trying to retrieve something from MacNeill's cancellation. All through that Sunday afternoon and evening, Michael McAllister of Swords Company recalled:

There was great coming and going of Battalion Staff Officers and it was quite apparent that something serious had gone wrong. We had got the Sunday newspaper and had seen MacNeill's countermanding order on it and we were busy surmising what had happened and, of course, there was the usual batch of rumours afloat.

In the weeks before Easter, Lord Middleton, a southern Ireland Unionist had called upon Lord Wimborne, the Lord Lieutenant of Ireland, at his London residence to discuss the very grave reports of an increase in volunteer recruitment and open threats of an early rebellion. Wimborne sought to reassure him in that MacNeill had laid it down that the volunteers were not to resort to force unless an attempt was made to disarm or disband them. Now with news that Casement had been arrested and the *Aud* sunk, followed by MacNeill's order countermanding volunteer exercises on Easter Sunday, the authorities in Dublin were convinced that no rebellion would take place. General Friend, commanding the Forces in Ireland, went on leave to England.

Meanwhile, Ashe sent Joseph Lawless to Dublin with a written and verbal message for James Connolly at Liberty Hall. Ashe informed Connolly that his battalion stood under arms in readiness and awaited orders. Lawless rode Ashe's Birmingham-made, two-stroke New Hudson motorcycle into Dublin, a journey of just twenty minutes. Weston reveals that there was 'an air of suspense' about the city. It was early morning. There were very few people about the streets and with very little traffic.

In Gardiner Street, a few pedestrians 'gazed curiously at the armed and uniformed Volunteer dashing wildly along as if on some hell-bent and desperate mission; my loaded British service revolver in holster was, I hoped, intimidatingly displayed on my belt.' Lawless rode up to Liberty Hall:

> Liberty Hall was a building I had never been inside before. I was rather surprised, if anything, to find a Citizen army man on guard inside the door. As everywhere had looked so deserted, I half expected to find no one there, but, with very little ceremony, he took me upstairs, along a passage, and announced me to someone in a room, returning himself to his post at the door. The other man went into a room or office next to his own, and almost at once James Connolly called me in...He shook my hand effusively before reading Ashe's note. I think this was the first indication he had from any Volunteer Commander during the day that sounded encouraging.

After a ten-minute briefing, Connolly instructed Lawless to tell Ashe that 'all was off for the moment, but to hold in readiness to act at any time'. Lawless reported back to Fingal. Equally concerned was Commandant Donal O'Hannigan, who was due to link up with Ashe in the master plan. He sent one of his junior officers, Captain Sean McEntee, to make enquiries. He was told to go to 21 Upper Dorset Street, the home of O'Hannigan's uncle, an IRB man. He directed him to Connolly at Liberty Hall. The message was the same; the Rising was off, but to hold the men in readiness. McEntee reported back to O'Hannigan, who like Ashe had assembled his men. At about 3am on Easter Monday, O'Hannigan sent his men home. McEntee was sent back to Liberty Hall to await further instructions.

In Liberty Hall early that Easter Sunday, there was total chaos following the news of MacNeill's cancellation. Earlier that morning, Connolly got word from his daughter Nora that something had gone wrong. She arrived at Liberty Hall having journeyed down from the north with news that the northern mobilisation had been cancelled. Then somebody brought in a copy of the *Irish Independent* with MacNeill's cancellation order. Connolly sent out a number of women as messengers to the other members of the military council, requesting their presence at Liberty Hall as soon as possible. The members duly arrived, and at 9am and until 1pm, they discussed the situation. The final decision was that in view of MacNeill's action, the Rising should go ahead, a day later, at noon on Easter Monday.

Chapter 3

Monday: Confusion and Certainty

Sunday evening passed, but no orders were received in Fingal. A little after midnight, instructed by Ashe, Dr Hayes and Frank Lawless drove to Dublin. Liberty Hall was locked up. The two then proceeded to call at the addresses of prominent volunteer leaders. At a house in North Richmond Street, they were admitted to the home of Michael O'Hanrahan. He, and those with him, were equally confused. Hanrahan's advice was that they should go home and disband their men but advise them to be ready to mobilise at any moment. Driving back to Fingal, Ashe and Captain Dick Coleman spent the night at the home of Hayes in Lusk.

The following morning, Joseph Lawless was woken from a deep sleep by a:

violent knocking on the front door, and heard my father going down to open it. Listening to excited voices in the hall below I recognized my Aunt Mary's voice, and felt that something had happened out of the ordinary to bring her here at this hour. Mary was my father's elder sister; she was a member of Cumann na mBan [the female auxiliary of the volunteers].

When my father came into my room holding a piece of paper in his hand, his eyes were alight with the excitement of joyful news, and with the announcement 'the day has come at last.' He handed me the note to read…I read the one line message – 'Strike at one o'clock today.'

Shouting to me from his own room, where he too was hurriedly getting some clothes on, Father directed me to take the message with all speed to Ashe.[1]

Shortly after 7am, having got just four hours sleep, Hayes and his two guests were awakened by heavy knocking at the door. It was Joseph Lawless who handed Ashe the dispatch from Padraig Pearse. The note read, 'Strike at one o'clock to-day.' Ashe shook Lawless by the hand, exclaiming, 'This will be the day to be remembered in Ireland for evermore.' Orders were at once issued to the four companies to mobilise at 12 noon at Knocksedan, a few miles from Swords.

At 9am that Easter Monday, Joseph Taylor arrived at the home of Kit Moran, urgently driving a pony and trap:

He took me with him, and we called on James Marks. Taylor now left me back at my house, with instructions to mobilise at Knocksedan crossroads at twelve noon that day. I arrived at Knocksedan about 11 a.m. There were about eighteen men from the Swords area there. Dick Coleman marshalled us and inspected us. He then detailed Joseph Taylor and me to act as sentinels on the Ballymun road, at the Boot Inn. Other men were sent out on the other roads. We received no specific orders as regards our duties. Taylor and I were at the Boot Inn, which is the better part of a mile from Knocksedan, for about an hour when Thomas Taylor came for us and brought us back to Knocksedan. When we were passing Bewley's house near the bridge, he said to us, 'It's on!' …Dick Coleman now sent the pair of us down to the main Swords–Rolestown road to cut the telegraph wire'.[2]

Mick McAllister of Turvey was out working in the fields when the summons came:

On Easter Monday morning Dick Coleman arrived with orders for a mobilisation at Knocksedan at once. My brother and I packed up the work we were doing on the farm and set out for Knocksedan on our cycles and, on arriving there we found men arriving from the other different areas. Doctor Hayes, Tom Ashe and Frank Lawless and his son Joseph, two brothers Ned and Jem were there amongst many others that I knew. Tom Ashe was in charge of operations. Every man had a cycle and was armed with a service rifle or a shot gun. Roughly about fifty men had mobilized. This was much smaller than the mobilisation on the previous day.[3]

Lieutenant Joseph Lawless rode over to St Margaret's on Ashe's motorcycle to mobilize the volunteers there. He was met with a rebuff:

Doubt was cast upon the genuineness of the call. Tom Duke was getting ready to open drills for potatoes when I called and he told me he was not going to be fooled by such false alarms again. This was a reference to the previous day's parade. However, after some words on the matter, he assured me that the St Margaret's men would be there when they heard the first shots fired and I had to be satisfied with this. Looking back on it, one can hardly blame a busy farmer intent on taking advantage of the fine weather, for not dropping his work to rush off on what he supposed might be another wild goose chase.[4]

When it came to it, Tom Duke and his brother Richard and a fair portion of the St Margaret's men answered the call and joined Ashe. Charles Weston, a stone mason by trade, following the order to stand down, had gone off to a local dance. He had got home about 5.30am and went wearily to bed. Two hours later there was an urgent knocking at his door:

> I was at home after the dance about two hours when I was mobilized again by Joseph Lawless. This was about 7.30 a.m. on Monday morning. We were to mobilise at Knocksedan at 10 a.m. I mobilized my section and proceeded to Knocksedan. Tom Ashe and Frank Lawless were there. Mobilisation was completed at 12 a.m. there were very few there, only Swords men. There were about 63 all present now.[5]

Elsewhere, Dr Richard Hayes was also rallying the local volunteers. On his way to Knocksedan, he was halted at the Post Office in Lusk:

> The postmistress, whom I knew very well, asked me to accompany her to her sitting room. There she told me that she had just received a wire in code from Dublin Castle to the Lusk police sergeant. She was familiar with the code from frequent messages. This particular one to the police sergeant was to the effect that he was to make immediate arrangements for the arrest of Ashe and myself. (I mention this incident because I think that similar messages were sent to various Volunteer centres in the country, and because it tends to show that the Rising leaders were right in their view that there was to be a general swoop by Dublin Castle on that day.)

In Dublin Castle, there had been some concern about the intended mass volunteer gatherings on Easter Sunday. However, with their cancellations, tensions were eased. It had given the British authorities something to think about though. As a precaution, the authorities decided to act, by arresting the volunteer leaders as a temporary measure. This suggestion has been refuted, but clearly arrests had been discussed in Dublin Castle.

The following day, Easter Monday, in Dublin and elsewhere in Ireland it was a Bank Holiday. It was a public holiday; a chance to have a day out. For Dubliners, undoubtedly the highlight of the day was the horse racing at Fairyhouse. Having been stood down, a number of the Fingal men went off to enjoy a day out with the rest of Dublin. Everyone seemed to be there, including a fair proportion of the British garrisons; officers and men alike, ready to have a flutter. Then suddenly in the early afternoon there was tension.

The word quickly spread round the race-going crowd. There were disturbances in Dublin. The Rising had started. In response, Bernard McAllister and his six companions set off immediately for home:

> On arriving home I got in touch with other men of our section and found that it had mobilised that morning. We decided to get off immediately and make contact with the Battalion or the Company. We took our rifles and ammunition and 24 hours' rations. We went to McAllisters of Turvey and there learned that the Company had gone to Finglas. We started off for Finglas – six of us. En route we found the Battalion at Knocksedan.[6]

At Rathbeale Cross, the volunteers were assembling. Joseph Lawless looked closely at those who were present:

> About fifteen to twenty men, including most of the officers, had uniforms. The remainder wore their equipment: bandolier, haversack and belt over civilian clothes. Most of the men of the unit owned bicycles. [Other transport consisted of] one horse and farm dray belonging to my father, was the only heavy transport…In addition there was a Morris Oxford two seater belonging to Doctor Hayes, and a motor cycle belonging to Thomas Ashe.[7]

They were about to take on the British Empire. Ashe informed the men of their task. It was to prevent British reinforcements from reaching Dublin. The main part of this plan was to blow the Rogerstown Viaduct Bridge carrying the Great Northern Railway between Belfast and Dublin. As prearranged, Charles Weston, Lieutenant of Lusk Company, was now ordered to do so. When originally told of the date of the Rising, that previous Saturday, Weston had requested to lay the charges at the granite buttresses that Saturday night at low tide. Ashe's response was one of caution. 'No,' he said. They 'had to be careful not to make any visible moves whatsoever, that everything was to start as a surprise. This surprise was vital, as if the military discovered anything, it would be detrimental to the whole plan of the Volunteers.' Now he had the go ahead – but circumstances had changed. Weston was accompanied in his task by Lieutenant Joseph V. Lawless. Some 50 pounds of gelignite, fuses and detonators were strapped on to Ashe's motorcycle, ridden by Lawless. Weston accompanied him on his bicycle. At Morganstown, they rendezvoused with half a dozen of Weston's Lusk Company, led by Ned Rooney. Amongst Rooney's men was a quarryman, John McCann, experienced in the use of dynamite. Weston now revealed the plan to Rooney. They were going to blow the bridge. The Rising was on. Arriving at the bridge, four men were posted to hold the northern approach to the bridge to warn the others of any attempt to impede their mission. Now came the change in circumstances as Weston revealed in his 1950s Witness Statement:

> When we got to Rogerstown the tide was flowing very strong through the arches and it was impossible to get the charges placed at the buttresses… We put the charges between the girders of the bridge. We set the fuses off, and the resultant explosion blew the rails out of position and made the line unserviceable. This was only of a temporary nature and it was easily repaired by railway engineers during the week.

Indeed, it was only a temporary measure. The line was damaged to the extent of £250. All traffic was transferred to the up line. There was an attempt made to blow up the down line between the middle arch at Fairview slob lands and the Wharf Road. The rails were damaged, but the traffic here was also transferred to the up line.

Meanwhile as the explosives were being put in place, the telephone and telegraph wires that ran alongside the line were ordered to be cut. After one unsuccessful attempt, Lawless himself mounted the pole to cut the wires. It was hard work with the cutter provided, but eventually he succeeded. Just then:

> A tremendous explosion shook the embankment and nearly swept me from the top of the telegraph pole which I clutched frantically with both arms. Looking up I could see rails, sleepers and all kinds of debris hurtling in my direction. One big baulk of timber came whirling and over end across me, to land about twenty yards away at the foot of the embankment. Hastily slithering down the pole without regard to splinters I joined the others in a sprint for the road and our bicycles and safety.

The men then returned to Knockscedan, cutting further telephone wires as they did so. Kit Moran from Swords Company, lacking a ladder to climb up the pole, used his ingenuity. He got a strong length of cord to which he attached a stone, which he then threw over the wire. By pulling down on both ends, the Volunteers broke the telephone cable, thus breaking communications between Dublin and the north.

On the return journey, Ashe's motorcycle, carrying Lawless, broke down when it ran out of petrol. Lawless continued on, on the back of Charlie Weston's bike, to Finglas, where the battalion had reassembled. They arrived about 4.30pm, having completed a sixteen-mile circuitous journey, avoiding any contact with the RIC or British soldiers. Here they discovered that the others were digging trenches along the road near the golf links, along the Ashbourne to Dublin Road, in accordance with fresh orders from Volunteer Headquarters. Their new orders were to hold the main road and ambush or fire upon on any enemy British troops that might appear. A camp had been established on high ground east of the Dublin Road. Any assault upon their position would not be easy. The only access from the road was by a gateway, which was heavily covered by the volunteers. On the north side was the village of Finglas, whose houses, walls and hedges would provide a succession of defences if any assault came from that direction. To the south and east were open fields across which any enemy could not advance unseen. Lawless and Weston reported their partial success to Ashe. Having achieved their original orders, Ashe informed them that he was now awaiting further orders from Dublin.

Ashe's original orders were to blow the bridge at Rogerstown and prevent any relieving British troops from the north reaching Dublin. He was also to link up with the 1st Battalion operating in the Four Courts area of the city, as Piaras Beaslai explained in his Witness Statement:

> Tom Ashe told me that his instructions were to establish touch with the 1st Battalion on Easter Monday and arrange some system of co-operation. In pursuance of this order he arranged for a (Fingal) Volunteer in uniform to wait at Cross Guns Bridge, at the time of our taking up our positions, for a messenger from us; but, though he waited a long time, no messenger arrived.

Within the city, Edward Daly, Commandant of the 1st Battalion was unable to establish contact with the Fingal men. All too quickly, at the outbreak of the Rising, the British had sealed off the city along the North Circular Road with field artillery and soldiers. It was impossible to get through the lines.

At about 6.30pm that Monday evening, Captain Sean McEntee, riding a motorcycle, having succeeded in eluding the British soldiers, reported back to Commandant Donal O'Hannigan at Lurgan Green near Dundalk. He had an urgent despatch from Pearse. It read, 'Dublin is in arms. You will carry out your original instructions.' Following the debacle of Easter Sunday, O'Hannigan was left with just 28 men. The volunteers from Ardee and Dunleer failed to turn up. Despite their shortage in numbers, O'Hannigan's men disarmed the RIC men who had accompanied them on their marches during the previous few days. Just then a big car approached. It contained six British Army officers and their driver, all in uniform. The car was stopped, and the passengers were forced to disembark. The volunteers commandeered it and more cars parked nearby, and set out on specific tasks, with the intention of rendezvousing eventually with their captain at Dunboyne. O'Hannigan with just nine men, proceeded to Dunboyne as instructed, with the intention of linking up with Captain Sean Boylan and his fourteen men (as it turned out), before proceeding on to Blanchardstown, where they intended to blow up a second railway bridge. There was no sign of Boylan and his men when they arrived at the agreed rendezvous point. He had been given fresh instructions to proceed to Leixlip and join with the men from Maynooth. Boylan, in his haste to comply with order, had failed to notify O'Hannigan of the change.

O'Hannigan carried on with his original orders to march on Dunboyne. He described the situation that now presented itself when he arrived on the outskirts: 'When we got near Dunboyne I halted and by using my field glasses I could see British soldiers on the railway over the road apparently holding the bridge.' Dunboyne was being guarded by, it was reckoned, 100 Lancers and 50 Infantry. The mission had to be cancelled. There simply were not enough volunteers to take them on. Nearby was a big house, the Red House on the Dunshaughlin Road, which proved to be deserted. O'Hannigan took over the outhouses attached to it and established his camp there, hoping that at some stage hearing of his location, Boylan and his men would join him.

Tuesday morning a young woman from Dunboyne, a Miss Mullally, arrived at the Red House. She had been sent by Sean Boylan. O'Hannigan sent her back with instructions that Boylan and his men should join him. Another scout previously sent by O'Hannigan the previous day managed to get through the British lines. He returned with a dispatch from Connolly, which read, 'To Comdt. O'Hannigan, Commandeer transport and move your men to Dublin where they will be rested and armed before being sent into action. Signed James Connolly, Comdt. General, GPO.' That evening, following the arrival of Boylan and his men, O'Hannigan called a conference of his officers:

> We discussed Connolly's order and decided it was impossible to carry out as (1) there was no transport to be got anywhere; (2) Cabra Bridge was in enemy hands and there was an enemy cordon around the city by this time. We decided to get in touch immediately with Tom Ashe and the Fingal Battalion with whom we had no contact so far and to join up with them or at least discuss the position with them.[8]

Previously, on the evening of Monday, 24 April, the men of the 5th Battalion ate their evening meal of sandwiches and tea. They discussed the events of the day. Now, for the first time, the men learnt of the occupation of the GPO and other buildings in Dublin. There were lots of rumours that followed; Casement had been arrested on the Kerry coast, the arms ship had landed guns; the rest of the country had risen up and the Germans were about to invade. All rumours and not necessarily true, but they hoped that some of them were. The battalion spent the night out in the open, with the rain continuing to fall. As he lay there, Weston recalled, 'We could hear the firing in the city quite plainly.'

Waking from a fitful sleep, Joseph Lawless heard Ashe and Captain Dick Coleman in discussion. He and Joe Taylor, lying next to him, went to investigate. They were told that twenty men were required on a mission. Lawless was told off to collect that number from those who were awake. There were twenty-two eventually. They were given their orders and set off on their bicycles, led by Coleman. Taking the road from Finglas, they rode alongside the River Tolka towards Blanchardstown. The object of their raid was to destroy the railway at Ashtown, to thwart British reinforcement arriving from the Curragh by train. It was a dark and rainy night with heavy clouds. Not familiar with the unlit roads, the party got lost. They were obliged to return to the camp, mission unaccomplished.

Chapter 4

Tuesday: Waiting for Orders

Having washed in a nearby stream, Joseph Lawless sat on the grass looking over Glasnevin Cemetery towards the city. The fighting was continuing there. 'What was happening over there in the city?' he pondered. 'And was anything happening in the rest of the country? What do we do now? Must we wait here to be attacked, or should we not start some attacking on our own account, and if so, where and when?…Here we were waiting for something to happen; we did not know what, but it would undoubtedly be easier to do something, whatever it might be.' Unknowingly, Thomas Ashe was thinking the same, as he awaited further orders.

That Tuesday morning, at about 11am, Richard Mulcahy and two other volunteers, Tom Maxwell and Paddy Grant, arrived at Finglas.[1] After being sent by James Connolly to Howth to sever the undersea telephone cable between Dublin and London, they found themselves cut off from their own unit and, hearing that Ashe was operating in the area, they set off to find the 5th Battalion men. Contacting them, the three agreed to remain with the 5th throughout the campaign; Mulcahy, a fellow IRB man, agreed to act as Ashe's administrative officer. He was already known to the other members of the battalion staff. To Joseph Lawless, 'It was soon apparent to everyone that his was the mind necessary to plan and direct operations. [He was] cool, clear-headed and practical, with tact that enabled him virtually to control the situation without in any way undermining Ashe's prestige as commander.'

Earlier that morning, Ashe had sent Cumann na mBan member Mary 'Molly' Adrien of Oldtown into the city as a courier with a request for further orders.[2] She returned with instructions to send forty men into the city to the GPO. Ashe could not afford to lose so many men. He sent twenty, under the command of Dick Coleman, captain of Swords Company. Volunteer Michael McAllister listed the names of the men in his Witness Statement:

Captain Richard Coleman, Swords
Dan Brophy, Swords
James Crennigan, Roganstown
William 'Beck' Wilson, Balheary
Thomas Peppard, Lusk

Jack Hynes, Lusk
Dick Kelly, Corduff
Peter Wilson, Balheary
Jack Kelly, Swords
John McNally, Lusk
William Doyle, Swords
Edward Lawless, Rathbeale
James Wilson, Balheary
Joe Norton, Mount Ambrose
John Clarke, Lusk
Patrick Caddell, Lusk
Patrick Kelly, Corduff
William 'Cooty' Wilson, Swords[3]
James Marks, Swords
William Meehan, Lusk

Volunteer Joe Taylor also went with them. He had orders to get fresh instructions from James Connolly, then return. By evening, Taylor had still not returned. He had got caught up in the fighting in Dublin. Tom Peppard, the Brigade's Intelligence Officer, gave a little more detail of the distribution of the men sent to Dublin in his 1950s Witness Statement:

> The late Richard Coleman took charge of this party. He was, I think, company captain of Swords Company. Daniel Brophy was next in command to Coleman. We proceeded into the city without incident and reported to the General Post Office in Sackville St., now O'Connell St. Some of our men were detailed to proceed to reinforce the garrison in Kelly's of Bachelor's Walk. Ned Lawless, a brother of Frank was one of this party. Another party was detailed for similar duty in the Mendicity Institution and I was among the party that went there. The garrison of Volunteers in the Institute was commanded by Sean Heuston, who was later executed. The position commanded the approach from the Royal Barracks and Kingsbridge along the Quays to the city centre.

Now with just forty men remaining of the 5th, their partial loss was made up later that night by the arrival of five or six stragglers cut off from their city units. The volunteers moved off in the early evening, the rain steadily falling, with a view to returning to Knocksedan, camping for the night at nearby Killeek. Charles Weston and his section acted as the advance guard. Along the way, they were halted when James Lawless raced up to them and claimed that horses had been heard upon the road. Were they British Army cavalry? They took up defensive positions. They waited, but no further sound was heard. Earlier that day, Brigadier General Lowe, commanding the Reserve Cavalry Brigade, had arrived at Kingsbridge Station in Dublin from the Curragh. He was leading a column of 1,500 cavalrymen and 840 men of the 25th Irish Reserve Infantry Brigade. The volunteers waited in silence, but no more was heard. Warily they continued to Knocksedan. Here they found a semi-derelict farmhouse, still partially roofed, and bedded down there for the night. Others were accommodated in the outhouses on beds of straw. As they settled down for the night, in the distance in the direction of Dublin, they heard the sounds of machine-gun and rifle fire.

Jim O'Connor, from the St Margaret's Company now turned up. It was just after midnight. He had been caught up in the confusion over the weekend:

On Easter Sunday the whole Bn. mobilized at Rathbeale Cross Roads. We had all the arms we had with us including shotguns and some rifles and rations for 24 hours. I had a shotgun and twelve rounds of ordinary shot, a haversack and a slouch hat… We were there until about 12 p.m. on Sunday night when we were told to go home and be prepared to mobilise again at short notice. I went home and went to bed.[4]

The following morning, he had gone off to the races at Fairyhouse like so many of his fellow Dubliners. That evening, he heard the Rising had begun. Dashing home, O'Connor collected up his uniform and his shotgun, and sought out the battalion. He found them at Killeek. 'I noticed Dick Mulcahy there,' O'Connor later related, 'He was not with us on Sunday'. Mulcahy, and a few others, had arrived during Monday. Richard Mulcahy, or Dick Mulcahy as he was more popularly known, had been sent along with Tom Maxwell and Paddy Grant, up to Howth Junction to cut telegraphic communications with Belfast and Britain. Cut off from re-entering the city, they sought out Ashe and his men. Dick Kelly remembered getting instructions from Ashe to go to a certain point where he would meet a man, whom he was to challenge and escort back to camp.[5] O'Connor, the late arrival, was put on guard duty up on a hill to watch the two roads that lead into the camp. 'My orders,' he confirmed, 'were to give the alarm if I saw the RIC or military coming but not to fire.' After being relieved, O'Connor bedded himself down in the straw-filled outhouse. 'We had plenty of food,' O'Connor stated, 'as they killed some lambs and they had a bread cart full of bread which had been commandeered. I think it was one of Kennedy's bread vans. It was a motor van.' After some thirty years, O'Connor's memory was not perhaps as sharp when he came to give his statement. Lusk Company's lieutenant, Charlie Weston, gives what seems to be a more descriptive account of what happened before O'Connor's arrival:

> On Tuesday morning a sheep was killed by Joe Taylor who acted as a butcher. We had rashers, eggs, tea and bread for breakfast. The Q/master had a horse van in which he carried rations and cooking utensils. It was driven by Vol. Norton.

Either way, the 5th Battalion were well catered for regarding rations, successfully living off the land and commandeering what they lacked.

The Skerries men were also absent on the second mobilisation. News reached them of the Rising in Dublin, late on Monday evening, when local residents returning home by the last train informed them. Volunteer Matt Derham spread the news, getting in touch with his fellow volunteers. By Tuesday morning, the Skerries men under Joseph Thornton were assembled and armed. However, the roads around Skerries were being patrolled by an increasing number of armed police and soldiers. Anyone venturing forth was stopped and questioned. Thornton sent out unarmed scouts in several directions attempting to locate Ashe and the 5th. Having found them at Killeek, the scouts were sent back with a message. Thornton's men were told to hold Skerries until Wednesday, when the battalion would arrive to attack the military wireless station. As happens in war, the plans were changed. To avoid being outflanked, the battalion turned west to attack Garristown RIC barracks instead. So, on the Wednesday, with support not arriving, the Skerries men individually passed through the British lines to meet up again as a depleted column on the other side of the cordon and set out the find Ashe.

From the British side, the presence of the Skerries Volunteers around the town that Tuesday caused some concern. The *1916 Rebellion Handbook*, published by the *Weekly Irish Times*, recorded:

> On Tuesday, 25th April, the police got word that the Marconi station recently erected by the Admiralty was to be attacked and some of the principal houses raided. There was consternation at this report, as the wireless operators were unarmed, and there were only seven soldiers to guard the station, while the police force, under Sergeant Burke, to whose energy and ability throughout the week a warm tribute must be paid, was wholly inadequate to protect the town. So great was the alarm that some of the townsfolk left their houses, and paced the shore as the safest place in case of a raid. The attack, however, did not come off.

On Tuesday evening, four of the Fingal Volunteers, including Kit Moran, were sent with a horse and cart to James Lawless's house at Cloghran to collect the arms and ammunition sent up from Dublin.

During the course of Tuesday night, the men of the 5th were joined by a number of volunteers from the 1st Battalion. They had been cut off by the British Army at Phibsboro'. They included Volunteers Jerry Golden, Paddy Holohan, Peter (later changed to Peader) and Tom Blanchfield, Anthony O'Reilly and Willie Walsh (a Liverpool Irishman). Their flight followed a fight in the Cabra suburb of north Dublin. The volunteers had erected barricades both on Park Road and on the Cabra Road near where Charleville Road connects both. Houses overlooking the barricades had been occupied by the rebels on Monday and held until the arrival of the Dublin Fusiliers from Templemore. They engaged the volunteers in a heavy fire fight, before some of them surrendered and others, like the above, escaped towards Glasnevin and Finglas. The British cautiously pushed up towards Glasnevin from the North Circular Road, as far as the Cross Guns Bridge, which commanded the canal and railway line running to the North Wall, Whitworth Road and the Finglas Road.

Jerry Golden explains how they came to join the Fingal men. On Easter Monday, Commandant Edward Daly, ordered men from B Company of the 1st:

> to proceed at once to the Nth Circular and Cabra Roads and take up positions of defence at the bridges, and if possible, demolish them. The Company started off about 65 strong via Queen St., Nth. King St., Upr. Church St., Constitution Hill and Phibsboro Road to the places we were ordered to. On our marching up Constitution Hill, opposite the King's Inns, we were subjected to a fusillade of rotten cabbages, oranges, apples etc. by a lot of women who were apparently wives of British soldiers. Our Capt. ordered us not to take any notice of them but to carry on. When we came to Doyle's Corner, at Phibsboro, we wheeled left towards the Park and at St Peter's Church, Phiboboro, Capt. Sullivan halted the Co. He sent about half of the men, under Lieut. Scollan, with orders to occupy the houses on Cabra Road beside the Railway bridge, while he took the remainder of the Co. up the Nth. Circular Road…It was about 3 p.m… the military opened fire on us with machine guns from the following points: Great Western Square, Broadstone Stn., Upr. Grange Gorman, and with shrapnel from artillery at the entrance to Connolly Norman's house, Grangegorman.[6]

The houses on Cabra Road now came under artillery assault. With the building falling apart around them, the only thing to do was to abandon their posts. Rather than try and break through, and return to the inner city, they decided to move north in the hope of joining with Ashe. The small group consisted of Golden, Paddy Holohan, P.J. Corless, Jack Price, Vincent and Dick Grogan, Peter and Tom Blanchfield, Arthur O'Reilly and one of the Liverpool Irish, Willie Walsh. Holohan, being a section commander, took charge. Golden, knowing that Ashe was at Finglas Golf Links, was all for making a dash across Glasnevin Cemetery, but Holohan urged caution, fearing that the British might have an outpost on the road. He was all for avoiding crossing open fields and for using the hedgerows for cover. It took much longer, but it was safer. They arrived at the River Tolka. Golden continues:

> We found it in flood, and as it had taken us over 45 minutes to reach the river I immediately entered the river with the water nearly up to my waist. When I got over the river I told the others to do likewise with the result that we were all washed out but otherwise uninjured.

Again, they circumnavigated the hedges of the fields, before entering Finglas Wood and near safety. It was slow and tedious, but it was as instructed in the British Army manuals, that they had been trained by. The group passed through the woods and arrived at the main road. Stopping at a cottage, they enquired as to Ashe's whereabouts. They were told that they had missed Ashe and his men, as they had passed by the cottage, by twenty minutes. They were last seen, the group were told, proceeding round the Beneavin Road that would take them to Glasnevin Village. By now it was dusk. At the Beneavin Convalescent Home, the little group cut the telephone wires, just in case the staff might telephone the police or military and give away their position. At 8.30pm, the six men made contact with an outpost of the 5th Battalion. The following morning, they continued on to Knocksedan where they found Ashe.

During the course of the day, following the departure of the twenty volunteers, a need for a reorganization of the remaining men now became essential. It was decided to divide the entire force more or less into equal sections of ten to twelve men, each section under the command of an officer, and with the remaining senior officers constituting the headquarters and command staff. The commanders of the sections were: No. 1. – Charles Weston; No. 2 – John V. Lawless; No. 3 – Ned Rooney; and No. 4 – Jim Lawless. Ashe would retain command of the whole force, with Mulcahy as his second in command, Frank Lawless would continue as quartermaster and Dr Hayes as Adjutant and Medical Officer. Each section would now act as a complete entity, and each section would act in daily rotation. Thus, one section would act as advance guard; one section as the main body with the commanding officer and staff; one section to act as the rear guard; and the last section would remain in camp and collect supplies each day and generally do the necessary fatigue work.

The new situation created meant the abandonment of the British Army organization in which they were trained. Due to the shortage of men, they had to evolve into a guerrilla army, and as is seen in the later War of Independence, a thirty-man unit was the ideal size of a guerrilla party. Ashe's new instructions, brought by 'Molly' Adrien from Connolly, were to go on the offensive and harass the government forces of police and army in order to relieve the pressure on the volunteers in the city.

That night Dr Hayes reflected upon the day, his thoughts later put down on paper some forty years later, 'On that day half a dozen stragglers from the city Batt[alion], cut off at Phibsboro' joined us. It was arranged on Wednesday that we would attack the police barracks at Swords and Donabate.'

Chapter 5

Wednesday: On the Offensive

Early on Wednesday further reinforcements turned up. Late arrivals James Kelly and Peter Ganley were accompanied by fourteen-year-old Jack McGowan. In the forthcoming struggle, Ashe knew that men would die. He did not want to be responsible for the death of McGowan, and so Ashe sent him home, telling him that his time would come.

The morning, as Lieutenant Joseph Lawless of the Swords Company remembered, 'looked more promising as far as the weather was concerned. The early morning was bright and sunny, though cool, and we felt inclined to laugh and make light of our miseries of the night before.'

On Wednesday, Miss Mullally and Miss Byrne, despatched by O'Hannigan, contacted Tom Ashe who sent word that he would meet O'Hannigan the following day. He was to send word later where they should meet. Things were now moving at a pace. Events were overtaking Ashe and his men. The instruction was never sent or perhaps never arrived. O'Hannigan was to comment, 'I waited all day on Thursday but got no word from Ashe.'

Ashe was still without precise orders from Connolly or Pearse. In conference with Dick Mulcahy, he decided to go on the offensive. He organized his forty-five men with a view to capturing the police barracks at Swords and Donabate, and destroying telephone communications as they proceeded. Lacking precise intelligence of the conditions around Swords, and wishing to avoid any surprises, Ashe divided his men up into the three units as previously described. Joseph Lawless, commanding that day's Advance Guard, was instructed to make the south-western approach along Forrest Road to Swords and to arrive a little ahead of the other two sections, which would arrive by the western and north-west approaches. They set off about 8.30am that morning. Charlie Weston's instructions were precise as he relates:

> I was to move on Swords via Rathbeale Cross Roads and the green, enter Swords and rush the Post Office, and smash all the instruments there, and take up a position in the row of houses opposite the barracks.[1]

The only other telephone in the town, the public telephone in Taylor's shop, was also destroyed.

The orders of Joseph Lawless, commanding the Advance Guard, were:

> to make a rapid and silent descent upon the town with the initial object of ascertaining whether or not the RIC garrison was in a state of defence there. If so, I would dispose my section for attack in rear of the barracks and send word to Ashe on the Rathbeale road, and if not, I could use my own discretion as circumstances might seem to warrant, though I think it was conveyed to me that further action could wait until Ashe arrived on the scene.

Lawless's section left first on their bicycles, the others cycled off a few minutes later, all with loaded rifles slung across their backs. They converged on Swords some fifteen or twenty minutes later. According to plan, Lawless's men cycled along the main street at speed, observing the barracks closely as they passed by. Lawless remarked, 'To my surprise, I saw as I passed, the RIC Sergeant, Sergeant O'Reilly, standing in a lounging attitude at the barracks door, his tunic half unbuttoned and his hands in his trousers pockets. He looked at us with a kind of mild curiosity as we flashed past him, and made no move to retire within.' The barracks seemed to be in no state of defence. The loop-holed steel plates fitted to the upper windows were still folded back against the wall. As planned, Lawless and his men turned down Chapel Lane and dismounted. Eight of his men moved forward to the rear of the barracks. A ninth was sent to tell Ashe on the Rathbeale Road and inform him of the situation. As leisurely as possible, Lawless approached the police sergeant who had watched the proceedings with a certain 'detached interest' and bid him a good morning. He responded in a friendly way, observing that the volunteers in Dublin were making fools of themselves. Lawless talked on, waiting for the arrival of the other units. Rooney's section with Ashe and Mulcahy then arrived on bicycles, which they proceeded to stack along the street or against the houses. As if on a friendly visit, Ashe and Mulcahy walked straight up to the barracks, which they entered. The rest of their unit followed on quickly and likewise entered, filling the downstairs office with volunteers. Ashe demanded of O'Reilly, the surrender of the barracks, and the six men under his command, even as his own men began seizing carbines, revolvers, ammunition and various bits of equipment. Six carbines and two Webley revolvers with a considerable supply of ammunition were seized. Seriously outnumbered, and completely taken by surprise, there was little that O'Reilly and his men could do. Outside, the other IRA units were destroying all communications, cutting telegraph and telephone cables. The raid on Swords RIC barracks was a complete success, and no one was killed or injured. In looking through the ammunition, Lawless made a disturbing discovery:

> I got some of the revolver ammunition for myself, as I was already armed with a .455 Webley as well as a long Lee-Enfield rifle. Some of the revolver ammunition I got was similar to that I already had, that is, the orthodox conical headed bullet; but a couple of packages of the ammunition had cylindrical flat-headed bullets of the dumdum type which we were indignant about.[2]

The claim that the volunteers used the illegal dumdum bullets was often levelled at them by the British authorities, but here was proof that the RIC at least had been supplied with them.

Just as they were about to move off with their booty, two large motor vans loaded with freshly baked bread arrived in the town, from Kennedy's Bakery on the north side of the city (this may possibly explain O'Connor's seeming former contradiction). The volunteers seized the vans and their contents, and sent them back to their camp at Killeek. The men then proceeded on to Donabate, to capture the RIC barracks there. Lieutenant Charlie Weston's section took the lead as the Advance Guard:

> We went via Batter Lane on the main road at Turvey and on to Donabate. At Turvey a civilian on a motor cycle passed – refused to halt. We did not fire as we did not like to shoot civilians. On reaching the railway bridge at Donabate we deployed round the railway line in order to cut the line. The police barracks was about 200 yards away. A few shots were fired here at a man on the railway who refused to halt. Mulcahy was very annoyed at this as it gave a warning to the barracks.[3]

Weston's section was ordered to take up positions covering the barracks. Ashe and one or two others entered the post office and dismantled the telephone and telegraph equipment there. The postmaster, a Mr Dunne, an ex-RIC man and in Weston's eyes a real blackguard, for he later joined the Black and Tans in 1920, agreed to go into the barracks and ask the sergeant to surrender. He did so but returned soon after to inform Ashe that there were two civilian workers within. The sergeant had refused to surrender but requested that the civilians be allowed to leave unmolested. Ashe agreed to this. Weston described what happened next:

The barracks was 50 yards from the road and approached by a gravel path. We were ordered to take a pickaxe, sledge [hammer] and crowbar and burst in the door. Six of us rushed up to the door and shouted at the police to surrender or we would break in the door. The answer was a revolver shot fired out of the top window. Immediately the window was riddled by bullets from our men. We proceeded to break in the door. After a few seconds the door frame gave way and the door went in. There was an inner iron door with a chain on it. When the door went in they immediately shouted that they would surrender. They could not get the iron door open, but one of them threw a rifle through the top window as a token of surrender. They eventually got the inner door opened and handed out 3 rifles (carbines) and a revolver and a small amount of ammunition. I got the revolver and 12 r[oun]ds of ammunition for the same. We went into the Barracks and Ashe took the Day Book and looked up the entries and pointed out entries about the Turvey Section of the Volunteers' parades, etc., and the names of the Volunteers on parade on various dates. We had a chat with the police who had got over their nervousness. After this the Battn. returned to billets at Killeek.[4]

During the brief exchange of fire, a policeman named Thorpe was wounded in the hand from a bullet coming through the loophole from which he was firing. This was sufficient excuse for the police to surrender without losing face.

Here at Donabate the column was joined by Bernard (Bennie) McAllister. At the time of the Redmondite split, he had thrown in his lot with the Irish National Volunteers. Like so many, he was at Fairyhouse Races when the rebellion started. Returning home, he was told that the 5th Fingal Battalion was on the move. He grabbed his Lee-Enfield and his ammunition pouch and set off to find them. He caught up with them at Donabate, where he joined them for the rest of the campaign.

Following the surrender of the barracks, while the others were gathering up arms and equipment, Joseph Lawless and Bartle Weston went off to carry out an experiment on the rails above the bridge using a few sticks of gelignite:

We had learned all about the methods of destroying rails with explosives from British text books on field engineering, but the explosive in the text book was gun cotton, and we wanted to see how gelignite would serve the purpose. Well, we tried several charges in different ways and they failed to produce the required result, so, feeling a bit disappointed about this, though we had certainly learned something, we trekked backwards towards camp at Killeek and a good dinner.[5]

On their return to camp, arriving at Turvey Hill, the volunteers received word that British troops had landed at Skerries and others were at Lusk. Indeed, they had. A destroyer had landed 200 men of the North Staffordshire Regiment, under the command of Captain Clay, at Skerries harbour. They had been marched off to the wireless station, where they dug trenches surrounding the station. Barricades of carts and sandbags were erected on all roads leading into Skerries. Two gunboats, including *Boadicea II*, had also arrived, their guns were trained on the coastal roads that the rebels were expected to arrive by. Some twenty persons with Sinn Fein sympathies were arrested and sent to Dublin.

The volunteers, meanwhile, proceeded back to their camp at Knocksedan. Later that afternoon, Molly Adrien entered the camp. She had arrived from the GPO and brought with her a copy of the 'Proclamation of the Republic' and a copy of the *Irish War News*. Molly also brought with her a personal account of the fighting in Dublin. She had ridden her bicycle through the streets of Dublin and argued her way through the barricades manned by British troops. She was lucky not to have been killed. About the same time, Margaret Skinnider, a soldier in the Irish Citizen Army, was shot at as she rode her bike:

> I had my first taste of the risks of street-fighting. Soldiers on top of the Hotel Shelbourne aimed their machine guns directly at me. Bullets struck the wooden rim of my bicycle wheels, puncturing it, others rattled on the metal rim or amongst the spokes. I knew one might strike me at any moment, so I rode as fast as I could. My speed saved my life, and I was soon out of range around a corner.[6]

Joseph Lawless, with the others, listened to Molly's account of the fighting. 'This was the first authentic account we had of the fighting in Dublin,' he remarked, 'and perhaps for the first time we, that is the younger ones of us, began to realise that all was not going well, and that there was no sign of the rest of the country rising in arms… However, we thought, the fight is only three days old yet, and, in time, the rest of the country must rise to our assistance.'

New arrivals now entered the camp, Mick Fleming and his sister Monica or 'Dot' as she was also known.[7] Mick Fleming belonged to the 2nd Battalion of the Dublin Volunteers. He had been sent around with MacNeill's cancellation order. Out of place when the Rising broke out, he was unable to join his battalion in Jacob's factory, so made his way north to join with Ashe. All thoughts of cancellation were now forgotten.

The senior officers, concerned that their position in the Knocksedan area might have become known to the police or military, decided to evacuate and relocate the camp at Baldwinstown. When it was night, an overcast one without moon nor stars, they set off, in one long column extended along the road in single file, with their transport wagons, a Ford van, Dr Hayes' car, and the horse and dray in the middle of the column. Avoiding the main road, they progressed along the minor roads and lanes. At about midnight, having travelled some twelve miles or so, they arrived before the village of Garristown. The column halted, and Ashe announced that he intended to attack the RIC barracks there. Dr Hayes would take the lead. A scout was sent into the village to reconnoitre. He reported back that the police had vacated the barracks. The IRA unit cycled down to the barracks. Very politely, they knocked at the door and called upon those within to surrender. The bolts were drawn back, and the door opened to reveal a lone barracks sergeant. He declared that his men and the rifles had been withdrawn, by the district inspector, to Balbriggan earlier that day as a precautionary measure. The barracks were searched but nothing was found. Jerry Golden (in his Witness Statement 521) relates that the commandant ordered some of the men to remove the Imperial Coat of Arms plaque from the front of the building. 'While the men were doing this one of them hoisted the tricolour on a broom handle to one of the high chimney pots.' Empty handed, the volunteers next went to the Post Office where they dismantled the telegraph equipment. Continuing on, the column made for Baldwinstown, where they found a deserted farmhouse and barns with straw for bedding. It was early morning. After a good meal of meat, bread and tea, exhausted by the day, with sentries posted, they slept.

A government communiqué was issued by the general officer commanding-in-chief in Dublin on Wednesday, 26 April:

> There is now a complete cordon of troops around the centre of the town on the north side of the river. Two more battalions are arriving this afternoon (Wednesday) from England. There has been a small rising at Ardee, Louth, and a rather more serious one at Swords and Lusk, close to Dublin. The last report I have shows the total of fifteen killed and twenty-one wounded, besides two loyal Volunteers and two policemen killed and six loyal Volunteers wounded.[8]

Chapter 6

Thursday: Controversy and Conviction

Despite their successes, there were some who questioned whether they should continue. Ashe heard the rumblings of dissatisfaction and called the men together. This would be a test of his leadership in holding the battalion together. He paraded the men and spoke to them. Ashe was as honest as he could be with the intelligence he had at hand. The argument of the dissenters concerned the 'legality' of their actions. The insurrection had not been sanctioned by the Volunteer Executive. Indeed, it had been expressly forbidden by its president, Eoin MacNeill. Also concerning them was the fact that the rest of the country had not also risen. Realising the danger that their argument was gradually creating unease, Ashe called upon those who were dissatisfied to step forward and air their grievances. One man stepped out and proceeded to set forth his argument that they were participating in an unauthorized and illegal war. He belittled the campaign so far as 'a foolish undertaking', as J.V. Lawless reported in his Witness Statement. A second man in the ranks supported the other's statement. Ashe tried to placate them. He gave them the facts as far as he knew them. The rest of the country outside Dublin had not risen as far as he knew but that they would rise. Ashe declared that he would not keep any man against his will and that anyone who wished to go home was perfectly free to do so. Ashe reminded them that twenty of their friends who had been sent into the city were even now in the thick of the fight. Mulcahy now spoke. He recapitulated the aims of the volunteers, and their duties as Irishmen. He said that he felt that most of them understood this. To those who felt uneasy, those who had doubts or scruples, he said that they could leave without reproach. Then he gambled and asked each section, 'Are you willing to go on? Any man who is not let him step out.' He called upon No. 1 section. Their response was 'Fight on'. So, it continued. Just five men from St Margaret's, led by Volunteers Duke and O'Reilly, decided to leave.[1] Ashe insisted that they leave their rifles.

Some further reorganization now became necessary. J.V. Lawless's brother Colm,[2] and Jack McGowan of Skerries, being too young (both were only about fourteen years old), and Bill Norton, who was too old, were sent home. The stragglers who had entered the camp were now allocated positions in the various units. That same morning a priest entered the camp. He was Father

Kevlehan, the son of an old Fenian. Ashe summoned the men and asked them to kneel down so that the priest might bless them. Then Father Kevlehan heard their individual confessions.

Meanwhile, the British authorities were not idle. Vulnerable installations were reinforced as and when soldiers or policemen became available. The *Rebellion Handbook* (p. 100) relates:

> On the 27th April, as soon as the troops became available, a detachment was sent by sea from Kingstown [Dún Laoghaire] to Arklow to reinforce the garrison at Kynoch's Explosive Works, and a small party was sent to assist the RIC post over the wireless station at Skerries.

At Slane Castle in the neighbouring county of Meath, Alexander Gray,[3] its RIC County Inspector, had received intelligence of the three RIC barracks that had been captured. It was a believable assumption, he contended, that the insurgents might well extend their activities into his district. He was responsible for thirty-six barracks and police stations. The smaller ones were no more than temporary huts, and these could be abandoned, moving the men to the larger and better fortified barracks. But then, being the nature of the man that he was, Gray decide to go on the offensive. By taking half a dozen or so men from the larger barracks, and the men from the indefensible police stations, he was able to build up a force of 100 men or so. His reinforcements included men from Navan, Trim, Kells, Oldcastle, Athboy, Dunshaughlin, Nobber, Duleek, Dunboyne, Summerhill, Ballivor, Moynalty, Crossakiel, Carnaross, Bohermeen Drumconrath, Longwood, Lismullin, Enfield, Kilnoon, Killyon, Carlanstown, Oristown, Kilmainhamwood, Robinstown, Ballinabracky, Moyglare, Stirruptown, George Cross, Parsonstown, Julianstown, Gormanston, Ticoghan and Ashbourne. Gray commandeered a fleet of fifteen cars from the neighbouring landowners and businesses to transfer his men quickly to wherever they might be needed.[4] In his preparations, Gray was ably assisted by his deputy, Harry Smyth, an Englishman.[5] While Gray became the coordinator, liaising with the local gentry and tradesmen in assembling the motorised unit, Smyth supervised the deployment of the men from the various RIC posts. On Thursday evening, a telephone call from Garristown informed Gray that the rebels were there and were going to camp at Borranstown, which was but a few miles north-east of Ashbourne. A second call announced their arrival in Borranstown. As a precaution, Gray sent a detachment of policemen under Harry Smyth to prevent the insurgents from crossing the bridge at Slane.

Earlier that Thursday afternoon, about 2pm, the IRA battalion moved off, making its way to Borranstown, by way of Garristown. In passing through

Thursday: Controversy and Conviction

Garristown, a bicycle that had been taken from the policeman in the barracks the previous night was returned to him as it was his own property and not government issue. It was a curious little war with such acts of honesty.

The men pitched camp at a disused farmhouse at Borranstown, about three miles south of Garristown. Ashe summoned Jerry Golden, one of the waifs and strays who had thrown in their lot with the men of the 5th:

> Commdt. Tomas Agas O.C. Fingal Brigade whom I had known for some years previous, spoke to me and said that as I was well acquainted with the towns and villages of Nth. Co. Dublin and adjoining C. Meath, but not known personally by the IRB, he would like me to cycle through the towns and villages and note any unusual RIC activity.[6]

Off he set cycling through the countryside. At each barracks, he now discovered that they were in a state of readiness to repel any assault. Standing at the doorways were usually one or two policemen, all fully armed with carbines and bayonets. He found the same in County Meath. Golden reported back to Ashe that the police were in a state of readiness.

At the new camp, they ate an evening meal 'with plenty of eggs and butter'. The senior officers now planned for the next day. Information had come in that a considerable force of troops was preparing to move from Athlone to Dublin by the Midland Great Western Railway. Ashe and Mulcahy decided to cut the railway line and thereafter to harass the troops which might be sent to investigate the breech.

Scouts were sent out to reconnoitre the immediate vicinity. Sentries were posted and defence positions were selected in case of sudden attack. Jim Lawless's section was responsible for the night guard. Because of this, his section would not accompany the others on their mission to Batterstown in the morning but remain to guard the camp and assist the quartermaster to replenish food supplies. The uncertainty of the early morning was now dispelled. The battalion was a unified force once more. That night there was good deal of humorous banter – or craic. J.V. Lawless recalled that they entertained themselves with song, with Paddy Brogan singing *Doran's Ass*.

> One Paddy Doyle lived in Killarney;
> He courted a girl called Biddy O'Toole.
> Her tongue was tipped with a bit of the blarney;
> The same to Pat was a golden rule
> Day and dawn she was his colleen.
> Pat was often heard to say,

'Arrah, what's the use of me walking faster?
Biddy, she will meet me on the way.'

Chorus: Whack fol loora loora lido
Whack fol loora loor I day

And so on until the song was complete. Then all became silent, as they settled down for the night. In the distance, they could hear the occasional rifle shot and short burst of machine-gun fire.

Chapter 7

Friday: The Attack on Ashbourne Barracks

The Friday after Easter Sunday, the great adventure was all but over. In Dublin, the GPO was surrounded and in flames. Volunteer Thomas Devine surveyed the interior of the building. The Rising was lost he acknowledged, but the spirit of freedom was still ablaze as he relates:

> bombardment had worked havoc in the building, especially in the roof and upper storeys which had got the brunt of the shelling. Daylight was visible in many places, twisted girders hung at queer angles, walls, floors and staircases were in a chaotic state. On such parts as still smouldered or burned the hoses were continually playing ... The garrison too showed traces of the ordeal. Down on the ground floor many wounded lay, sat or stood by, whilst those active went about their tasks. I state the simple truth when I say that on that eventful Friday, discipline and the morale of the defenders was without exception splendid.[1]

The truth was that now completely surrounded and pounded by field artillery the defence of the GPO and indeed the Rising in Dublin was all but ended. From within the GPO, James Connolly issued a defiant message:

> Soldiers, this is the fifth day of the establishment of the Irish republic, and the flag of our country still floats from the most important buildings in Dublin, and is gallantly protected by the officers and Irish soldiers in arms throughout the country. Not a day passes without seeing fresh postings of Irish soldiers eager to do battle for the old cause…Our commanders around us are holding their own…The men of north Co. Dublin are in the field, have occupied all the police barracks in the district, destroyed all the telegram system on the Great Northern Railway up to Dundalk, and are operating against the trains of the Midland Great Western. Dundalk has sent 200 men to march upon Dublin, and in other parts of the North our forces are active and strong.[2]

At Slane Castle in County Meath, its active county inspector, Alexander Gray, viewed with some concern the activities of the volunteers in neighbouring

County Dublin. He strongly suspected that they would march on Slane. On the afternoon of 25 April, he mobilised a strong force of policemen for sentry duty in and around Slane. On the afternoon of 27 April, Constable Bratton, who had been scouting the area on his motorbike, reported that Ashe and his men were camped near Kilmoon, not far from the RIC Barracks at Ashbourne. That evening, Gray despatched District Inspector Harry Smyth, a former British Army officer, with 15 men to arrange an ambush at Slane Bridge, the most likely point of entry into the county. At 2am the following morning, with no sign of volunteer activity, the police were recalled. Gray now decided upon a proactive campaign against the insurgents. An unspecified number of men from Navan, Dunboyne and Slane RIC Barracks were sent to reinforce the garrison at Ashbourne and ensure its safety. Inspector McCormack was put in charge. Under his instruction, Barrack Sergeant Tully set up a perimeter defence on the minor approach roads around Ashbourne. On the morning of 28 April, fifteen commandeered cars, containing fifty-five men, led by Gray and Smyth, set out for Ashbourne. Along the way, the rear car containing Smyth, Sergeant William O'Connell and Constable Bratton suffered two punctures, causing delay.

Out in the countryside of north County Dublin, the Rising was about to witness its greatest triumph. Unaware of the true situation in Dublin, Joseph Lawless, an eternal optimist, spoke of the early morning:

> Friday, 28th April 1916, was a beautiful spring morning, with brilliant sun in a cloudless sky and a sufficient coolness in the light breeze to add zest to the joy of living.

About 7am, all the sentries around the volunteers' camp were called in for breakfast. Soon it would all begin. There was a degree of excitement as Ashe explained their mission that day. Jerry Golden lists his companions of that day:

> Commdt. Tom Ashe, Vice Commdt. Frank Lawless, Capt. James V. Lawless and Capt. Dr. Richard Hayes with about 35 of the Swords, Lusk, Skerries and St Margaret's Companies together with Lieut. (afterwards General Dick Mulcahy) and Tom Maxwell and Paddy Grant members of the 2nd Batt. Dublin Brigade and 5 members of 'B' Co. 1st Batt. Dublin Brigade, namely Paddy Holohan, Peadar Blanchfield his brother Tom, Arthur O'Reilly and myself together with one of the Liverpool Irish known as Willie Walsh with Miss Mollie Adrien of Oldtown of the Cumann na mBan.

About 9.15am, Ashe ordered two sections of 21 men to get their arms, ammunition and cycles and proceed with him and Lieutenant Dick Mulcahy. Advancing in spaced-out groupings, Charlie Weston's unit formed the advance guard, Ned Rooney's section formed the main body and Joseph Lawless formed the rear guard.

It had occurred to Ashe that the Ashbourne RIC Barracks, which was on the route, might not have been evacuated, as some others had as a result of the IRA raids. Scouts were sent out who returned with word that the barracks were in a state of defence, and that a barricade was in the course of erection across the main road in front of the barracks. At about 10.30am off the volunteers set, cycling down the lanes towards the Dublin-to-Slane road at intervals of about 200 yards between sections.

Michael McAllister was in a group of eight, under the command of Charlie Weston, as they cycled towards Ashbourne. They reached a bend in the road, about a quarter of a mile from the junction with the main road, when they came across a policeman armed with a rifle, guarding a temporary barrier consisting of nothing more than a pole on two boxes. Confronted by the eight determined and armed volunteers, he calmly handed over his rifle, ammunition and handcuffs when requested to do so. Perhaps fearing that he might be shot, he attempted to calm the situation, by asking if he could smoke.

This was permitted, and the policeman was led away with an escort to the volunteer camp at Borranstown. Onward, the unit now continued to their destination.

When the volunteers were about five yards away from the Rath crossroads, Ashe raised his hand, and they came to a halt. It was about 10.40am. They dismounted and parked their bicycles. They approached the barracks in single file. Ashe then directed eleven of the men under the command of Joseph Lawless and Charlie Weston to enter the field on the north side of the road. Their orders were to proceed with caution using the hedges and ditches as cover, until they came to the nearest hedge to the rear of Ashbourne Barracks, which was about 200 yards down on the left-hand side of the road to Ashbourne.

As Jerry Golden's group waited for the other groups to get into position, they espied three RIC men cycling towards them. As they approached, Ashe ordered five of his men to capture and disarm them. Out of the field and onto the road they leapt, calling the surprised policemen to surrender. The two constables leapt from their bikes, dropped their arms and ammunition to the ground, and raised their hands in surrender. The sergeant was made of sterner stuff. Sergeant Brady of Dunshaughlin leapt to the ditch and began to reach for his revolver. As Jerry Golden approached him, he called out, 'Golden, I'll get you before I die!' Golden, armed with a Martini rifle with a long bayonet, raised his rifle to fire with the intention of wounding the policeman, but the cartridge jammed in the breech. Instead, he lunged at the sergeant with his bayonet. Brady avoided the lunge, and to his dismay, when Golden withdrew his rifle, the bayonet remained imbedded in the ground. Brady grabbed the barrel of the gun, pulling Golden down upon him. The volunteer released his hold on the Martini and grabbed at Brady's throat.

Meanwhile, the police sergeant had drawn his revolver and was about to fire when Bartle Weston went to Golden's assistance and struck the policeman over the head with the butt of his rifle. The sergeant dropped his revolver, and in terror called out, 'Don't kill me.' Brady was dragged to his feet, and having regained some composure, he was taken prisoner.[3] As all this was going on, one of the two constables, Roche by name, who had come from the Dunboyne Garrison to reinforce Ashbourne, made good his escape. Charlie Weston ordered Bernard McAllister and Jim Rooney to go after him. McAllister briefly relates the chase that followed:

> Rooney and I were told to follow up the policeman that got away. Less than half a mile from the Cross on the west side towards Ratoath we found his bicycle and rifle on the side of the road. We saw a gap in the hedge which he had made and traced him to a farmer's house about 300 yards away. We asked the farmer's wife if she had seen a policeman. She denied any knowledge of him. We searched the house and found him under a bed in a top bedroom. He had discarded his tunic and cap and was dressed in shoes, pants and a shirt only. We took him back to the Cross at Rath.[4]

The police in the barracks were now aware of the approaching rebels. John Austin, a local man, was standing at the barracks talking to one of the policemen, Constable Tully, and, on looking up towards the Cross of Rath, saw some of the rebels, as he described them, arriving on bicycles with guns on their shoulders. McAllister and Rooney having handed over their prisoner began to move off to take up their designated positions for the attack on the barracks. As they were doing so, a policeman was seen crossing the fields towards Ratoath, evidently sent to get aid. Either Ashe or Dr Hayes (the accounts vary) called out, 'Get that fellow!' Off the two volunteers set in pursuit. The policeman had a good 500-yard start on them. Across country the policeman ran, with the volunteers in hot pursuit. They fired a few shots at him, but he succeeded in getting away and was able later to summon help. By the time McAllister and Rooney had returned, the other volunteers were in position.

Friday: The Attack on Ashbourne Barracks

The barracks at Ashbourne, as the witness John Austin described them, was situated about 160 yards on the south-east side of the Cross of Rath, which is about half a mile north of the village of Ashbourne. It was situated on the main road from Dublin to Slane. The barracks was a detached building, set back about twenty yards from the road. It was two storeys high with gable ends on which there were no windows. The barracks had two doors, one to the front and one to the rear. There were windows on the front and back. The sergeant's married quarters took up a portion of the building, with its own separate porch entrance, constructed of wood and iron, at the rear. Between the barracks and the road, on either side of the path leading up to the barracks, there was a high bank of earth with a thorn hedge. On the other side of the road was a similar bank and hedge. Behind the barracks and on the north and south ends, there were a series of small fields with hedges and ditches. In normal times, the barracks was staffed by just a sergeant and four men. Aware that the rebels were in the vicinity, Sergeant Toomey sent out a request for additional men. Early that Friday morning an unspecified number of extra police arrived from Navan, Dunboyne and Slane, to reinforce the garrison.

Sergeant Brady and the other constable were brought before Ashe and Mulcahy, who persuaded them to act as go-betweens and get the garrison to surrender. Under an improvised white flag, the two men were escorted by Volunteer Paddy Holohan down to the barracks. As directed, and seemingly acting in good faith, Brady called out to the defenders to surrender. It was to no effect. The policemen were brought back to Ashe. Brady suggested that he be allowed to go down to the barracks and speak to his colleagues. Under the improvised white flag, a stick with a handkerchief tied to it, Brady walked down the path. But before he reached the door, he jumped through a gap in the ditch and ran off, using the hedgerows to aid his escape.

As instructed, Charlie Weston led his section up the field on the south side of the main road, to a position behind the hedge and ditch, facing the barracks. Ashe and Mulcahy joined them. They were within twenty-five to thirty yards from the front door of the barracks. The door was shut and the steel shutters on the windows were also closed. The garrison was called upon to surrender. There was no response. Ashe, then very bravely or perhaps foolishly, dressed in volunteer officer's uniform, got up onto the bank and demanded that they surrender. He informed them that the place was surrounded, and if necessary, he would destroy the barracks with the men inside it. Joseph Lawless, the Swords company's lieutenant reveals that Ashe:

> spoke with an authoritative assurance in his voice that no doubt inhibited the defenders from firing on him for a time; but an anti-climax was

reached when at the end of his speech no move was made to comply with the demand, and the next minute some shots came in his direction from the loopholed steel shutters.[5]

For his own safety, Ashe was pulled down from the bank to the ditch, as the volunteers returned fire on the front door and windows of the barracks in response. The little squad of volunteers with Ashe were then ordered to redeploy along the ditch, extending the range of fire. Charles Weston described the initial response of the volunteers: 'Our fire was heavy and the windows were quickly shattered.' Joseph Lawless described the response, though, as no more than a 'desultory siege of the barracks'. Bullets were not going to penetrate the steel shutters over the windows or the heavy-duty door. What was required was a more positive action. One policeman had escaped, and he undoubtedly would summon aid. Now it was a matter of time before police reinforcements arrived. In an attempt to forward the situation, Ashe handed Volunteer James O'Connor a sledgehammer and told him to follow him. His instruction was that he was to break in the barrack door. As they stealthily approached from the blind-sided gable end of the building, the RIC opened fire from the upstairs windows. The fire now became more intense, and Ashe and O'Connor withdrew for fear of being accidentally hit by their own side. Firing continued for half an hour as Dr Hayes indicated, but with little result.

More immediate action was required. In their armaments, the volunteers had two home-made canister bombs. They were two-pound size cocoa tins packed with four two-ounce sticks of gelignite and packed with shrapnel. The bombs had a ten-second fuse sticking out from a hole in the lid of the tin, which was soldered on. The man selected to throw them was Peter Blanchfield,[6] as Joseph Lawless informs us in some light-hearted detail:

> Few, if any, of the other men had ever seen one of these bombs exploded, and so no one quite knew what to expect from it, but it was with a keen interest those nearby watched Blanchfield as he peered cautiously above the bank to estimate the range and direction. They stood clear of him while he settled himself for the throw; then, the fuse is lit and, quick as a flash, the bomb is hurled high in the air and across the road, but alas, not high enough. Someone whose curiosity got the better of his caution peered over the top of the bank to see the result and noticed with horror that the bomb struck the top of a bush on the other side of the road and there seemed a chance that the whip of the bush top might return the bomb to its point of origin; but no, it went through, though at a reduced velocity, so that it fell in the middle of the front garden. To the listeners

crouched in the ditch the sharp percussive noise of the detonation, and the appearance high in the air of earth, stones and cabbage stalks was encouraging.

However, as Michael McAllister relates, it 'made a terrific noise and let off a lot of smoke but otherwise did no damage'. The volunteers followed up the explosion with a terrific burst of rifle fire. The noise from the bomb had made an impression on the garrison within the barracks. Fire from the barracks lessened. Within minutes, a makeshift white flag tied to a rifle barrel was pushed out through one of the upper windows. The garrison had agreed to surrender. A cease fire was ordered, and Ashe called out to the policemen to come out unarmed, with their hands held up. The attack had lasted half an hour.

Chapter 8

The Battle of Ashbourne

News arrived at Slane Castle that Ashbourne RIC barracks was under attack. The news was brought by the RIC man who has escaped at the start of the assault. Constable Eugene Bratton recounted what happened next:

> On Friday morning a force of police were assembled in Slane under the command of Co. Inspector Gray and District Inspector Smith [sic]. All the police except myself carried rifles. I was in civilian attire as I was driving a car. I think each policeman who was armed carried twenty rounds of ammunition. I would say there was about sixty police all told. We acquired a number of cars belonging to the 'gentry' of the surrounding areas. Cars at that time were only found in the possession of the very well-to-do, and had not come into general use as they are today. The cars acquired were driven by civilian drivers who were employed by their owners.... We knew what we were about and did not consider it was going to be an easy task.[1]

The convoy of cars, conveying about sixty policemen in all,[2] left Slane en route for Ashbourne. The constables were armed with Lee-Enfield Mark 1 Carbines, while their officers sported the double-action revolver, which because of its use with the Irish police was known as the Webley RIC. District Inspector Alexander Gray rode in the first car. He was supremely confident that they would prevail. The convoy passed through Balrath and on to Kilmoon, where there was another small barracks, a short distance from Ashbourne. Trailing behind them, having suffered two punctures to their car's tyres, Smyth, O'Connell and Bratton were just about to start off again when they were approached by an old man. He informed them that the rebels were up on their left at the Cross of Rath. Off they set, to catch up with the convoy to warn them. The police convoy was now some way ahead. In sight once more, Smyth ordered O'Connell to blow his whistle and have the leading cars stopped. Unable to get them to hear, all they could do was to try and catch them up. They caught up with them just as Gray called a halt. The site chosen to halt was on an eminence, and at the foot of which was a small road branching off. All was silent up ahead. The official government account according to the report given to the *Irish Times*, was that the intention of County Inspector Gray was 'to get out of the cars and march to Ashbourne', just a short distance away.

Dr Hayes with two other volunteers, Bernard McAllister and Christy Nugent, were stationed at the Cross to watch the main road, guarding the flank of Weston's line. Their attention was temporarily turned towards the barracks, as the shooting subsided and the garrison surrendered. Looking back towards the main road, Nugent cried out, 'Look! Look!' The other two turned to see a long line of motor cars approaching.[3] The first reaction of the volunteers was to drop to their knees and open fire, but Hayes shouted at them not to. The cars had come to a halt about 100 yards away. Hayes thought at first that they were the Dunboyne Volunteers who they believed were coming to assist them. He was quickly disabused of that when he recognised the police uniforms. They were RIC men riding in the cars. At the rear of the police convoy, Sergeant O'Connell recalled:

> We immediately left the cars, Mr. Smyth and I getting on the fence facing the Garristown road. Two shots rang out from the rebels, I should say at the C[ounty] I[inspector]'s car, which was stopped...We had observed four rebels at the gateway on the Garristown road.[4]

Volunteer Christy Nugent, armed with a Martini carbine had fired on the convoy, only to discover that he could not extract the spent case to reload.[5] With a useless weapon, Hayes sent him to inform Ashe of the developing situation, as Hayes and the other volunteer, Bernard McAllister, returned fire. Sergeant O'Connell continues:

> The officer directed me to fire. I did so, and immediately a bullet touched my moustache, and in rapid succession, roughly about seven bullets buried themselves in the fence between Mr. Smyth, a few constables, and I.

Having run down the road to the RIC barracks, at the point of its surrender, Nugent informed Ashe of the arrival of police reinforcements. His response was immediate. Charlie Weston heard Ashe call out to the men around him, 'Stop them cars!' as he pointed up the road. Looking up the road towards Slane, Weston saw the cars that had come to a halt just breasting the top of the hill:

The first cars pulled up short of the Cross Roads and I saw police jump from them with helmets and rifles. We jumped across the ditch into the field in front of the Bks. And in a few seconds Mulcahy came to me and ordered me to go up to the cross and see how many police were in it, and where they were. I got to the Cross and had a quick look up the road. I estimated there was a hundred police there and I returned to Mulcahy and reported this to him. He said, 'It does not matter if there is a thousand, we will deal with these fellows. Get your men along the road to the Cross and hold the police from the Cross. Keep them under fire and don't waste ammunition.'[6]

Bernard (Bennie) McAllister was relieved to see the arrival of reinforcements coming up behind him. There were some twenty volunteers now. The order was to hold the crossroads at all costs. Weston, the section leader, led the party. His order to the men was to use volley fire. Hardly had the police got out of the cars than a fusillade of bullets was sent into their midst. Sergeant J. Shanagher of Navan was shot through the heart (other accounts suggest that it was the head) almost as he was leaving his car. The police at the front of the convoy took what cover they could behind the cars and in the ditches. The others followed suit, behind and underneath the cars, as the firing began in earnest. Some attempted to charge the rebels. As they did so, the volunteers fired upon them. McAllister noted in their first charge, 'I noticed several fall and in one case I saw four out of a party of five get hit and fall.' One of them was Sergeant Young of Kilmoon. A chauffeur named Kepp, who worked for the Marquis Conyngham of Slane Castle, was shot in the leg as he dismounted and looked for shelter. He later died of his injury.

The result of Ashe's rapid response was that the convoy was halted before reaching Rath crossroads, and thus contained within one short, enclosed stretch of road closed in by hedges, for the whole of the ensuing action. If they had been soldiers, rather than policemen, they would have been dispersed by their officer into the fields either side. But they were policemen and not trained in field craft. This in essence, lacking any experience, is why they were eventually defeated. Some policemen sought shelter by the side and under the cars. Others dived into the ditch along the road, but these were killed or wounded in the early stages of the fight.

As if from the British Army manual that he had studied during training, Mulcahy now put that training into practical action:

The Attack: Preliminary measures: 'Each commander who issues orders should assemble his subordinate commanders, if possible, in view of the ground over which the troops are to operate, explain his orders, and satisfy himself that they thoroughly understand their respective tasks.'[7]

Mulcahy ordered two groups of volunteers to advance across the fields on both sides of the road and enfilade the police position. Near the rear of the police convoy, observing the rebel movements, Sergeant O'Connell said to Smyth:

> I am afraid we are surrounded, sir. He agreed. We went back along the fence for some distance, and potted for roughly half an hour at the rebels. Mr Smyth had but a revolver. He kept repeatedly saying, I wish, O'Connell, I had a rifle. We experienced trouble from our rear all along; a good many bullets were hitting very close to us. I said I'd rush across the road to see where the bullets were coming from. He acquiesced. I did so, and spotted a young fellow about seventy yards behind the road fence. I found his dead body here when all was over. His brother, a rebel, was crying over it. There was another further down about 400 yards away – I fired four shots. I could not say I got him. I had to leave off the firing it became so desperate.[8]

Mulcahy, meanwhile, had turned his attention to the other sections. Joseph Lawless had remained in the ditch on the north side of the barracks, where he had been told to remain until further orders. One of his men pointed out the approach of Mulcahy. Lawless saw the oncoming Mulcahy from about 200 yards away. He was shouting something and waving his arm in some sort of signal, but Lawless could not hear or understand amidst the shooting. Then Mulcahy moved away to rejoin Weston's section. Lawless sent one of his men, Ned Stafford, after Mulcahy to find out what it was he wanted. He had selected Stafford because he was in volunteer uniform, so there would be no danger that he might be mistaken for an RIC man. The order from Mulcahy was that Lawless was to outflank the police by crossing the fields, go past the volunteers already in position and get behind the police to cut off any retreat by them. Of equal importance was that they should look out for police reinforcements coming down the road.

Meanwhile, Ashe ordered those of the men who were on the front of the barracks to get up to the crossroads and try to stop the RIC men from reaching it, or climbing into the fields, possibly outflanking the volunteers already committed to the fight. Jerry Golden was one of those so ordered:

> We rushed up and three of us, Mich. Fleming, Dick Aungier and myself lay down in a gully on the left hand side of the road to Slane and about

7 yards on the Ashbourne side of the Cross Roads. Mich. McAllister, Bartle Weston, Bennie McAllister threw themselves along the bank on the right hand side of the road the remainder of the men took up their positions about 6 or 7 feet behind us three and we all opened a rapid fire.[9]

Mick McAllister, advancing to join with them, remembered thinking:

There seemed to be a mile of cars halted north of the crossroads. Rumours had been prevalent during the preceding days, one of which was that a British Naval brigade had landed in Dundalk and we now concluded that this was this Brigade coming for us.[10]

McAllister's fears were not realised. They were not the naval brigade that he had feared, but he could see 'that it was a big force of RIC we were up against'.

Meanwhile, the men at the rear of the barracks were ordered to take up positions in order to attack the police on their left flank. Mulcahy took command of this group, leading them in an attempt at outflanking the policemen. Using the banks and water cuttings along the fields, Mulcahy and his section were able to get up to the crossroads unseen. Here, they could see the police taking cover along the road, beside and under the cars, and into the fields on the western side of the road. With the police in some disorder still, the volunteers put down heavy fire on their positions. McAllister recorded:

We opened up with rapid fire on them and soon my rifle was burning my hands. This pinned the police to the ground and what fire was coming from them now became very erratic.

At an early stage in the fight, the 57-year-old Inspector Gray, standing prominently by the lead car, was directing his men to take up positions. A discharge from a shotgun at fairly close range tore into both his hands. Then he was hit in the stomach. Wounded, but not fatally at this stage, he staggered for cover in a ditch. From there, he attempted to rally his men. As Gray was the obvious leader, fire was directed at him. Weston notes, 'We were careful not to waste ammunition and only to fire when targets presented themselves.' Gray was an obvious target. McAllister added, 'After the initial burst of fire by us, our men settled down very calmly and, although this was our first experience of being under fire, they were behaving as veterans. They were not firing wildly or wasting their ammunition but deliberately picking their target and dealing with them very cooly in their own time.' The battle developed into fighting amongst small groups as the police moved from one sheltered position to another, with the volunteers moving into position to pin them down.

Sergeant William O'Connell and the men about him, though badly positioned initially, were fighting back:

> I got on to the middle of the road. I could see Mr Smyth above me, rapidly firing with his revolver, apparently at close range. He was without his cap, and was a good deal exposed over the fence. I meant to shout to him not to expose himself, but I had not time. The firing was desperate now, and I and three other Constables (McKeon, Shane, Cunningham) were engaged with rebels in front of us on the road. We wounded or killed three or four of them, and they disappeared off the road. I got on a ditch slightly lower down than Mr Smyth. He was deliberately firing towards his left-hand side, still wearing no cap. There were some Constabulary near him. He was between me and them. His firing ceased somewhat, and I got back again to the centre of the road, and for a second time the rebels appeared on the road in front of us. The motor car near us was smashed up. The fire was very severe. We got the rebels off the road a second time, but not before Constable McKeon was wounded, a scalp wound. I had two small scratches, one on the second finger right hand and one immediately over the hip. Some men round us were moaning heavily.[11]

Then occurred one of those bizarre incidents of combat. Two civilians arrived in a small two-seater car during the fight. Apparently, as Bernie McAllister relates, 'the police thought those were Ashe and Dr Hayes as their car was similar to the one used by them, and they shot both of them. No one in our unit knew who they were.'[12]

Up near the Cross, Ashe issued an instruction to Mulcahy, 'Bring down the camp reserve. Charge the police line from the Slane end. I'll support you from the Cross.'[13] In the volunteer camp, Frank Lawless registered the approach of Mulcahy across the fields. He noticed the occasional strike of a bullet in the ploughed field. It did not appear to be directed fire; the police had no idea where the attackers were but were firing in the general direction in hope. Arriving at the crossroads, Frank Lawless and his men were joined by Ashe. After a brief consultation between the two senior officers, and a reassurance by a supremely confident Mulcahy 'that the police had not a chance of success. They had walked into a trap,' they were led off by Mulcahy.

Meanwhile, now behind the RIC lines, beyond the last car of the convoy, Joseph Lawless (Frank's son) and his unit had been ordered to prevent the police from escaping. Impatient for action, Joseph Lawless decided to act under his own initiative There was heavy fire on his right flank:

> It occurred to me then that if, in fact, the police were to advance upon us from where they were, they would meet the right flank of our line, enfilading our position from which we could bring no fire of any consequence to bear upon them. Whereupon [Ned] Rooney and I, in consultation, decided to move our sections forthwith into the ditch at right angles to our left flank and fronting the field which had hitherto been in our rear, while in the meantime, another messenger had been sent to find Ashe or Mulcahy and ask for instructions.[14]

The plan as outlined to Lawless initially was that the unit under Weston, strengthened by Ned Rooney's section and half of his own men, were to launch a 'vigorous assault' on the police position from the crossroads. Lawless and his remaining team were to manoeuvre to a position in the rear of the police position on the main road. There they were to conceal themselves until the attack was launched from the other side of the position. Their job was to see that none of the police made good their escape. Ashe personally led Joseph Lawless's group to the position they were to hold on the main road, about 100 yards north-west of the rearmost police car. Lawless listed his men in his Witness Statement. They were Peter Blanchfield ('our grenadier' with the remaining bomb), Johny Devine of Lusk, Paddy Brogan of Lusk, Jack Rafferty also of Lusk, Jimmy O'Connor of St Margaret's and 'a young lad' as Lawless describes him, also from St Margaret's named Teeling. This was Nicholas Teeling. To reach their designated position, they travelled along the bottom of ditches in single file, through the briars and brushwood, wading in water and mud. They were two fields away from the police position, their sound muffled by the hedges. Having reached their position and being given final instructions, Ashe left them to return to the main body of the volunteers. It was about one o'clock that afternoon. In his statement, Lawless described the terrain:

> The main Dublin–Slane road, upon which we then were, is a wide straight road at this point, descending in a very slight incline towards Rath crossroads. Immediately north-west of our position this incline culminated and dropped slightly in the opposite direction, so that at a point about seventy yards further back than we were one could kneel on the road and be out of view of the police position...[the hedges either side of the road rose to] four to six feet high, which has a thorn hedge on

the field side…It was at a junction of one of the lateral ditches with the road ditch that we were placed.

Cautiously looking down the road Lawless could see the end of the line of police cars. The last one was about 80 to 100 yards away. Then, to Lawless's complete surprise, a very tall man in civilian clothes stood up from behind a bush on the other side of the road. Lawless naturally assumed that he was a policeman. 'I swung my rifle, but I held fire as he seemed unarmed and had his hands raised over his head.' He identified himself. His name was Quigley, and he was the County Surveyor for Meath. He informed them that he had tried to get to them ahead of the police to warn them but had been unsuccessful. Lawless thanked him and sent him on his way.[15]

While all this was going on, down on the road near the Rath crossroads, the police were under heavy fire. A number of them, in the middle of the police convoy, who had dismounted from the cars now sought shelter in the ditch on the right-hand side of the road. Others were lying underneath the cars or by their side. Michael McAllister recounted:

> We continued to engage the enemy whose firing now became very spasmodic. They occasionally hit the bank we were behind but did not injure any of us and there was little or no movement on their part. They were, apparently, hugging mother earth for dear life. Some of them had realised their mistake in getting under the cars and tried to get out of that position but were promptly dealt with by us.

Mulcahy had taken more men across country in an attempt to outflank the police. Michael McAllister alleges that just 'eight of us were holding up this big force of RIC' at the cross. RIC man Eugene Bratton records that Sergeant Shanagher, as previously mentioned, was one of the first policemen to fall; he was shot through the heart. He had leapt from the car and was seeking some form of shelter. Jerry Golden ascribes the killing to Michael McAllister:

> I think the first casualty to the enemy took place; we were about two minutes at the motor cars when we saw one of the Police, Sergt. Shanaher, step out of the front one and attempt to cross the road to a cutting in the bank which would give him cover to fire on us. He was just in the middle of the road when I saw Mick McAllister step out on the footpath and raise his rifle and fire at the man who staggered into the cutting and fell against the side of it with his rifle pointed down the road at us who were at the Cross roads and only about 60 yards from us.[16]

Golden records in his Witness Statement that he, Michael Fleming and Dick Aungier had all fired at Shanagher but without result.

Weston and his men now received orders from a runner that they were to pull back to reinforce the others at the Cross. As they began to do so, a countering order came through, that they were to return to their former position. The situation in their intended position had improved with the addition of more men. 'After we got back to our position,' Weston revealed, 'we discovered the police under the cars by the dust that would rise when they fired. This was caused by the blast or vacuum set up by the police rifles when fired. We put down heavy fire on the police where we thought they were and also under the cars. Some of the police rolled out from under the cars and I would say there was a number of them hit at this stage.' The police were now under fire from the Rath crossroads and an enfilading fire from across the fields at the Garristown Road. Out on the road, in and around the parked cars, a number of the policemen now lay dead or wounded.

Following the surrender of the RIC barracks, Mulcahy placed Dr Hayes and a small section of men behind a hedge, some 100 yards at the rear of the barracks. His orders were to prevent the garrison escaping from the building or joining in the fight. Hayes, as a doctor, was also attending to the wounded. The fight had now lasted for an hour.

With the arrival of the men from the camp, Mulcahy then led Frank Lawless and the reserve, using all shelter available, up along the inside of the hedge to the road, to a position on the extreme north side of the police position. On the other side of the road, with Gray being incapacitated, District Inspector Smyth, a former British Army officer, was now directing the police action near the rear of the motor convoy.

Frank's son, Joseph Lawless, whose men were positioned to cut off any retreating policemen, began moving his men around to cover all eventualities. His men were too close to the road, the hedges limiting their vision to a few yards. However, if he placed them out on the road, they would in turn not only give away the position of the volunteers but would also make them targets. Lawless moved Jack Rafferty and Paddy Brogan to the corner of the field, from where, without being seen, they could look down the road to where the police lay concealed in the ditch. They were then in a position to warn of any movement by the police. Lawless placed Peter (or Peadar) Blanchfield (the company's 'grenadier') who had the second of the cannister bombs behind a large tree, cut off at a height of about eight or ten feet, which leaned towards the road. Given notification of any police retreat by Rafferty or Brogan, he could lob his bomb at any car that tried to pass. To avoid being surprised in the rear by police reinforcements, Lawless placed James O'Connor and Nicholas

Teeling to watch. Seeing if any advantage could be gained by placing men on the other side of the road, Lawless, bending double so that he could not be seen by the police, crossed the road and went into the field. The bank was thickly covered by a hawthorn hedge. From there, he could see, down below, the policemen in the ditch on the other side of the road. None of them had succeeded in crossing the road to the side he was on, nor had they entered the field below where his men were situated. As fire from the volunteers at the Cross had prevented them from moving, there would be no retreat along that hedgerow, and the possibility of his men being outflanked or attacked was negligible.

Lawless returned to his men. Here, he discovered that Jack Rafferty had received a serious scalp wound in his absence. Peter Blanchfield had taken him to the volunteer dressing station for the attention of Dr Hayes. How he received the wound was not explained. It would appear that it had been a random volley fired by the police to keep volunteer heads down, while Constable Eugene Bratton escaped. Bratton seemed to think that this was the case, as he contends in his Statement. So, there they were, just five volunteers under Joseph Lawless, who were ordered to prevent the withdrawal of the police and to ensure that the main body were not surprised by police reinforcements arriving. To add to the challenge, Blanchfield, escorting Rafferty, had also taken the bomb with him. As they watched and waited, young Teeling called out that a man was advancing towards them. Joseph Lawless looked down the road. 'It seemed that there was some movement among the long grass and small bushes of the shallow channel between the cars on the roadside and the bank beyond, and I believed I could see someone sprawled under one of the rearmost cars, but obviously the bulk of the police were in the deep ditch beyond the bank bounding the road on the north-east side.' What he was witnessing along the ditch of the road, appears to have been the escape of Constable Bratton to summon reinforcements.

It is not clear whether Bratton was acting under orders from District Inspector Harry Smyth or, being isolated, was acting under his own initiative. He does not make it clear in his Witness Statement. Crossing a field away from the road, he made his way northwards about 200 yards before he was discovered. Bratton relived what happened next in his Statement:

Firing was continuous and general now. I was not armed and in civilian clothes. After some time I moved back towards Kilmoon and after travelling about two hundred yards I was held up by a party of rebels who were behind the road ditch in our rear. Just at this moment a volley was fired in our direction. The rebels ducked for cover and I ducked too and out of that position, showing them a clear pair of heels. I kept going towards Kilmoon and, after travelling some distance I got out on to the road. I secured a bicycle from a house there and cycled to Balrath barracks and from there I 'phoned Navan and Drogheda RIC Barracks and told them what had happened.[17]

It was now 2pm, Lawless and his five companions were becoming restless to be involved. They could hear the shooting down around Rath crossroads. Further down the road from there, the men from the camp under Frank Lawless, Joe's father, had arrived. There were just six of them, but they were good shots. Under orders, they crossed into the fields, with the intention of manoeuvring to get behind the police. One of their number, Tommy Rafferty of Lush, stood up on the bank in an attempt to locate the enemy. He was seen by the police on the road, about 150 yards away, and was shot. He was mortally wounded and taken away to a nearby cottage by some of his comrades. Frank Lawless's men, now five in number, worked their way along the inner hedges of the fields on the right-hand side of the road until, unseen, they got behind the police's position. Frank's son, Joseph, meanwhile, impatient with doing nothing, decided to move out onto the roadside. They were seen by some of the police, sheltering near the last car in the convoy, who opened fire. 'I'm hit!' cried Patrick Bogan from the Lusk Company, as they all dived back into the ditch and relative safety. Brogan was clasping his waist, now in obvious distress. Lawless got him to remove his hand from his waist in order to examine him. Bogan had been hit all right, but miraculously for him, it was not serious. The bullet had struck the buckle of his belt and had been deflected. Lawless opened his shirt but there was no sign of blood, just a red weal above his hip to show the path of the bullet. It had penetrated the belt in front, then travelled through his clothing above his hip, barely touching the skin. It exited without causing any further injury, save for a hole in his shirt.

The position of the volunteers to the rear of them had become known to the police. Lawless and his men were now committed to the battle as gunfire was directed against them. A firefight began. While some began firing from the hedgerow, Volunteers John Devine and Joseph Lawless got out onto the road. Lying flat, they began returning fire. Lawless described their intention, 'There were no individual targets in view, but we agreed to spread our fire discriminately…Devine and I raking the outer channel and the cars on the roadside.' They shot the petrol tank of the rearmost car, thus preventing any attempt at a sudden evacuation. Somewhat emboldened, Joseph Lawless got up from his prone position along the road. He raised himself onto one knee, which gave him a full view of the enemy. John Devine joined him.

Together, they raked the enemy position. Now, going against orders to remain in position, the two volunteers advanced further forward towards the police position, emptying a magazine each, into the police position. Resuming a kneeling position to reload, a bullet from return fire struck the roadside about a foot in front of Lawless. The grit hit him full in the face. Such was the force, Lawless was convinced that he had been shot. He rolled over into the ditch where Patrick Brogan attended to him. There was no blood. The grit was wiped away with the aid of a handkerchief, and Lawless's sight was restored. A fierce firefight had developed at the rear of the police column, with neither side having the other in full view. Then, to Lawless's alarm, Jimmy O'Connor warned him that there were men on the other side of the road, behind the hedges, moving opposite their position. Lawless peered through the hedge and saw crouching figures approaching. Believing he and his group were being outflanked, Lawless fired across the road at one of the figures, now barely twenty yards away. Fire was returned. To his dismay, Lawless now discovered that he had run out of rifle ammunition. It was the same for the others. Only Johnny Devine had some, but it was for his Howth Mauser and was of no use to the others. Lawless decided to withdraw. Emptying his revolver in the general direction of the men across the road, the group moved off. Devine agreed to give covering fire as they evacuated.

Arriving back at the little road leading from Garristown to the Rath crossroads, Joseph Lawless found Dr Hayes. The battle had been going on for two and a half hours. Lawless reported that he and his remaining men had come under fire from across the road and running out of ammunition had been obliged to withdraw. Lawless feared that police reinforcements had arrived. Ashe now arrived to hear what was happening. Accepting the interpretation, Ashe considered withdrawal of the volunteers. It was decided to assist the getaway of the men by moving all the bicycles and Hayes's car, which had been parked on the roadside near the crossroads, to the rear. Accordingly, the bicycles were all removed about 600 yards back in the Garristown direction where a slight bend in the road concealed them.

Mulcahy now arrived, puzzled at what was happening. Hayes explained the situation. Understanding the confusion, Mulcahy informed the group that the 'enemy force' on the other side of the road was in fact himself and the unit left behind at the camp at Borranstown that had been called up to join the fight. This section contained Lawless's father and his uncle James. What had happened was that following a delay, Mulcahy went to meet the men and conducted them to the position across the road from where District Inspector Harry Smyth and his men were putting up a strong resistance. Mulcahy knew that Joseph Lawless and his men had been placed at the rear of the police column. But Joseph Lawless was no longer there. A scout should have been sent on in advance to make contact, but it was deemed that there was not sufficient time. There had been a complete breakdown in the plan, caused by Joseph Lawless, who disobeyed orders to remain where he had been put. By his repositioning, he had now put his comrades in danger. The fierceness of Joseph Lawless's men's fire that followed convinced Mulcahy they had stumbled upon police reinforcements. It was not until Mulcahy saw a uniformed Joseph Lawless fleeing the scene on the other side of the road that he realised each party had been firing on each other. He ordered his men to cease fire. To his horror, having discovered what had happened, Joseph Lawless now realised that he might have killed his father or his uncle James – and they him.

Elsewhere near the front of the police convoy, a private duel was being enacted. The 32-year-old Matt Kelly of Corduff was fighting it out with a lone policeman in the field opposite. Kelly was sheltering behind a stone gate pier. He had been wounded in the left forearm. Every so often, he took an occasional shot at the concealed policeman and faced the incoming shot that struck the bars on the iron gate or the stone pier he was concealed behind. Lawless, now re-armed made his way back to his men. He came upon the little private war. He sent Kelly back to Dr Hayes to have the wound attended to. Aware that he could not just leave this sniper, and thus endanger the lives of unsuspecting volunteers, Lawless decided to take him on. He needed to pinpoint the exact position of his adversary. He waited until the policeman showed himself and fired once more. The bullet struck the iron gate. Lawless now knew exactly where he was. He returned the fire, then fired again at the position. Lawless waited, uncertain of his marksmanship. He waited, but there was no reply. He tested the policeman in the field opposite by placing his hat on the point of his bayonet and let it be clearly seen. There was no reply. Lawless had either killed him, or the policeman had withdrawn.

Lawless now returned to the fight proper. He met up with Charlie Weston, bringing in one of his wounded men. Lawless agreed to join with Weston as he returned to his section at the crossroads. They had retraced their steps to the gateway where Lawless had continued Matt Kelly's duel. A little way off, the battle was continuing but at a slackened pace. Then suddenly Lawless heard the snapping of twigs. Was this it? Was it their turn to be killed? From the hedgerow, suddenly, as Lawless describes:

> I saw the black figure of a policeman clambering up from the ditch behind, and standing up amidst the bushes of the hedge on top of the bank within ten paces of where I stood. I had my rifle hanging by its sling from my right shoulder and, consequently, could never have brought it into action

in time had the enemy been anxious to shoot first...It gradually dawned on me that the policeman appeared to be unarmed and was raising his hands above his head while he called out to me not to shoot.[18]

He wanted to surrender. Lawless and Weston could not believe it at first. Both pointed their rifles at the man. Then, other policemen emerged with their hands in the air. 'Eleven stalwart, mud-spattered and thoroughly demoralized RIC men climbed through the hedge and formed up in two ranks on the road before me,' Lawless added. Leaderless, and cut off from their comrades, they were surrendering. Lawless and Weston studied their captives. One of them, a youngish fellow, had a rather bad scalp wound where a bullet had made a perfectly straight furrow laying bare his skull from forehead to crown and right in the centre. Lawless could not help but see the funny side to this, observing, 'The scar that will leave will make a perfect parting of his hair in future.' It was a ludicrous thought in the middle of a battle. Most of the other policemen were also wounded. Lawless led them off to the makeshift infirmary, where Dr Hayes attended to them.

Weston had returned to the fight. Lawless replenished his ammunition supply and moved forward up towards the crossroads to join him. The main action was now concentrated around the rearmost number of cars. Police morale elsewhere was cracking. Isolated from the rest of the RIC, District Inspector Harry Smyth, the former British Army officer, had taken control of a small group of policemen. To the rear of them, and anxious to engage, was Jim Lawless's section, which included his brother, Frank. They moved to within ten or fifteen yards of the rearmost police car.

Meanwhile, down near the Rath crossroads, emerging from the side road and onto the main road, Joseph Lawless found Weston engaged in his own little fight, with an isolated pocket of policemen in front of the cottages on the other side of the road. Weston informed him that he had wounded at least one of the RIC men as they attempted to reposition themselves in one of the cottages. The two men opened rapid fire. There was no response.

Much further up the road, to the rear of the cars, the fight continued. Sergeant O'Connell described its intensity:

There was a systematic fire both sides of the road. Explosive bullets were freely used, and a good deal of grape, something in the form of buckshot. This systematic fire was having its effect; the men were getting wounded. It was impossible to stick it. Mr Smyth came on past me partly running back-ways and repeatedly firing into the field with his revolver. I shouted at him 'For God's sake, sir, don't expose yourself so much.' He passed on and said something I could not catch. He got over the fence and fought from the drain for a time. He fought openly from this point for a considerable time.[19]

The exploding bullets were in fact the very large bullets fired from the dated Mausers. By their size, they caused terrible wounds amongst their victims.

Facing Smyth and his men were Frank Lawless and his unit, including his brother James. Closing in on the police, the company lost its second volunteer, John (Jack) Crennigan, who was killed outright. Joseph Lawless tells the story of what happened, as related to him by his father:

> They could hear a voice loudly berating the police for skulking in the ditch and calling for them to get up and fight like men. Moving out to get a better view of the speaker, he saw the police officer (whom we subsequently were told was District Inspector H. Smith [sic] standing on top of the bank and waving his revolver towards them, as he reviled the police for their cowardice in his effort to get them to stand up and fight the closing enemy. Smith was undoubtedly a brave man who stood exposed, to show the police that they need not fear to get up there also. Hearing the movement of my father towards him, he fired at him on the instant, and his bullet missing my father, penetrated Crennigan's heart, killing him instantly. My father's shot at the same time hit Smith on the forehead and smashed his skull. He still lay as he fell – as I came along – feet on the bank and head near the edge of the roadside, and, although his brain matter spattered the grass beside him, he yet lived, his breath coming in great gasps at long intervals, in the minute or so I watched him. Then he was still, and the muscles of his face relaxed.[20]

Crennigan's death was personal to Joseph and his father. Young Crennigan was not only a comrade but also a friend. The 21-year-old had worked on the Lawless farm for a number of years. He and Joseph Lawless had gone to school together. Young Crennigan was almost family.

It was now about 4pm. Mulcahy's section were slowly driving the police down to Ashe's position at the Cross. James O'Connor 'thought Dick Mulcahy was a very brave man as he went up to the middle of the road disregarding any cover and firing at the RIC as he went'. Mulcahy called out to the panic-stricken policemen, urging them to surrender. 'Will you surrender by [God]. If you don't we will give you a dog's death,' Charlie Weston recalled. Mulcahy had now made a decision to end the fight. He would undertake a bayonet charge as per the British Army training manual:

A bayonet assault should preferably be made under cover of fire, surprise, or darkness. In these circumstances the prospect of success is greatest, for a bayonet is useless except hand-to-hand.

The bayonet is essentially a weapon of offence which must be used with skill and vigour; otherwise it has but little effect.

Jerry Golden was with the volunteers down at the crossroads. During a lull in the firing, Golden heard a shout, 'Charge!':

Looking up the road we saw about 300 yards away Lieutenant Mulcahy and about seven men charge down on the police with fixed bayonets. When the police saw them, those who were unable to run threw their arms on the road and rushed into a labourer's cottage which was just about fifty yards from the crossroads on the right hand side towards Slane. We immediately opened fire on the police as they huddled together trying to get into the cottage and after about ten minutes we heard the shout, 'We surrender,' and they marched out on the road…The commandant [Ashe] then ordered firing to cease.

Elsewhere, Michael McAllister recorded the surrender of his group of policemen:

The police now came out from their positions with their hands up and we herded them in together to a central position where we were joined by Mulcahy and Ashe and the remainder of our men. Their arms and equipment were now collected up and Doctor Hayes, who had now come up, set about tending to their wounded. They seemed to have a big number killed and wounded. I remember the District Inspector Smith [sic] was sitting in a car with what appeared to be half his hand blown away.

This in fact was County Inspector Alexander Gray, wounded at the start of the battle. McAllister continues, 'While Doctor Hayes was treating him he never winced and I remarked to Doctor Hayes that he was a brave man. The Doctor agreed with me.' Gray, a widower, was taken to the County Infirmary in Navan for further treatment. Here he died of his wounds on 10 May 1916. Gray was 57 years old at the time of his death. He was buried in Lucan Old Cemetery in County Dublin.

Up at the tail end of the convoy of cars, with the shooting of Smyth, police resistance crumbled completely. The men who had been with him were driven down towards the crossroads. 'Some were running and taking cover after having discarded their rifles,' as Golden testified. Confronted by more armed Volunteers, the policemen threw up their hands and surrendered. 'They were astonished to find their attackers so youthful and so few in number,' Sean O'Luing wrote in his biography of Ashe:

> One of them, [a policeman] showing signs of frenzy, shouted to the others, 'Are you going to surrender to a lot of schoolboys?' But his colleagues pacified him.[21]

After a five-and-a-half-hour battle, it was all over. The police had been defeated. The Republicans had triumphed. Along the road, District Inspector Harry Smyth lay dying. Sergeant O'Connell was to write:

> I did not actually see him being hit, but when all was over and I got released, I found the poor man in the drain breathing his last. I removed him with the aid of a few Constables to the roadside. He lived roughly three quarters of an hour. I almost broke down when I saw him, and his words of the night before when we were together at Slane Bridge came back to mind. 'I would much prefer, O'Connell, to be killed by a German bullet than one from these fellows.' It was wretched. Poor Mr Smyth was dead, he who had gone out with us that same morning full of life and vigour.

The firing ceased; the battle was over. Police Sergeant William O'Connell had timed the battle. It lasted from 12 noon to 5.50pm. 'I happened to look at my watch,' he clarified.

Ashbourne resident and witness to battle, John Austin, was asked to assist in removing the bodies of the dead policemen from the road:

> I got a horse and cart and proceeded down the road...Two of the policemen who had not been wounded helped me to collect the dead policemen into the cart. I had eight dead men in the cart when I had finished. Included in this number were Sergeant Shanagher from Navan and Sergeant Young. Two of the dead men were civilians whom I believe were drivers of the cars. The bodies of the County Inspector of Police and the District Inspector had been taken away before I got on the scene, and the wounded men were also taken away.[22]

Regarding Sergeant Shanagher, Austin reveals that 'he was shot right between the eyes as he left the car and slumped into a small depression on the side of

Patrick Pearse, the son of an Englishman, had overall command of the Irish forces during the Easter Rising.

The Irish Volunteers poster summoning Irish Nationalists to an inaugural meeting at the Rotunda in Dublin.

A membership card was issued to all Irish Volunteers upon joining.

An advertisement depicting the uniform of an officer in the Irish Volunteers. In reality, few men were as fully equipped as this. Some of the ordinary volunteers had no more than an arm band.

Revolt of the Sinn Feiners. A misnomer that was adopted by the British press. The rising had no direct connection with the political party.

Commandant Thomas Ashe proved to be a highly competent guerrilla leader.

Captain Edward Joseph Rooney.

Richard Hayes became Ashe's adjutant after releasing command to him.

Lieutenant Charlie Weston.

Frank Lawless, a senior officer under Ashe, organized the purchase and storage of the brigade's arms and ammunition.

Joseph V. Lawless.

A group photograph of some of the members of the 5th Brigade who served under Ashe.

The Military Sunbeam

Single Speed—
Nett Cash
£10 10 0

The Military Sunbeam bicycle, first used by the British Army from 1910. Ashe adopted their use for quick transport.

POBLACHT NA H EIREANN.
THE PROVISIONAL GOVERNMENT
OF THE
IRISH REPUBLIC
TO THE PEOPLE OF IRELAND.

IRISHMEN AND IRISHWOMEN In the name of God and of the dead generations from which she receives her old tradition of nationhood, Ireland, through us, summons her children to her flag and strikes for her freedom.

Having organised and trained her manhood through her secret revolutionary organisation, the Irish Republican Brotherhood, and through her open military organisations, the Irish Volunteers and the Irish Citizen Army, having patiently perfected her discipline, having resolutely waited for the right moment to reveal itself, she now seizes that moment, and, supported by her exiled children in America and by gallant allies in Europe, but relying in the first on her own strength, she strikes in full confidence of victory.

We declare the right of the people of Ireland to the ownership of Ireland, and to the unfettered control of Irish destinies, to be sovereign and indefeasible. The long usurpation of that right by a foreign people and government has not extinguished the right, nor can it ever be extinguished except by the destruction of the Irish people. In every generation the Irish people have asserted their right to national freedom and sovereignty; six times during the past three hundred years they have asserted it in arms. Standing on that fundamental right and again asserting it in arms in the face of the world, we hereby proclaim the Irish Republic as a Sovereign Independent State, and we pledge our lives and the lives of our comrades-in-arms to the cause of its freedom, of its welfare, and of its exaltation among the nations.

The Irish Republic is entitled to, and hereby claims, the allegiance of every Irishman and Irishwoman. The Republic guarantees religious and civil liberty, equal rights and equal opportunities to all its citizens, and declares its resolve to pursue the happiness and prosperity of the whole nation and of all its parts, cherishing all the children of the nation equally, and oblivious of the differences carefully fostered by an alien government, which have divided a minority from the majority in the past.

Until our arms have brought the opportune moment for the establishment of a permanent National Government, representative of the whole people of Ireland and elected by the suffrages of all her men and women, the Provisional Government, hereby constituted, will administer the civil and military affairs of the Republic in trust for the people.

We place the cause of the Irish Republic under the protection of the Most High God, Whose blessing we invoke upon our arms, and we pray that no one who serves that cause will dishonour it by cowardice, inhumanity, or rapine. In this supreme hour the Irish nation must, by its valour and discipline and by the readiness of its children to sacrifice themselves for the common good, prove itself worthy of the august destiny to which it is called.

Signed on Behalf of the Provisional Government,
THOMAS J. CLARKE.
SEAN Mac DIARMADA.   THOMAS MacDONAGH.
P. H. PEARSE,   EAMONN CEANNT.
JAMES CONNOLLY.   JOSEPH PLUNKETT.

The declaration of Irish independence.

The Irish Republican flag.

The formidable Marxist James Connolly was commandant of the Irish Citizen Army.

General Sir John Maxwell, commander of the British forces, put down the Easter Rising.

A poster depicting the Irish Republican leaders, issued after the surrender.

Molly Adrien acted as a courier between the 5th Brigade and rebel headquarters in Dublin.

The highly competent Richard Mulcahy. He became Ashe's active adjutant during the campaign. Later, he went on to command the revitalised Irish Republican Army.

Ex-British Army officer, Harry Smyth, took command of the RIC force at the Battle of Ashbourne following the fatal wounding of Alexander Gray.

County Inspector Alexander Gray initially led the police attack against the rebels at Ashbourne.

SERGT. JOHN YOUNG, R.I.C.,
Killed in action at Ashbourne, Co. Meath, during the rising. The Inspector-General, R.I.C., sent a message of sympathy to his wife on the death of her "gallant husband while bravely performing his duty in pursuing the rebels."

RIC John Young and James Gormley fought at the Battle of Ashbourne.

A street barricade erected by the rebels in Dublin during the Rising.

Sackville Street in Dublin, scene of the most intensive fighting in the Easter Rising.

Prisoners being marched away to captivity following the surrender of the Irish forces.

Another photograph showing Irish prisoners being marched along Bachelor's Walk, Dublin, under British guard following the Easter Rising.

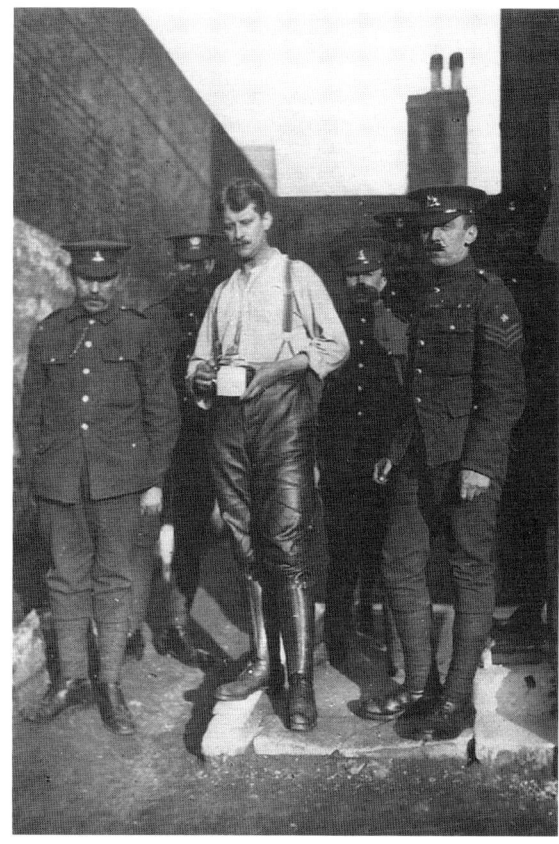

Thomas Ashe as a prisoner. Even in captivity he had a presence.

A lone Irish prisoner from the 5th Brigade is taken under armed guard into captivity.

The grave of Harry Smyth, who was killed at the Battle of Ashbourne.

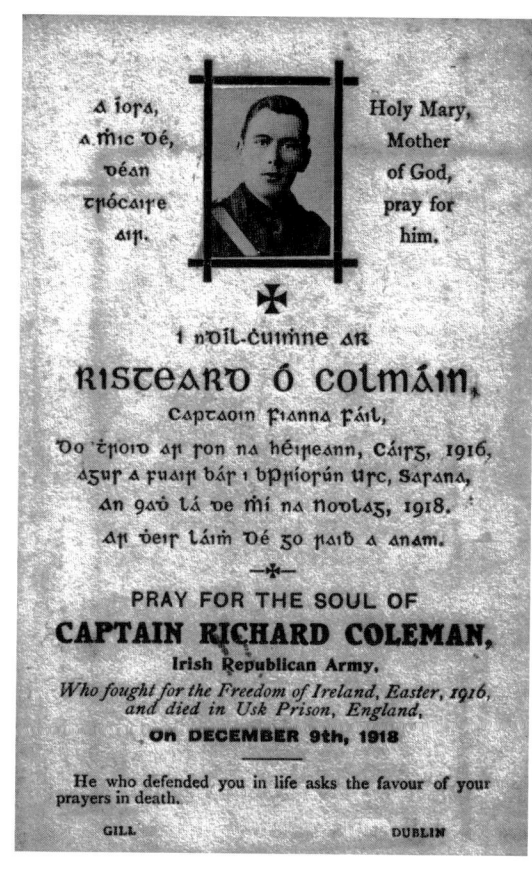

Memorial card of Richard Coleman.

The North Camp of Frongoch Internment Camp. Most prisoners here were released at Christmas time in 1916.

The Ashbourne 1916 Memorial.

the road. The road that evening was a terrible sight with blood and bandages strewn on it…We put the dead men in the washhouse at the end of the barracks. And the following day coffins arrived for them and they were taken away in a lorry.'

Official government reports, loath to admit the facts, claimed that the police surrendered only when they had practically used up all their ammunition.[23] From the various volunteer accounts, this was plainly not so. They collected up arms and ammunition following the surrender. Gray's successor as County Inspector, George B. Heard, sought to blame Gray without having the full facts. He mistakenly described the battle as an ambush:

> no precaution was taken to guard against surprise with the result that within 200 yards of the barracks the cars ran into an ambuscade and the police were under fire before they could leave the cars.[24]

The fault, if there was fault, was with Gray in his impetuosity. He was the wrong man leading the wrong force. The RIC were experienced in dealing with riots – actions against unarmed disaffected persons, but this was different. He came up against an armed British Army trained, albeit reduced in numbers, battalion. Mulcahy, perhaps more than Ashe, had fully absorbed the teachings of the British Army manuals and was ruthless in his application of their teachings. If the volunteers had been confronted by a British Army battalion, the end might have been completely different.

Chapter 9

After the Battle

Ashe now returned to the barracks with a small group of volunteers in support. When they were about eighty yards or so from it, twelve unarmed policemen emerged from the barracks; their hands in the air. They were led by Inspector McCormack. Michael McAllister remembered the incident, some thirty-five years later, because of its slight eccentricity. McCormack, he recalled, 'was wearing a white-crowned yachtsman's cap over his RIC officer's uniform.' From its holster, Inspector McCormack retrieved his revolver and presented it to Thomas Ashe in surrender, saying, 'Allow me to present you with my revolver Commandant.' Ashe thanked him for the gesture. The garrison was then taken back up the road where the other prisoners were. The arms from the barracks, and those laid down upon the road, were now collected up. 'All told,' as McAllister reflected, 'the police numbered seventy-five including the dead and wounded.'

Jerry Golden chipped in, 'They were all armed with 5 shot magazine carbines of Lee-Enfield pattern, bayonets, revolvers and 250 rounds of .303 ammunition and 50 rounds of either .45 or .38 revolver ammunition.' Inspector McCormack, Golden added:

> handed his revolver to the Commdt. When the Commdt. broke it he found it contained six soft nosed cartridges with the tops cut away . The D.I. also handed over 2 pouches of similar ammunition and when the Commdt. asked him was this the ammunition he would have used on us he replied that it was the ammunition issued to him on the previous day.[1]

Joseph Lawless in his Witness Statement records that the Volunteers had also previously found dumdum bullets at Swords RIC Barracks. It would appear that the RIC Headquarters in Dublin Castle had issued the illegal ammunition to some, if not all, of its police stations. The bullet took its name from the British Army arsenal at Dum-dum in Northern India (now Pakistan) near its border with Afghanistan. It was a soft-nosed or hollow pointed bullet. The bullet was a fearful weapon. Entering the body, it expands, tearing apart organs and body tissue. The bullet was secretly adopted by most European nations and used against the native populations in their colonial wars. The Hague Convention of 1899 rightly outlawed the use of the dumdum.

The enemy weapons were gathered up. They numbered, as Joseph Lawless records, 'about ninety-five Lee-Enfield carbines, with between 2000 and 3000 rounds of ammunition, some half dozen .455 Webley revolvers with a supply of ammunition for these, and sundry rugs, belts, pouches, coats and suchlike items of equipment.' They were loaded aboard a bread van brought up by Frank Lawless and driven off to the volunteer camp.

As the uninjured policemen waited for a decision over their fate, Joseph Lawless studied one of the policemen, Sergeant O'Reilly. He was in a bewildered state. Lawless conceived the notion:

> I think... finding himself at middle age in the service of the enemy now at war with his countrymen, was seriously disturbed by his latent sympathy for their efforts, but yet felt bound by his contract of service as well as his dependence on it for the welfare of his family.

There indeed was the pity; Irishmen fighting Irishmen. So many of them would have known each other if not by name, then by sight. In the *Memoirs of Constable Jeremiah Mee*, edited by A.J. Gaughan, Mee remembered the story of Constable James Gormley who was killed at Ashbourne. His brother was an active member of the volunteers in Ballintogher:

> The Gormley family was very popular in the district and nearly all the people, including local Volunteers, turned out to attend a requiem Mass for the dead constable.[2]

Ashe addressed the defeated policemen from the top of the roadside bank. He warned them that should any of them again be found in arms against the Republic they would be shot out of hand. The policemen were then allowed to march off towards Slane. The wounded, meanwhile, were attended to by Dr Hayes, assisted by Molly Adrien. With the limited medical equipment available, they managed as best they could. Sergeant William O'Connell, slightly wounded himself, was treated by Dr Hayes. Then O'Connell returned to the head of the police convoy to speak to County Inspector Gray:

> I called to Mr Gray's car; he was sitting in the car [his wounds] dressed. He asked me about Mr Smyth. I said I am afraid sir, he is rather badly wounded. He practically collapsed, and the poor man seemed in terrible pain. Mr Smyth was dead at this time. Mr Gray was hit at the very outset (about half an hour after the start). He lay on the road during the whole encounter, speaking and directing the men around about. I understand

> Mr Gray was actually looking through his [field] glasses when he was hit first.[3]

Volunteer Tom Rafferty was also mortally wounded.[4] He was treated by Dr Hayes, but he was too far gone. His death was inevitable. Rafferty was made as comfortable as possible in a nearby house, along with another wounded volunteer, Captain Eddie Rooney. Michael McAllister reflected upon the police casualties:

> I cannot remember now what the police casualties were, but from what I saw they were heavy. There were quite a few dead and a large number wounded…Meanwhile, the services of a Priest had been procured for the wounded police and a couple of civilian Doctors had also arrived and were tending them. Father Dillon was the priest's name and he was very displeased with us and told us so in no uncertain manner.[5]

James O'Connor gives the unvarnished comment. The priest called them 'murderers'. A number of other parish priests also spoke out against the volunteers who had taken part in the action. Father Kelly of Ratoath condemned, 'the feeble attempt [that] had been made to establish a toy republic under the jurisdiction and by the liberty of Liberty Hall'. This was perhaps a reflection on James Connolly, a Marxist but also a Catholic. He made his confession and received communion before his execution.

The official British casualty list, as appears in the *1916 Rebellion Handbook*, gives the names of two officers and six other ranks killed, with fifteen policemen wounded. Joseph Lawless gives the volunteers' side as two killed, Jack Crennigan and Tom Rafferty, and five wounded, Joe Taylor, Jack Rafferty, Willie Walsh, Matt Kelly and Ned Rooney.

Constable Bratton, who had escaped the battle in an attempt to get reinforcements from the nearby RIC Barracks, then returned to Ashbourne. Here he was met by the sad scene of the police defeat:

> When I arrived back at the scene of the fighting, the first thing I saw was the D.I.'s whistle on the road. I knew then that all was up with him. The next thing I saw was the dead bodies of seven of our men on the side of the road.

Bratton approached Tom Ashe and requested that he be allowed to take District Inspector Smyth's body back to his home. Ashe readily agreed. The body was carefully placed in a 'T' Model Ford. It was a private car, which belonged to Spicer's of Navan. Bratton continues:

> I got the D.I.'s body into the car and travelled back to his house outside Navan with it, where I handed it over to his unfortunate wife. As far as I can remember, Mrs Smith had no previous knowledge of the death of her husband until I arrived. A policeman's wife came out with me to Mrs Smith's house.[6]

After the battle, Dr Hayes while dressing the wounds of one of the policemen got into conversation with him. The policeman revealed that on leaving the barracks that morning the orders were that 'no rebels were to be taken prisoner, but that all were to be shot on sight'.

An hour or so after the surrender, with all the police casualties attended to and their weapons and ammunition gathered up, the volunteers returned to the camp at Borranstown. They were hungry. They had not eaten since breakfast. Apart from the hunger, as Charlie Weston eulogized, 'Everyone was now in great spirits as a result of our victory and we felt ready now for anything that might come. We had gained great confidence in ourselves and felt that given an equal or nearly equal chance we were match for any force that we would meet.' The police rifles and ammunition were redistributed amongst the men, with 50 rounds of .303. Following the adrenalin rush the mood of the camp calmed down. Joseph Lawless described it as being 'remarkably quiet. There was, of course, a certain amount of chattering talk, with occasionally a loud laugh at the narration of some funny incident of the day, but, on the whole, men spoke quietly in small groups and, once fed, soon sought out a place to sleep.' He reflected upon the day:

> Today had been our baptism of fire; five and a half hours of extreme nervous tension during which we had not eaten, and during which there was a fair amount of physical exertion, notwithstanding the static character of the fight. Now had come the reaction when body and mind needed rest. One could not bother to think very much except in a mechanical sort of way, and then only of the practical things that had to be done at the moment. Sleep tended to overcome tired bodies the moment they sat down anywhere.[7]

Donal O'Hannigan, still anxious to link up with Ashe and his men, and unaware of the fight, despaired:

On Friday I got a further message from Ashe to the effect that he would send me word where and when he would meet me. No word arrived on Friday. On Saturday morning I got a message that Ashe would meet me at Dan McAllister's house at Turvey at 11.a.m. on Sunday morning.[8]

Saturday morning, just after 7am, the Fingal men broke camp. On their bicycles, the column moved off in sections. The two sections in front supplied the advance guards, the ammunition cart and commissariat van, which had been loaded up with spare carbines and provisions, followed on behind, with two other sections acting as the rear guard. With its now heavy load of additional arms and ammunition, the weight on the van was too great, its springs were compressed, and its engine was sounding laboured. It was halted, and its load was lightened. Each bicycle-mounted volunteer was ordered to take at least one additional rifle or carbine. Off they set once more, proceeding towards Oldtown, bypassing Garristown. Jerry Golden remarked:

> I am sure if any person could have taken a photo of the Column on the march it would have been an unique one, as most of the cyclists had three rifles or carbines slung across their shoulders or strapped to their bikes, and nearly all had not shaved since the previous Monday. We certainly looked some of the brigands or pirates you would read about in some adventure story.

After passing through Oldtown, the column turned south-west and arrived at Newbarns near Kilsallaghan. The place was occupied by a herdsman and his family. The volunteers found quarters in the outhouses that had straw on the floors. Outposts were established on the surrounding roads to mitigate against a surprise attack. Fatigue duties fell to Joseph Lawless and his section. A sheep was killed and cooked. A girl who lived locally, a Miss Hickey was her name Lawless believed, brought a bucket full of fresh eggs to add to the volunteer's commissariat.

That evening Molly Adrien arrived at the camp with dispatches. They contained information that a cavalry force of the 5th Lancers was searching for them. It was now dusk. It was unlikely that any attack, if there should be one, would take place before daybreak. Some of the volunteers discussed what use the cavalry would be against them. In the communiqués brought by Molly Adrien, they heard of the futile dash of cavalry along Sackville Street. They were totally ineffective against defended buildings. The victors of Ashbourne were supremely confident in themselves that the cavalry would not fare any better in the countryside, where concealed riflemen could pick them off long before the cavalry could engage them. But what about dismounted troops? Ashe arranged fresh sentries for the next twelve hours to mitigate against any surprise assault. Jerry Golden was sent on sentry duty. He and his fellow sentries were given the password 'Rath Cross'. Golden and fellow volunteer Paddy Grant were instructed to watch the road from Balbriggan and the Naul, and also the road from Swords. Now aware that an attack might be imminent, the sentries were nervous, anticipating a possible attack on their watch. There was a false alarm during the night. One man challenged an imaginary enemy and getting no reply opened fire. Other sentries nearby now shot into the darkness. The mistake was soon discovered, but not before the rest of the men were roused from their sleep and were standing by ready for action. The men were stood down and returned to a restless sleep.

About 11am the next morning, Sunday, 30 April, an RIC car driven by Sergeant Reilly of Swords, and with Head Constable Kelly of Balbrigan as a passenger, was intercepted driving along the road, coming from Swords. They came with a message for Thomas Ashe. The policemen were brought into the camp. The message was presented to Ashe. It was an order signed by Pearse to lay down their arms and submit to the enemy terms. Pearse's signature was all too familiar. There was very little doubt of the authenticity of the document. It seemed surreal to the men of the 5th. Joseph Lawless summed up the general feeling:

> We could not accustom ourselves all at once to the idea that we who were so far victorious in our fight should surrender even before we were attacked…This seemed to be the complete crashing of all our hopes; the shaming of all our boasted valour, and, with only a bare seven day's fighting to the credit of our organisation, it was unbelievable; and yet we felt it was true. We needed time to think, to consider the situation in all its aspects, and the various implications of the unconditional surrender ordered by Pearse. Doubt of the genuineness of the document was, therefore, expressed to the police emissaries who, after some further talk agreed to take Mulcahy to Dublin to interview Pearse at Arbour Hill and have the order confirmed by him. Sergeant O'Reilly to remain with us as a hostage pending Mulcahy's return.[9]

It was all over for now, but Ashe realised that given the momentum, there would be another rising and sooner rather than later. He decided to dump some of the arms and ammunition for that future day. Jerry Golden listed what was dumped. Not everything because suspicion would be aroused, and a search would be made. It was mainly the volunteers' own rifles and handguns. They included six Howth rifles and Howth ammunition, four or five American-made shotguns and their ammunition, three or four Lee-Enfield rifles and about 200 rounds of .303, six Webley and Scott revolvers, and about 60 rounds of .45 ammunition, together with gelignite and dynamite. They were packed into three large wooden boxes. All the munitions were soaked in three-in-one oil to prevent rusting and wrapped in sacking, which had been soaked in three or four tins of cart grease found in the cart sheds. The arms were buried in a trench three feet deep and nine feet long. The pit was hidden by several large shrubs.

While waiting Mulcahy's return, some of the men were talking amongst themselves. Jerry Golden approached Ashe, informing him that some of the men were refusing to surrender. They intended to make off and return home. Ashe warned them that on their first visit home they would be arrested as they were all known to the local RIC of North Dublin. The only ones who had any chance of escaping were the city men. As a Dubliner, living in Botanic Avenue, Golden decided to take his chances:

> As I was about to leave Peter Blanchfield asked me if I would try and get his brother Tom into town. Another brother of theirs who was not a Volunteer was working in the Clontarf Pumping Station, and as this place was outside the city proper I said I would leave Tom down there if there was no military cordon to pass through. Another man, Arthur O'Reilly, who lived in Millmount Place, just off Millmount Avenue, Drumcondra, also decided to go with us and take his chances…We started for Dublin about 9.45. We came up the road from the camp which brought us on to the main Finglas-Ashbourne Road just at the Ward RIC barracks… we saw 3 or 4 RIC men standing outside the barracks but they took no notice of us so we continued on our way.[10]

Meanwhile, arriving in Dublin, Mulcahy, escorted by Frank Lawless, was taken to Arbour Hill. Mulcahy recalled:

> We proceeded to the military prison at Arbour Hill. Inside the prison, on the right, the door of the second or third cell was noisily opened by a soldier who shouted harshly 'Get up!' Pearse, in his uniform, was lying on bare trestle boards at the back of the cell; on a small table alongside was a glass of water and some biscuits. He rose and moved quietly a few steps towards us.
>
> Slightly behind my left shoulder was the officer and, behind him, the soldier. When movement ceased I turned to the officer and said that I

wished to speak to Commandant Pearse alone. I was not surprised that this request was refused, and that in a manner which alerted me to the full realities of the position. I was in the presence of my Commander-in-Chief; both of us in the hands of the British Army authorities. I could be nothing but the most perfect soldier; it was a moment for standing to attention.

'Is this your order sir?' I asked, as I held it out before him. Pearse answered 'Yes.' 'Does it refer to Dublin alone or the whole of Ireland?' 'It refers to the whole of Ireland.' 'Would it be of any use,' I asked, 'if a small band of men who had given a good account of themselves during the week were to hold out any longer?' And Pearse replied, 'No.' My lips moved to frame 'Beannacht De agat,' but the sound was stifled, absorbed in the solemnity of my salute which closed the scene.[11]

Mulcahy and Lawless were then driven to British military headquarters at Parkgate and taken into a room to meet Major General Sir Lovick Friend. Mulcahy remembered Friend as a gentlemanly character who was standing in front of a fire, surrounded by half a dozen senior officers. Mulcahy asked what Ashe's men should do. Friend agreed to supply a cavalry unit to escort the Fingal Battalion into captivity.

Upon Mulcahy's return to Newbarns, he gave them Pearse's message. 'It's all up boys,' he said sadly. His return to camp with that message dispelled any vague hopes that they had entertained. Resignedly, Joseph Lawless recalled:

We were told that the Volunteers in Dublin city had already surrendered unconditionally, and that the enemy authorities had now been informed that we also were ready to obey the order of our Commander-in-Chief to lay down our arms and await their orders.

Bernard McAllister recorded the reaction of the men. 'On hearing this some of the men broke down and cried bitterly, and some of them wanted to fight on.' Some of the men said they would not surrender. One of those men was Joe Kelly. 'I took my rifle,' said Joe Kelly, 'and I think I was going to smash it against a wall. One of our officers told me that would do no good. Then I think I broke down.'[12] Mulcahy addressed them and spoke to them of their duty as soldiers to obey all lawful commands. He reminded them that they had come out as soldiers, had behaved as well-disciplined soldiers of Ireland and that Pearse, whom he had seen, was proud of them. It was his orders that they should now surrender as soldiers. 'Are you going to desert your officers now?' Mulcahy asked. This had a quietening effect on the men and was the end of the threat to ignore Pearse's order. The men dispersed to their various duties. In the quietness that now hung over the camp, Michael McAllister reflected upon the notion that if any of their leaders had stood up and said, 'We won't surrender', there would have been a rousing cheer and the men would have grabbed their arms again and rushed to follow him. 'But our leaders had too much honour, discipline and respect for higher authority to do a thing like that.'

Sometime later, Ashe approached some of the younger men and told them that they could leave. This is confirmed in Dr Hayes's Statement. 'A few youthful Volunteers in their teens were ordered home.' James O'Connor was one of them. 'I left for home immediately without my bicycle; he would not let me take it, but told me to keep to the fields,' he wrote. Allowing them to escape was all very well, but it was to no avail. Over the years, the local RIC had made assiduous notes as to the members of the local volunteers. Their names and addresses, who they had been with, were all meticulously written down. Luckless O'Connor dictated in his Witness Statement:

> On the following Monday the RIC from Glasnevin came to the house and arrested me and brought me to Glasnevin Police Bks. That night I was brought by some of the Berkshire Regiment to Trinity College, Dublin, and put into a room there under guard. There were a few other fellows there that I did not know. Tuesday evening the Guard Commander told me to get out and I got out and went home. When I was in bed that night I was arrested again, this time by the police from Santry and taken to Santry RIC Bks.[13]

The same fate befell Kit Moran, who become ill before Ashbourne and was sent home by Ashe:

> On the Monday following the surrender or collapse of the rebellion, I was arrested at my home by a party of British cavalry. There was a large force of cavalry operating – equivalent to a brigade – and made up of detachments of lancers, Yeoman and Royal Horse Artillery and so forth. They had a motor truck with them, loaded with forage, and four or five others who had also been arrested and I was put up on this forage and taken along with them.[14]

At Newbarns, the remaining Volunteers waited for a British cavalry escort to take them away as prisoners. By 2pm, frustration had set in. Michael McAllister approached Ashe. He told him that he intended to make a getaway before the escort arrived. Mulcahy who was standing next to Ashe urged him not to take anyone else with him. There was little more the officers could do to prevent any departures. McAllister took his brother and cousin, Tom Weston. They left with their rifles. Joseph Lawless was of the same opinion, as were comrades James Kelly and Mick Fleming. They too decided to leave. They packed a couple of revolvers and ammunition as well as a few other bits and pieces and began to walk away from the camp. Lawless was confronted by his father, Frank Lawless, as he tells us:

> 'Where are you fellows off to?' he said. We told him our ideas, and he listened for a while then he put another view of the case. He opened by saying that we had as a body given implied bond in our formal surrender, and that if we hoped to be treated by the enemy as honourable foes, we must honour our word by, initially at any rate, placing ourselves at their disposal. 'Besides,' he added, 'the smaller the number that remain here, the harder it will be for them.' He also referred to the hardships it would entail on the people at home consequent on the inevitable searching for the missing men.[15]

Joseph and the other two took the older man's advice and returned to the camp. As they lay on the grass awaiting captivity, an RIC head constable and a sergeant arrived. They began taking names and addresses. Indolent, or perhaps just not caring, nobody seemed to bother about food. Breakfast had been prepared and eaten while they awaited Mulcahy's return, but now nobody could be bothered to prepare lunch.

The escort arrived about 5.30pm – a squadron of the 5th Lancers. 'They were a rather truculent swaggering lot,' Joseph Lawless felt. 'I think the feeling was general amongst us that these fellows would have been sitting ducks to us had they ventured to attack our camp.' Bernard McAllister witnessed what amounted to a formal surrender. Ashe handed over his revolver to the police sergeant as a token of surrender. He then formally called the men to order, and they fell-in, two files with their bicycles. The cavalry came up and were placed on either flank of the prisoners. They were marched off to Swords. Joseph Lawless saw the light-hearted side of the march from the camp to Swords:

> I shall always remember that five miles march to Swords, if only for one thing. The soldier on my right was a rather beefy red-faced sergeant, and his indignation at our preposterous attack on the Empire knew no bounds. Almost the whole way along he cursed us fervently and went into all the gory details of what he would like to do to us if he had his way. 'Here I am', said he, 'having come safely through two blankety years in

the blankety trenches in France, come here for a blankety rest, and then run the chance of getting a blankety bullet from a lot of blank-blank-blanks like you.'

They arrived in Swords at dusk; the town was deserted. Outside the barracks were three motor lorries with open flat bodies. Milling around was a crowd of soldiers and police. The order was given by a British officer, 'Stack your bicycles.' Having done so, the prisoners were put aboard the lorries. Off they set, a lorry load of troops to the fore, and another to the rear. Dublin seemed like a dead city, Joseph Lawless remembered, as they arrived. They passed through a number of checkpoints before reaching their destination, Richmond Barracks. The gates were opened, and the convoy started to pass through the massive granite gateway. The driver of the second lorry, the one with the prisoners, misjudged the turn. Joseph Lawless, his right hand grasping the edge of the lorry, had the little finger of his right hand crushed as the lorry scraped through the gateway. A civilian doctor was brought in to attend to the injury.

Unaware of the surrender, Donal O'Hannigan cycled off to meet with Ashe at Dan McAllister's house as arranged. He took a local man with him, Volunteer Madden:

We got to Turvey without incident. Dan McAllister came out of the house very excited and shouted 'Go away. You will be caught at any moment.' I said 'Where is Tom Ashe?' and he replied, 'He is a prisoner and they are looking for you. Go away at once.' I succeeded in calming him down somewhat and he informed me that Ashe and his column were now all prisoners, having surrendered.[16]

Now O'Hannigan was on the run. He and Madden cycled away. On the road, coming towards them, was a troop of cavalry. The two held their nerve and cycled on. They saluted the troop who responded and allowed them to pass on without even stopping them. This was the advance party of a much larger column. Near Swords, they came across the main body who also allowed them to cycle on. At Blanchardstown, they stopped at a public house for a drink and to pick up any information. The publican, suspecting who they were, whispered, 'Don't stay, you are known here.' He did not take any money for the drinks. Acting as normally as was possible, the two drank their drinks, and left. They passed the RIC Barracks without being stopped and proceeded back to their camp at Tyrrellstown. Here the men were dismissed and returned to their homes. But, of course, the local RIC men knew who they all were, and if they had not gone on the run, they were rounded up and deported to English prisons and eventually to Frongoch Internment Camp. In all, some 114 individuals were interned from north County Dublin, not all of them had participated in the Rising. Some had just fallen foul of the local RIC. One such was William Ganley from Skerries, then aged 64 and far too old to be traipsing around the country. The home locations of the interned are given below:[17]

Lusk	26
Swords	25
Skerries	20
Castleknock	7
Donabate	5
Artane	5
Howth	4
Finglas	4
St Margaret's	3
Sutton	3
Baldoyle	3
Cloghran	3
Ashtown	2
Blanchardstown	2
Balbriggan	1
Malahide	1

Chapter 10

Prisoners

Richmond Barracks, situated on the outskirts of the city centre of Dublin, was built between 1810 and 1814. The barracks enclosed 22 acres of ground, with two entrance gates (north and south), each with a guard room. Within the enclosure were two parade grounds. The barracks could house upwards of 1,600 soldiers. Following the surrender in Dublin, the women soldiers were housed here overnight. Annie Cooney, a member of the Inghinidhe branch of Cumann na mBan, recalled her night in the barracks. They were housed in the married quarters:

> We marched right into the big square, where we were halted. There we were separated from the men who were put into a separate building. We were all – 22 of us – brought into a large building up the stairs and we were first put into a rather small room, where we were divided up for the night, eleven of us in each of two rooms. A British military sergeant had charge of us and brought us tea in a bucket and some hard biscuits which he called dog biscuits. We ate and drank what we got, as we were hungry. The sergeant apologised for the sort of food he had given us.[1]

The treatment of the men was altogether different. Upon entering Richmond Barracks, the prisoners were searched. Some watches and money were stolen but later returned following the prisoners' complaints of theft. The men were put into a large bare room. No provisions had been made for them. No food or drink; there were no beds nor furniture. For the first night they slept on the floor, making themselves as comfortable as possible. After treatment to his hand, Joseph Lawless was taken to join his comrades:

> The barrack room in which we were confined was just an ordinary barrack room on the ground floor, about the middle of the east block. The two windows facing west looked out on the barrack square, and on the veranda outside sentries paced up and down, warning us now and then to keep away from the windows.
> There were other prisoners from the various city garrisons similarly housed in adjoining barrack rooms, but all the Fingal contingent, as

far as I can remember, were placed in one room which was therefore very overcrowded. There were no beds or bedding; nothing except a few blankets, which scarcely allowed one each to the prisoners, but I expect that the sudden demand was more than the Barrack Quartermaster could supply, and other barracks would hardly help him out under the circumstances. A large iron tub in one corner of the room provided the only latrine facilities available to the occupants.[2]

That night spirits were low. Ashe tried to raise morale by singing an old country song, the *Cottage by the Lee*. Paddy Brogan sang a song in Gaelic called *Kilmurry*. Richard Hayes and others joined in. Soon spirits were raised. They had lost the battle this time, but there would be another time – and soon they believed.

Monday, 1 May, after a breakfast of biscuits and bully beef, and buckets of tea, groups of men were taken to the gymnasium for interrogation. Their inquisitors were army officers, G Men (the Intelligence Section of the Dublin police) and senior RIC men. Crossing the barrack square, Joseph Lawless espied 'a tall, spectacled Volunteer officer in uniform, wearing field top boots and slouch hat, and having a bandage around his neck. He was being marched under escort to the dressing station across the square. This officer was identified by some of those in the room, who knew him, as Joe Plunkett, one of the signatories of the Republican Proclamation.' Led into the gymnasium the prisoners were lined against the wall. Joseph Lawless looked about him:

> I recognised Sean McDermott, Eamon Ceannt, Sean Heuston, Willie Pearse, Michael O'Hanrahan, Con Colbert, Tom Clatrke, John McBride and Thomas McDonagh…It was clear to us then, that these men across the room had been selected from the general body of prisoners, and that the purpose of our entry to this building was for similar selection.[3]

The new arrivals were lined up along the opposite wall. Three RIC sergeants and a military officer approached them and proceeded to walk slowly up and down the line, pulling out the officers. Tom Ashe, Dr Hayes, and Frank Lawless were pulled out of the crowd and lined up with the prisoners on the other side of the gymnasium. Unbeknown to them, they were marked for execution. The remainder were marched back to the barrack room. As they were being taken back, they looked across the square and saw Pearse, accompanied by three soldiers, walking in what they took to be exercise. He looked towards them, and they saluted.

Having separated the 'sheep from the goats', an official government statement was issued from Irish Command Headquarters in Dublin in May 1916:

> Rebels considered suitable for trial are being tried by Field General Court Martial under the Defence of the Realm Act in Dublin. As soon as sentences have been confirmed the public will be informed as to the results of the trial. Those prisoners whose cases could not be immediately dealt with are being sent to places of confinement in England. Their cases will receive consideration later.

Elsewhere, outside in the country, the volunteers who had escaped before the arrival of the cavalry to take them off to Kilmainham, were now being rounded up. The RIC had kept meticulous records of all their names, addresses and activities over the years. James O'Connor, rearrested, was held at Santry RIC barracks for a few days, before being marched off by a party of the Berkshires to Trinity College and from there on to Richmond Barracks. Kit Moran, having spent the night as a prisoner, was the next morning:

> loaded up again, and proceeded towards Dunboyne in Co. Meath. En route, they arrested Thomas Condron and also Mr. Quigley who was then county surveyor to the Meath county council. Quigley was on the road, apparently attending to his normal duties. He was subsequently tried by court martial for having taken part in the fight at Ashbourne. That evening, we were taken to the gymnasium in the Richmond Barracks at Kilmainham, Dublin.[4]

All prisoners had previously been briefed, that when questioned by the authorities, that in going out on Easter Monday 'they were obeying as Volunteers the orders of their leaders to mobilise in the ordinary way for manoeuvres.'[5] This response, hopefully, would get them off on a more lenient sentence, for a jail sentence was inevitable.

There were some of the Fingal men who evaded the authorities. Jerry Golden and his party of Peter Blanchfield and his brother Tom, safely made their way back into the city, where they lay low. Michael McAllister, his brother John and Tom Weston kept together for about a week, sleeping in barns and in the shelter of hedges, getting food where they could. They did not know who they could trust. Every County Council was bending over backwards to show their loyalty to the British crown. They were busy passing resolutions condemning the rebels who had taken part in the Rising. Virtually every priest in the country condemned them from the pulpit. After a week or so, Michael

McAllister and his brother risked going home. They learnt that the military and the police had been at the house looking for them. Not daring to sleep at home, after a month on the run, they received word from John Joe Keane, a forage contractor at the Haymarket in Dublin. He told them that a number of men who had escaped arrest were going to America. If they wanted, they could join them:

> I got in touch with Keane and he sent me down to the North Wall, Dublin, where I was smuggled on board a Liverpool boat by a man called Kavanagh who took me to Liverpool. Here, through the good offices of a man called Kerr, I got signed on under the name of Bergin which was my mother's name, on the SS *Baltic* as a coal trimmer. All the trimmers on the *Baltic* were men who were escaping to America to avoid conscription.
>
> When we got to New York we all deserted the ship…I made contact with the late John Devoy and he sent me to Judge Cohalan, who is also dead now, and he got me employment in a seed store in New York.
>
> I was in my new job until April 1918 when I received a telegram informing me that conscription was being enforced in Ireland and that all the boys were returning there for the fight which was about to take place.[6]

McAllister eventually returned home to Turvey – where he was arrested:

> One day I was in the house for a short period and, on looking out the window, saw that a force of military and police had surrounded the place. I went to the front door and opened it and was confronted by Lieutenant Small. Small was the Intelligence Officer for Swords where the British Army had now established an outpost. Small said, 'Come on, I want you.' I asked him what he was arresting me for and he replied 'Murder,' to which I replied that I had not murdered anyone.

McAllister was sent to Belfast Prison and from there to Ballynlar Internment Camp, where he remained until after the War of Independence and the Treaty of 1922, which ended the war.

Back in Richmond Barracks on the evening of Sunday, 30 April, the prisoners witnessed the arrival of more prisoners. Joseph Lawless looked briefly through the window down onto the yard. He recognised the tall figure of Éamon de Valera. They were the last of the rebel garrisons to surrender. Within the barracks, amongst the men of Fingal, there still remained an element of resistance. Richard Mulcahy had not been picked out in the gym, as had Ashe and the others. He naturally became their leader. Lawless was to write:

> We had a feeling that though we must now depend entirely on his advice and guidance, we must be careful to make no display of his leadership lest we should draw the attention of the army to the omission in his selection of leaders.[7]

About 4.30pm in the late afternoon of Tuesday, 2 May, the prisoners became aware that something was in the offing. There was an unusual bustle of preparations and the shouting of orders outside in the yard. Just before 6pm, the prisoners were given extra rations for their tea. It became clear that they were about to be moved. The order came. They were led out and formed up on the square, where they were numbered off and names checked by a list. Now the speculation started as Lawless related:

> either through information received from the soldiers, or intelligent speculation, the rumour went around that we were being placed aboard a ship for some overseas destination. Of course this led on to more speculation, the most popular being that we were to be used as forced or slave labour units in France, where we would be compelled to make our contribution to the British war effort in expiation of our sins.

Dusk was falling as the men were marched out of the barracks, with troops with fixed bayonets on either side of the column. Joseph Lawless expressed his heartbreak as he passed through the desolate city:

> It was only when we got to Bachelor's Walk that a sense of tragedy added itself from the appearance of the shell holes in the walls of Kelly's shop, and as we reached the corner of O'Connell St. the scene of desolation that met our gaze there brought home a realisation of the tough fight made by the Volunteers in the city, which necessitated such wholesale destruction to compel their surrender.
>
> The gaunt ruins of the GPO were outlined against the twilight sky, and still smoking heaps of masonry were all that remained of most of the shops and buildings on either side of that once proud thoroughfare, while the street itself was littered with debris.

Bernard (Bennie) McAllister takes up the narrative:

> We were paraded with other prisoners, about 300 strong, and marched from there to the North Wall. While going through the city to the Docks we got a very bad reception from the civil population. They boohed us, called us ugly names and were generally hostile. This crowd represented the rabble of the city and not the ordinary citizen. At the North Wall we were marched on to a cattle boat and put down in the cattle pens. We got no food on board. We sailed to England and thence to Knutsford Jail.[8]

Landing at Holyhead in north Wales during the night, the prisoners were packed aboard a specially commissioned train. Joseph Lawless contrasted the attitude of their guards in Ireland with those they now met:

> In contrast with this hostile action of some of the escorting troops was that one of them, who sat in our railway carriage with us. There were one or two in each carriage with the prisoners. This fellow shared his cigarettes with us and, while the train was stopped at Crewe or Chester, or some other place, where V.A.D. ladies came running along the platform with tea for the troops, he claimed several cups from them which he passed behind him to the prisoners who would not be given tea otherwise. We thanked him for his generous impulse, and forgave the others because of him.

The Fingal prisoners had been broken up by the alphabetical listings. Some went to Knutsford in Cheshire, others went to Wakefield in Yorkshire, while a third party were sent to Wandsworth Prison in London. They would all meet up again at Frongoch Internment Camp in Wales. In Kilmainham, the leaders awaited their fate.

Chapter 11

Executions and Deportations

On 27 April 1916, Prime Minister Herbert Asquith announced in the House of Commons that martial law was to come into effect immediately all over Ireland. That same day, General Sir John Grenfell Maxwell sailed for Ireland to take over command of British troops. All civil functions were set aside. Maxwell to all intents and purposes held absolute power in Ireland. On 11 May 1916, Maxwell issued a directive from British Headquarters, Parkgate, Dublin:

> In view of the gravity of the rebellion and its connections with German intrigue and propaganda, and in view of the great loss of life and destruction of property resulting there from, the General Officer Commanding-in-Chief has found it imperative to inflict the most severe sentences on the known organisers of this detestable rising and on those Commanders who took an active part in the actual fighting which occurred. It is hoped that these examples will be sufficient to act as a deterrent to intriguers, and to bring home to them that the murder of His Majesty's liege subjects, or other acts calculated to imperil the safety of the Realm will not be tolerated.[1]

By the date of Maxwell's statement, twelve leaders of the Irish Volunteers had already been sentenced by court martial and executed by firing squad; Patrick Pearse, Thomas McDonagh, and Thomas J. Clarke (executed 3 May), Joseph Plunkett, Edward Daly, Michael O'Hanrahan and Willie Pearse (4 May), John McBride (5 May), Cornelius Colbert, Eamon Ceannt, Michael Mallin and Sean Heuston (8 May). The day after the proclamation James Connolly and Sean MacDermott were executed. That Maxwell's statement was issued after the executions of many of the above suggested that more would take place. These would be the commanders of the various garrisons and others.

Maxwell found justification in executing the signatories of the 'Proclamation of the Republic', having been handed Pearse's final letter to his mother. As a postscript to her, Pearse wrote, 'P.S. I understand that the German expedition which I was counting on actually set sail but was defeated by the British.'[2] This almost throwaway comment sealed the fate of the leaders of the Rising.

It enabled Maxwell to charge further insurgents with aiding the enemy. Given the power, and without reference to the government, Maxwell exercised that power without thought of the repercussions that might accrue. Now the Republican prisoners like Tom Ashe were brought before the court-martial board on 11 May. The charge presented was iniquitous in that two charges were presented as one:

> You did act, to wit – Did take part in an armed rebellion and in waging war against his Majesty the King, such act being of such a nature as to be calculated to be prejudicial to the Defence of the Realm and being done with the intention of acting for the purpose of assisting the enemy. Or, You are charged with having been one of a party at…from which shots were fired occasioning casualties amongst His Majesty's troops, and you are further charged with conspiracy with His Majesties enemies.

His response was like many of his co-defendants, while not denying his involvement in waging war, he vehemently denied the charge of assisting the enemy. However, the judges sitting on the court martial ruled that there was but one charge and to plead guilty to one part of the charge was to plead guilty to the other. From the framing of the charge, it was fairly obvious that he, Tom Ashe, and the others so charged, would be found guilty of the charge, but he, like the others, never suspected that they would incur the death sentence. The majority had fought in uniform as soldiers and, therefore, believed that they would be treated as prisoners of war in accordance with the Hague Convention. Later that day, having been returned to his cell, the door was opened, and the question was put to him, 'Are you Thomas Ashe?' He replied that he was. To which the British officer announced, 'You have been found guilty and have been sentenced to death or to be shot.' Then there was a pause to see what effect this would bring. There was a stoic silence. Then the officer continued, 'The sentence has been commuted to penal servitude for life.'[3]

Ashe took the sentence in his stride. He put his affairs in order, in a letter to his sister Nora:

> Dear Nora,
> I am sure you are very much troubled over me for the past few weeks. I expect you know before this of my presence here. The term looks long, but I am facing it in a most optimistic mood. Prison life, so far anyhow, is not so bad as one views it from the outside.
> Be sure and write home as soon as you get this. They [his parents] must be in a queer state. Let them go on with their business as if nothing happened to me.[4]

Ashe then goes on to list a series of bequests; books and small amounts of money to various people, and his treasured motorcycle to Dan McAllister of Turvey. And, of course, his resignation as headmaster of Lusk National School.

Both Frank Lawless, and his brother James, were likewise sentenced to death, but had their sentences commuted to ten years imprisonment. James Marks of Swords, prisoner number 108, a labourer, had his death sentence commuted to three years penal servitude. Dr Richard Hayes, even though he had assisted the wounded policemen after the battle at Ashbourne, was sentenced to twenty years imprisonment.[5] As it was most unlikely that he would be available to attend to its patients, the local Board of Guardians dismissed him from his position with them:

> The Local Government Board wrote, noting an entry contained in the minutes to the effect that Dr. Richard Hayes, medical officer of the Lusk dispensary district, had absented himself from duty without leave during the previous fortnight and had been suspended from office by the guardians. It appears from the official statements published and verified by the military authorities that Dr. Hayes has been convicted by court-martial, due to his having taken part in the recent rebellion, and has been sentenced to 20 years penal servitude.[6]

Ashe was later transferred to Dartmoor Prison, one of England's harshest prisons, on 23 May 1916. Likewise imprisoned in Dartmoor for his part in the Easter Rising, Captain Paul Galligan of C Company, 2nd Battalion, described life within the prison:

> On arrival in Dartmoor Prison we were allocated to cells…My convict number was Q216. We were issued with convict clothes which included a jacket, knickers, long stockings, leggings and bailed boots, shoes, cap and a smock for wet days. All were stamped with the broad arrow which was the Government brand for prison materials. We were kept in single cells, no intercourse was allowed, but we were kept separate from the ordinary criminals. We were housed in the west wing of the prison. The heating system was antiquated and seemed to be there from the time the prison was built. No heat reached the cells. Bedding consisted of a mattress placed on the cell boards which was only three inches from the concrete floors. Two blankets in the summer, three in the winter, and a bedspread. The mattress was a very poor one. Food was ordinary prison diet and on most days was very poor. No food was allowed to be sent in to us. We were allowed one letter in and one out, I think every three

months. We had exercise around the ring in the morning before work, but no intercourse. We worked in the shops making mail bags, but no conversation or smoking allowed while at this. We had a haircut and a bath once per week.[7]

Galligan makes an oblique reference to Ashe being there:

> Our cells were on the top or third floor. De Valera was on the second floor. Tom Ashe and [William] Partridge [of the Irish Citizen Army] were on the ground floor.

Shortly before Christmas 1916, 125 of the Irish prisoners condemned to death but reprieved were transferred in handcuffs from Dartmoor to Lewes Prison. Though the rules were stringent, the prisoners were allowed to talk to each other and associate during exercise time. This proved to be an opportunity to compare notes on the rebellion and also to organize. Éamon de Valera became the recognised leader. He and the other leaders of the volunteers imprisoned here, Eoin MacNeill, Eamon Duggan and Thomas Ashe organized the men and drew up proposals for their treatment as political prisoners. Peadar Doyle, Quartermaster of F Company, 4th Battalion, listed the proposals in his Witness Statement:

> 1. We were to refuse to work, except for our own comfort and cleanliness.
> 2. We were to refuse to exercise with criminals or associate with them.
> 3. Our hair was not to be shaved.
> 4. The abolition of certain rules.[8]

The matter was referred to the Home Office, the government department responsible for prisons. There was little hope of them conceding terms simply upon request. The response was that prisoners would be punished for non-observance of rules. De Valera issued an order to the men to refuse to work. In the exercise yard, de Valera presented his demands for political status. Ignoring them, the Governor then instructed the warders to put the prisoners back in their cells. To avoid further mutinies, the leaders were dispersed to other prisons. Ashe and some of the others were sent to Portland Prison in Dorset. Peadar Doyle, recorded the grimness of Portland:

> We reached Portland Prison about 7 p.m. that evening and were immediately paraded in the Reception Hall and the Riot Act was read to us. Several of the warders here were half-castes and offered us very

little consolation. We were committed to our cells and given a change of clothes, which consisted of a buff coloured jacket, a boat cap, corduroy breaches with a broad arrow prominently displayed all over in zig-zag form, black and red stockings and black shoes. For the first month we were in solitary confinement making sacks in our cells. Portland Prison was looked upon as the principal prison in England for discipline and cleanliness. Several of the warders were very strict and some of our men were frequently punished by being confined to the 'Clink,' a dark cell and bread and water for the trivial offence, such as talking.

The Governor was a very critical man and never lost an opportunity of abusing any prisoners who were brought before him. There are many strange stories regarding him.

The whole 57 Irishmen were stationed in one wing of the Prison. Our daily exercise consisted of half an hour after breakfast and half an hour after dinner. Letters were permitted once a month and in lieu of a visit.

From Portland, the prisoners were again transferred, this time to Pentonville in London, from which Ashe and the others were released on 18 June 1917 in a general amnesty.

Of the junior officers, Frank and James Lawless were sentenced to death, but their sentences were commuted to ten years imprisonment. Thomas Peppard of Lusk, who had been sent by Ashe into Dublin at Connolly's request, was sentenced to death, but this was generously commuted to three years imprisonment. Likewise was Captain Richard Coleman. Joseph Lawless was sent to Knutsford Prison in Cheshire. He and the other prisoners disembarked at the railway station. He was impressed at the surrounding countryside and lyrically wrote of it:

The sun was rising as we formed up on the road outside the station, too early an hour for any curious sightseers, but we viewed it at its best and with appreciation this English country town which bore on its face the stamp of centuries of assured and undisturbed occupation by its inhabitants. The impression I had was that the rich growth of spring in the hedgerows was as carefully tended as the neat dwelling houses and trim lawns.[9]

The party was marched along to the prison. Lyricism gave way to harsh reality. Knutsford Prison was like so many Victorian prisons; wings containing three tiers of cells, radiating from a central block that contained the administrative offices, kitchens and baths. A narrow walkway linked the cells of each wing and communicated with the ground floor by an iron stairway at each end. The balustrade along the gangways by the cells and the stairs was topped by a polished steel rail, while across the open space between the gangways of the opposite sides of the wings was stretched wire netting to 'discourage any ideas of suicide by jumping over the handrails on to the flagged hall below', as Lawless described. Like Joseph Lawless and Bernard McAllister, Richard Mulcahy and Charles Weston were also sent to Knutsford. Weston was less than enamoured at the conditions:

> On arrival at Knutsford we were put in single cells with bed board and a stool, but no bed. Next evening I got a pillow. After three days I got a very worn blanket. I was about a fortnight there before I got a mattress. We got only half an hour or twenty minutes exercise each day and were not allowed to talk. Food was very bad and the ration was about quarter enough. After a week we had a bath and a severe haircut. I was never abused though.[10]

Knutsford was formerly a prison for criminals but was now converted to a military detention centre for deserters and people who had committed military offences either in France or England. It was completely in charge of the military. The non-commissioned officers in charge of Knutsford had been invalided from France having been gassed or wounded. The prison was subject to military discipline. In some cases, this involved bullying. Some ten days later, following questions in the House of Commons by an Irish MP regarding the ill-treatment of the prisoners, a delegation of British Army officers and some civilians arrived at Knutsford. The prisoners were lined up and the prison governor asked for any complaints that the prisoners had. Those who had were later interviewed. All complaints were dismissed. The whole procedure appeared to be nothing more than a paper exercise. Surprisingly though, a week later, prison discipline was relaxed slightly. Letters home were permitted, though subject to strict censorship. Visitors arrived and strict regulations broke down when the visitors intermingled with any number of prisoners. A short time after the first visitors, there was a noticeable change in the attitude of the guards. Joseph Lawless briefly takes up the story:

> A few days later we were all assembled in the hall and informed by the Governor that the Government had agreed to relax the ordinary prison discipline, and to treat our confinement as internment.[11]

Here in Knutsford, and the other prisons, the Irish prisoners had acquired political status. Early in June, there was a rumour that the prisoners were going to be moved to an internment camp. The news was confirmed by the visit of Alfred Byrne, Member of Parliament for Dublin. Lawless again:

> I think the first confirmation of the internment camp rumour came from Mr. Alfred Byrne, one of the members of Parliament for Dublin, who came to visit us at Knutsford about this time. Alfie was a well-known figure to most Dubliners, and it was characteristic of him to seize the opportunity of adding to his popularity with his constituents by visiting the imprisoned Dublin men. In England. Alfie claimed the privilege of his membership of the British House of Commons in making this visit.

In his Witness Statement, Joseph Lawless now brings us back to his comrades in Fingal because this is their story:

> It may be noted that in my description of life in Knutford I have made little mention of my comrades in arms from Fingal, and I hasten to assure the reader that this is not because they had lost any of their significance or fallen in my esteem. When we arrived at Knutsford, and, in fact, before our arrival there, the general body of prisoners had become split up into groups, the composition of which was largely accidental or following on our roll call in alphabetical order at Richmond Barracks. Thereafter the Fingallian prisoners met and discussed matters as individual members of the larger body of prisoners, rather than as a territorial group. We were proud of ourselves and of each other, from our achievement of Easter Week, and feeling no necessity to stand apart as a body, each individual formed his own circle of intimate friends.

Chapter 12

Frongoch

> After six weeks in Knutford we were moved to Frongoch in Wales. Frongoch was good. We were all together here in a big loft in an old distillery. We had straw mattresses and fairly good bedding. Food was better and camp routines were good. We had our own Camp. Comdt. there and were organised in Coys. We had plenty of hot water for baths and washing. We had football games, concerts, card playing was the principal pastime. Language classes and other subjects were taught there.

This was Charles Weston's appreciation of the new internment camp.

Fingal comrade Bernard McAllister was in the first batch of Irish prisoners to be sent there:

> We were the first party of about 20 to arrive there. Further batches began to arrive there until the camp (North) filled up and there was about 1,500 all told. At first rations were bad, but when the camp filled up conditions improved.[1]

Frongoch Internment Camp was situated near Bala in North Wales. It had formerly been a whisky distillery, the only one in Wales, but production had ceased at the outbreak of the First World War. The site was requisitioned by the War Department and used initially as a camp for German prisoners of war. After the decision was made to imprison the Irish prisoners together, Frongoch, in its isolation, was the site chosen. It was a quiet, out-of-the-way place, with a stark beauty all of its own. It was blessed with a railway station, formerly used by the whisky company, situated along a branch-line of the Great Western Railway, running between Bala and Blaenau Ffestiniog.

Upon arrival at the railway station, the prisoners were marched down the road to the entrance gate of the camp. Here, they were counted once more as they walked under a big archway and entered an inner yard. Then, they were addressed by the British Army camp commandant, Colonel F.A. Heygate Lambert, who read aloud the rules of the camp. They were told in no uncertain terms that if they tried to escape, they would be shot. The sentries up in their gantries were armed with buckshot. This same speech was issued to all new arrivals, thus earning the colonel the nickname of 'Buckshot'. The men were then addressed by Sergeant Major Newsome. He was given the name 'Jack Knives'. His was a much-repeated speech too. New arrivals were asked if they had concealed weapons (particularly jack knives) in their possession. He was not a bad man, certainly not a bully. IRA prisoner William Daly wrote of him:

> Jack Knives, although stern, became very popular with us. He tried very hard to discipline us and we defeated him on every occasion and he took his defeats in good part.[2]

Frongoch consisted of two camps, north and south. The buildings were arranged around two yards. The western side of the square of buildings was occupied by a huge three-storied grain store. The three floors had been turned into dormitories. The buildings on the northern side of the square were pierced by a huge central gateway, which acted as the entrance to the camp. The right-hand side was utilised as a hospital and the censor's office. The left side was occupied by an electric power plant, furnace and prisoners' drying room. Attached to this block was a corrugated iron structure used as the prisoners' latrines during the day. The building on the eastern side, formerly the distilling and vat house, was converted into a coal depot and a carpenter's and engineer's workshop. The lower end of the block was the prisoners' cookhouse. A long one-storey building completed the square on the southern side. This was the dining hall, capable of seating 1,500 men at one time. Part of the lower portion of the building was used as a wash and shower bathhouse. Surrounding the yards was a ten-foot high, barbed-wire fence, with double apron entanglements of barbed wire, over which sentries on raised towers kept watch night and day. Beyond the wire, there was a securely wired playing field, where the prisoners, weather permitting, had access for a couple of hours each day. When the south camp was full, having then over 800 prisoners, the north camp was opened to receive further contingents amounting to a further 1,600 men.

Joseph Lawless and his group joined some prisoners already there from some of the other gaols, such as Wakefield, Stafford and Wormwood Scrubs. They introduced the newcomers to the camp routines and showed them where to find the dining hall and other essentials. Lawless details the camp routines:

> There was a roll call in the dormitories at nine o'clock each evening, after which we were locked within the dormitories until roll-call again at 7.30 in the morning. In the meantime we had the comparative freedom of association with each other, and even though subjected to

a continuous surveillance by roving Provost Sergeants and other NCOs as well as officers to control the discipline of dormitories, cook-house, dining-hall, and such like. Brennan-Whitmore was Camp Commandant at first, but when the camp had filled up there was a new election of officers, and Michael Staines, a Dublin Volunteers officer, was elected Camp commandant.[3]

There arose the question as to who should run the camp on behalf of the prisoners. The secretive IRB thought that it should be them. A move was made, therefore, to contact the members of the IRB in the camp and a meeting was held one day in a small dormitory or attic above the canteen to organize a forthcoming election of camp officers. Liam Tannam, a captain in E Company, 3rd Battalion, was not happy at this attempted coup:

> One party thought ranks as they existed during the fight should be adhered to, and the remaining prisoners organised and commanded as far as possible by officers. The other party succeeded in having a committee appointed to run the camp, this committee being composed entirely of members of the IRB. Although I was an IRB man I sided with the military idea and came in conflict with [Michael] Collins over this.[4]

Tannam was not the only one who came into conflict with Collins. Frank Henderson, who had served in the GPO during the Rising, seems to have personally disliked the man. Though there is no suggestion of this in his Witness Statement, in conversation with Ernie O'Malley he spoke as he felt:

> Henderson commented that Michael Collins was unpopular in Frongoch Internment Camp 'and seemed to be looking for power'. Henderson gave a graphic description to O'Malley of Collins in pre-Rising days wearing a hard hat, carrying an umbrella and speaking 'bad Irish.'[5]

Collins was already positioning himself to rise within the ranks of the IRB by establishing a support basis within Frongoch. Being only a captain though, he lost the argument, due to rank. Following a stormy meeting, Colonel 'Ginger' O'Connell[6] stamped his authority on the assembly and told them that this was a military camp, and they all were soldiers – 'and we'll all be treated as soldiers'. A military structure was set up. Within the structure, the men were divided up into companies with commanders. Captain Dick Mulcahy was appointed to command 'D' Company. There was nothing for Collins. This did not stop the IRB from recruiting new members from amongst the prisoners though. Each of the company commanders undertook to perform the duties of orderly officer to oversee fatigues relating to the cleanliness and well-being of the camp.

Sometime into their incarceration at Frongoch, the camp authorities issued an order. Joseph Lawless in his detailed Witness Statement relates:

> An order was issued that the wearing of Volunteer uniforms by the prisoners was no longer to be allowed, and that, in fact, those who had uniforms were to surrender this in exchange for a civilian suit. Up to this I and a number of others were still wearing the uniforms we had on us during Easter Week, though we had, in the meantime, acquired some change of clothing. It had been a matter of pride with us to display ourselves in uniform at all times, but now we preferred to retain our uniforms hidden than to surrender them, and so collecting a very motley suit of tattered duds I handed in these in exchange for a new suit of 'hand me downs,' which type of clothing became known to us as 'Martin Henrys'. My uniform I still had with me on my release.

Rather than some sort of conspiracy, it was an attempt by the authorities to give the men more 'fresh' clothing. By this time, their uniforms smelt. The new clothes appear to have been issued prior to the men attending the Sankey Enquiry. An Advisory Committee was set up in London under the chairmanship of Mr Justice Sankey (afterwards Lord Sankey), whereby all interned Irish prisoners were to be brought before this committee and given an opportunity of establishing their 'innocence of complicity in the Rising'. The intention was to give the impression that, as Joseph Lawless indicates, 'only an insignificant fraction of the population of Ireland favoured the Rising'. Contingents of about 300 prisoners at a time were selected every week or two and sent by train down to London. They were lodged overnight in one of two London gaols (Wandsworth or Wormwood Scrubs). Joseph Lawless again:

> A few draughts had come and gone before my name was called one day, and I set off on what was my first visit to London. The escort...were a pretty decent lot on the whole, so they chatted to us about the war and about ourselves, and swapped cigarettes as we travelled on, across England and towards the great metropolis. ...It was late afternoon or evening when we arrived at Wandsworth Prison, where we were ushered into cells and given a meal, after which we were locked up for the night.

Within the prison, there were a large number of conscientious objectors. Lawless described the brutality that they suffered:

> Later in the day we heard the 'Conchies,' as they called them, being put through a gruelling course of squad drill in the exercise ground outside our cells, the NCOs in charge fairly revelling in the sadistic joy of making life an 'appropriate hell' for these poor beggars. I climbed up on my table and stool to get a peep through a small ventilator pane in the window of my cell, and for a while watched those near me being doubled up and down, turned right, left and about, to the accompaniment of blistering epithets, when, in their bewilderment, they became confused in the rapid fire of apparently contradictory commands....On the other hand we found the prison staff of Wandsworth quite decent to us, perhaps because they looked upon us as fighters, however misguided.

On the following morning, the Irishmen in groups of twenty or thirty at a time were marched into the main hall of the prison to await being interviewed by the panel. As Lawless remarked, 'There was something of the air of the confessional about it, though I fear the element of contrition was conspicuously absent.' Lawless's turn came:

> I marched boldly into the centre of the room and halted, stiffly at attention. Sankey was smilingly affable, suave, and even friendly as he motioned to me to be at ease. My name, age, and activities during Easter Week he read out to me from a sheet he held in his hand, now and then requesting my conformation or denial of these facts, and as he came to the end of the recital, he suggested in a sort of sympathetically confidential way, 'but of course you could not know what you were being led into when you took up arms.'

A sensible man would have agreed with him and been released in July – but not Lawless:

> Respecting his very affable manner, I avoided hyperbole or flamboyant attitude, but told him quietly and formerly that when I had first joined the Volunteers in 1913 I had done so with the sole purpose of taking up arms against England sooner or later. I said that I had known of the preparations for the Rising long before Holy Week, and had helped to make them.

It was not perhaps the response that Sankey was looking for, but he managed to laugh off the comment. 'Joseph is a bit of a firebrand,' he said to those around him on the table. He smiled and nodded 'to me to indicate the termination of the interview,' Lawless declared. When the draught [*sic*] of his fellow prisoners was complete, the prisoners were returned to Frongoch. About the middle of July, the first releases began. Every other day or so a list of names was called out on a general parade of the prisoners. About 1,000 were released in this way. As Lawless came to realise, 'The Advisory Committee had apparently made its decision as to what was wheat and what was chaff; who were the sheep and who were the goats.' Now with fewer numbers, the prisoners were all moved into the south camp.

One day, Charlie Weston was talking to Dick Mulcahy. He reminisced about the boat journey from Dublin to Holyhead in Wales. He brought up the comment of Mulcahy's, 'I am as happy as the day is long, everything is working out grand.' Weston asked him to explain. 'By sending us to prison,' Mulcahy said, 'they have made heroes out of us. We will have men with us in the future who would never have touched us if they had sent us home after we surrendered.'[7] This was very true, and at the time, a great change had come over the people of Ireland. Margaret Skinnider who had served as a sniper in the St Stephen's garrison during the Rising commented of the time:

> When I went back to Dublin in August, it was to find that almost every one on the streets was wearing republican colours. The feeling was bitter too – so bitter that the British soldiers had orders to go about in fives and sixes, but never singly. They were not allowed by their officers to leave the main thoroughfares, and had to be back in barracks before dark – that is, all except the patrol. The city was still under martial law, but it seemed to me the military authorities were really nervous persons. Much of this bitterness came from the fact that people remembered how, after the war in South Africa which lasted three years instead of five days, only one man had been executed. After our rising sixteen men had been put to death.[8]

In Frongoch, there were rumours of an early release for the remaining inmates. Joseph Lawless pointed out in his statement that Britain was facing a critical stage in its war with Germany:

> America was still a neutral state. Britain was consequently very sensitive to adverse propaganda in the United States, and the big Irish population in the United States was very concerned over the reputed conditions of

the Frongoch prisoners. As Beasley [in his biography of Michael Collins] puts it, 'The Frongoch internees had become a greater source of trouble and danger to the English Government in custody than they could possibly be at large.'

As the month of December wore on we had heard some rumours of the agitation for our release then in progress at home and abroad, but I am afraid our minds had by then settled into a rather cynical disbelief in the efficacy of such efforts. We had no real hope that the British would even consider our release while the war was still on.

On the afternoon of 22 December, an order was issued that all prisoners were to assemble at once in the dining hall. There was a healthy degree of scepticism that good news would be imparted. The camp adjutant entered the hall and, without any preliminary comment, announced, 'An order has been received from the Home Office for your immediate release.' The release would be in stages. The first batch of prisoners were released at 6pm on Friday, 22 December. One hundred and thirty of them landed at Kingstown (Dún Laoghaire) by the mail packet steamer from Holyhead on Saturday morning. Sixty-three of these travelled by the mail train, which enabled them to proceed by the Great Southern and Western Railway to the south and the Midland Great Western to the west of Ireland. A tram arriving in Westland Row, Dublin, at 7.40am discharged sixty-seven of the freed men in the city. They carried their personal belongings in small bags on their shoulders. The men formed into line and marched along Great Brunswick Street into Sackville Street. Forty of the released prisoners arrived at the North Wall on Saturday morning at 6.30am by one of the London and North Western Company's cargo boats. Of the Dublin men at their departure from Frongoch, Joseph Lawless in his very detailed account, revealed:

> I pass over the details of our entrainment, and the rail journey to Holyhead. There was little regret at leaving the camp where so much had happened to us in the months just past. We had not yet come to look upon it as a bit of our past, and I do not remember any head turned to look back at it as we marched out or as the train left the station. Our eyes were on the future and our minds concerned with thought of home.

The ship they sailed in from Holyhead was a cross-channel cargo vessel. The men from Frongoch were its human cargo. At daylight the next morning, the outlines of the Wicklow mountains could be discerned. Then the lighthouse beams of Baily, North and South Bulls, and Rockabill were reflected across the water. They entered the Liffey and were home. The ship docked, and each man with his bundles of personal belongings strove to be first to the gangway. Despite the attempt by the authorities to make the return low-key, there were crowds there, but nothing in the way of a demonstration, to meet the returning prisoners. As the word spread, even more people gathered. Given the final word, Joseph Lawless celebrated the return:

> The rest may more easily be imagined than described. We were submerged in a riot of joyous welcome, each of us becoming the object of so much promiscuous handshaking, hugging and kissing, that we were glad at last to get away. Mick Fleming and I, with his sisters and mine who were there to meet us, and also Jimmy Kelly and Joe Taylor, went to Flemings at 140, Drumcondra Road, where we breakfasted and spent some hours in the enjoyment of our new freedom before I went home to Saucerstown.

On Sunday (Christmas Eve) some 130 released prisoners arrived at Westland Row by the 7.40am train from Kingstown, having come across by the mail steamer from Holyhead. Upwards of 300 men from Frongoch Internment Camp came by steamer to the North Wall. On Christmas morning, twenty-eight of the released men arrived at Carlisle Pier from Holyhead. The men were home.

Chapter 13

The Aftermath

The men from Fingal returned home. It was an unsettling time. The great adventure was over. Now they returned to their humdrum lives. Joseph Lawless, who always had something to say, put a positive spin upon his return. 'In the following month or two there was plenty to keep me busy in looking after the work on the farm. My father, with the other sentenced prisoners, was still held in prison in England, and I therefore had to do my best to get the work done at home.' Kit Moran, optimistic of the future, remarked:

> I now returned to my home in Swords. Although the people seemed very depressed, there were already signs that the country was awakening to a new sense of nationality. I was still a sick man, as well as a man without a job, and it was not until the following year, 1917, that I succeeded in getting work at the construction of the aerodrome at Collinstown which the British War Office was building there.[1]

George B. Heard, County Inspector for Dublin, reported to his masters in London:

> Those who a few weeks previously were openly hostile to Sinn Feinism began to show sympathy towards it and for a time this change of feeling spread rapidly. However, there are no leaders in the country to organise the movement, and it is in abeyance, but the seeds have been sown and it would not require much energy on the part of a clever organiser to create a dangerous organisation.[2]

Unbeknown to George Heard, the volunteers had already become active once more. Following a meeting of the IRB in late June 1917, in the following month, general manoeuvres of the various battalions of the Dublin Brigade restarted.[3] It had begun much earlier than this. James Crennigan, brother of Jack Crennigan killed at Ashbourne, testified:

> I was released from Lewes Jail, England, about March 1917 where I had been detained consequent on my activities in the 1916 Rebellion,

and returned to my home at Roganstown. There was nothing doing in Volunteer circles then and the movement seemed to be dead. There were quite a number of men in the area who had participated in the Rebellion and it was evident that they were anxious to keep associated with the movement, so, in order to fill this desire in some way, we started a football team. This proved to be a success as it brought the lads together and gave them an opportunity of discussing Volunteer matters amongst themselves and with other individuals who were sympathetic to us.[4]

In 1917, the Fingal Battalion was brought together on two sad occasions when they acted as the escort at the funerals of Thomas MacDonagh's widow Muriel, and their commandant, Thomas Ashe. Muriel McDonagh, aged 31, the mother of two young children and sister of Grace Gifford, the widow of Joseph Plunkett, was drowned on 9 July 1917, off the coast of Skerries while swimming on holiday. Following a requiem mass in the town, her coffin, draped in the Irish tricolour, was carried to the train station by Irish Volunteers from Skerries, Lusk and Rush. Her body was removed to the Pro-Cathedral in Dublin, before continuing on to Glasnevin Cemetery for burial. In September of that same year, the Fingal Battalion men acted as an honour guard following the death of Ashe, from the effects of being force-fed in Mountjoy Prison.

Spared execution after the failure of the Rising, Ashe was separated from his men. With some sixty-five other officers such as de Valera, Harry Boland, Desmond Fitzgerald, Thomas Partridge of the Irish Citizen Army, and later Eoin MacNeill, he was sent to Dartmoor Prison. Ashe was entered on the prison register as 'Q.102.Life'. In December 1916, Ashe was transferred to Lewes Prison. Following the amnesty of the Frongoch prisoners, only the convict prisoners, sixty-five in Dartmoor and fifty-seven in Portland Prison remained in British custody. The prisoners now demanded to be treated as prisoners of war. Denied by the authorities, the prisoners went on strike, refusing to work. They broke cell windows and furniture. The Home Office responded by separating them. Ashe was sent to Portland in Dorset. At the time of leaving Lewes, Ashe had been elected President of the IRB Supreme Council. Following his arrival in Portland, the Irish Volunteer prisoners were quickly organized into a disciplined body. They refused to abide by prison rules. As a punishment, they were placed in individual punishment cells, but their spirit was not broken.

British Prime Minister David Lloyd George, concerned at Sinn Fein's successes in by-elections in Ireland, called for 'a convention of Irishmen of all parties for the purpose of producing a scheme of Irish self government'. Redmond, still a force to be recognised with, agreed on the basis that the prisoners should be released as a good-will gesture. On 15 June 1917, Andrew Bonar Law announced in the House of Commons that the Irish political prisoners would be released. The Fingal Volunteers welcomed the return of Ashe and Dr Hayes when they came home. Comrade in arms, John Devine, wrote:

> The day Tom Ashe and Dr. Hayes came home after their release we met them outside the village and had a crowd there to welcome them. We had bought a lot of cartridges at bargain price from a decent man named George Carton. I showed them to Dr. Hayes and Tom Ashe. Tom Ashe said with approval, 'so you're tearing to be at it again.'[5]

Within weeks of being freed Ashe went on the campaign trail to promote Sinn Fein candidates in a series of by-elections. Good speakers were in great demand, and Ashe proved to be a great orator. In August, Ashe made a short visit to Fingal. Writing from the Greville Arms Hotel to James Kelly, he wrote:

> I have been in Fingal once or twice since my return, on a flying visit, but I am going there next Sat. and will speak at an apricot [sic] at Donabate on Sunday I intend spending the week among the boys…I am very busy since my return, but of all welcomes we get wherever we go, and all the honours showered on us I would prefer to be among the good men and true of the fighting 5th.[6]

Following a speech he gave at Ballinalee on 25 July 1917, a warrant was issued for the arrest of Thomas Ashe by the British Authorities in Dublin. The charge was one of sedition under the Defence of the Realm Act. As a consequence, Ashe was arrested in Dublin, on Saturday, 18 August. The controversial point, which appears to have got him arrested, was his stated opposition to recruitment for the British Army. Ashe delivered the speech at the rath where Roger Casement had been arrested. Thousands of Irish citizens walked and cycled to listen to him speak. It was the largest single gathering of nationalists since the 1916 Rising. Alice Stopford Green paid for the printing of a small pamphlet containing Ashe's emotive speech.[7] In normal circumstances, such a comment would have been ignored by the authorities, but the size of the crowd alarmed the authorities. Sinn Fein was on the rise and might prove unstoppable. Measures had to be taken to prevent this. The government in Ireland embarked on a campaign to coerce Republican leaders. Ashe was arrested. He had been free for just eight weeks. Other prominent men within Sinn Fein were also arrested. They were taken to the Curragh

Camp in County Kildare to face a court-martial. The evidence against Ashe was presented by two RIC men who had been at the Ballinalee meeting. Ashe was charged 'with doing an act prohibited by Regulation 42 of the Defence of the Realm regulations namely, attempting to cause disaffection among the civilian population'. The evidence by the two policemen was a little shaky. It was based on 'mental notes', rather than written testimony. Though he put up an adequate defence, the verdict was a foregone conclusion. Ashe was found guilty and sentenced to twelve months imprisonment. Ashe and the others, some forty in number, including Captain Richard Coleman of Swords, a comrade in the Fingal Battalion, were transferred to Mountjoy Prison. Here, the prisoners demanded prisoner of war status. They had been prosecuted for their political actions, not for any crime, and as such should be afforded special treatment as political prisoners. To emphasize their status, they refused to do any work. They refused to observe silence during exercise, which was expected of criminal offenders. As a punishment, the forty were deprived of their mattresses and personal possessions. As a final resort, on 20 September, the prisoners went on hunger strike in the pursuit of their claim. The newspapers got hold of the news of the hunger strike, and day-to-day accounts were published. Forcible feeding was resorted to. Protests took place concerning the treatment of these men. Éamon de Valera, Cathal Brugha and Constance Markievicz spoke at a huge demonstration in Smithfield; the large open area off Arran Quay. On 23 September, Ashe was taken from his cell to the infirmary. Here he was secured to a high wooden chair by leather straps that bound his wrists and ankles. His mouth was prised open with a wooden spoon, and a doctor inserted a tube down his neck and into his stomach. The other end of the tube was inserted into a pump, and the end of the pump was put into bowl containing a mixture of milk and eggs. The pump was hand operated. The process of forced feeding lasted between five and ten minutes. A degree of vomiting usually occurred when the tube was removed from the stomach. Ashe endured the force-feeding five times. On 25 September, Ashe had a reaction to the feeding. He collapsed and was taken to the prison infirmary. Here his condition deteriorated, and he was removed to the Mater Misericordiae Hospital. Laurence Nugent, who knew Ashe, was strongly of the opinion that 'he had been removed from Mountjoy Prison by the authorities when they saw that he was about to die; they did not want the death to take place in the prison.'[8] On the night of 25 September 1917, Ashe died. He was thirty-two years old. It would appear that the food was pumped into his lungs rather than his stomach. An inquest was held, at the end of which the jury agreed on the verdict:

We find that the deceased, Thomas Ashe, according to the medical evidence of Professor M. Weeney, Sir Arthur Chance and Sir Thomas Myles, died from heart failure and congestion of the lungs on the 25th September 1917; that his death was caused by the punishment of taking away from the cell bed, bedding and boots and allowing him to be on the cold floor for up to 50 hours, and then subjecting him to forcible feeding in his weak condition after hunger-striking for five or six days.

We censure the Castle Authorities for not acting more promptly, especially when the grave condition of the deceased and other prisoners were brought under their notice on the previous Saturday by the Lord Mayor and Sir John Irwin.

That the hunger strike was adopted against the inhuman punishment inflicted and a refusal to their demand to be treated as political prisoners.

We condemn forcible and mechanical feeding as an inhuman and dangerous operation, and which should be discontinued.

That the assistant doctor called in, having no previous practice, administered forcible feeding unskillfully.

We find that the taking away of the deceased's bedding and boots was an unfeeling and a barbarous act and we censure the deputy governor for violating the prison rules and inflicting punishment which he had no power to do.

That we infer he was acting under instructions from the Prison Board and Castle, which refused to give evidence and documents for.

We tender our sympathy to the relatives of the deceased.'[9]

The body of Thomas Ashe was taken to the Pro-Cathedral and then on to Dublin's City Hall where it lay in state for two days. Michael Collins, a fellow IRB Supreme Council member, donated an Irish Volunteer uniform to be worn by Ashe and his body was dressed in it as he lay in state.[10] Collins, very much a protégé of Ashe, succeeded him as President of the Supreme Council of the IRB, and in essence the successor of Padraig Pearse, the first proclaimed President of the Irish Republic.

Ashe was guarded by volunteers in their now illegal uniforms. Some 30,000 people, the great and the good of Dublin and the rest of the country, passed before it. Many were dressed in black; many were in tears as they left. In the days after his death, the city was tense. In the streets, hawkers sold photographs of the dead hero of Ashbourne. Others sold copies of his poem written in Lewes Gaol in Sussex, *Let me carry your Cross for Ireland, Lord*. In a well-planned procession, his body was taken to Glasnevin Cemetery. The coffin was draped in the Irish tricolour of green, white and orange. Crowds lined the street and public houses were closed. Fifty volunteers marched in formation before the coffin in uniform and carried rifles with bayonets fixed. Two rows of volunteers in uniform walked alongside the hearse, their rifles reversed. Behind it a horse pulled a cart carrying dozens of wreaths. Trailing behind the carriages that carried family members and friends were two hundred Catholic priests led by two Capuchin fathers who had given the last rites to the executed leaders of the Easter Rising. Following on were brass bands, from the Dublin Fire Brigade, the boys from Na Fianna, the women of Cumann na mBan, hundreds of primary school teachers, reflecting Ashe's calling, followed by representatives of the city's trade unions, members from the Gaelic Athletic Association carrying hurley sticks over their shoulders. Thousands of men and women lined the pavements, the men removing their hats as the cortege passed. The British military was confined to barracks for the day to avoid any tension, and the police were noticeable by their absence on the streets of Dublin. The procession reached Glasnevin Cemetery shortly before 4pm. Volunteers controlled the entrance, and only those with permits were allowed to gather around the newly dug grave. After the tricolour was removed and folded, the coffin was lowered into the grave. The priests intoned the *Miserere Benedictus*. Then, Michael Collins in his vice commandant uniform issued a command in Irish to the captain of the firing party lined up by the graveside. Raising their rifles, they fired three volleys into the autumn sky. A bugler sounded the *Last Post* and Collins standing at the head of the grave announced in a clear voice, 'Nothing additional remains to be said. That volley is the only speech it is proper to make above the grave of a dead Fenian.'

On 8 October 1917, the castle authorities conceded full political or prisoner of war status to the remaining prisoners in Mountjoy.

Of the others who made up the Fingal Battalion, Richard Coleman died in Usk Prison in December 1918 from the flu pandemic then sweeping through the world. Of the other comrades of the 5th, and those with them at Ashbourne, Frank Lawless was elected to the First Dáil for the new County Dublin constituency. He was re-elected to the Second Dáil of 1921–22. Lawless voted in favour of the ratification of the Anglo-Irish Treaty on 7 January 1922. He tragically died three months later from injuries sustained when the horse and trap he was driving overturned. A year and a month later, in February 1923, Ned Stafford died. After release from Frongoch, he went on to serve in the War of Independence and in the National Army during the Civil War. His obituary appears in the *Irish Times* for 26 April 1923:

The funeral took place to Swords cemetery yesterday with full military honours of Vol. Edward Stafford, The Green, Swords, who died in

Peamount Sanatorium, from Tuberculosis contracted on active service. The brass and reed band and a firing party and Guard of Honour under Capt. T. O'Doherty, attended from Collins Barracks, as well as a large party of troops from Dublin. Staff Capt. Stafford, St Brecan's Hospital, had charge of the funeral arrangements. All business was suspended in Swords as the cortege passed through.

Joe Taylor, born in 1896, died in March 1932. He took part in the full campaign under Ashe. During the War of Independence, he served as a lieutenant and later as company commanding officer. He took part in a number of attacks on RIC barracks and in an attack on British forces near Santry. He was arrested in December 1921 but freed at the end of the war. Taylor took the Free State side during the Civil War.

James Vincent Lawless, brother of Frank and uncle to Joe, died in December 1939. He was sixty years old. After the surrender, he was sentenced to death, but this was commuted to ten years in prison. Like a number of other volunteer officers, he was freed in June 1917. Lawless worked for Dublin County Council during the War of Independence. He supplied Irish Intelligence with details of British military and police activities. After the war, he worked on the Dáil Éireann Commission on Local Government.

Peter Moran and William Norton both died in March 1940. Moran was with the column throughout the campaign. During the War of Independence, he was involved in intelligence work. Moran was briefly interned but released at the time of the Truce. He took no part in the Civil War. Norton was forty-six years old at the time of the Rising. Quite old for a soldier, but he likewise served throughout the campaign. He is not recorded as taking part in the War of Independence nor the Civil War.

Tom Seaver fought with the Fingal Battalion throughout the Easter Rising. He was interned until Christmas 1916. Seaver served throughout the War of Independence. He died in April 1948.

Tom Maxwell of E Company, 2nd Battalion of the Dublin Brigade fought with the 5th after having been cut off from his unit. He went on to fight in the War of Independence and served the National Army during the Civil War. He left the army in 1924. Maxwell died in March 1953.

James O'Connor (Connor) and Thomas Blanchfield both died in 1955. O'Connor was sent home by Ashe just prior to the surrender but was arrested and interned a few days later. Upon release, he rejoined the volunteers and took part in the War of Independence. He did not take part in the Civil War. Tom Blanchfield, brother of Peadar, served in the 1st Battalion, Dublin Brigade. He joined Ashe after being cut off from his battalion. He later went on to serve in the War of Independence and in the National Army during the Civil War. Blanchfield retired from the Defence Force in 1950.

Thomas Patrick Duke of the St Margaret's Company was sixty-three years old at the time of his death in May 1956. He fought throughout the Easter Rising, and during the War of Independence he served as officer commanding the company. Duke fought throughout the war, and during the Civil War, he fought against the Free State Army.

Charles Weston, Section Commander of C Company, 5th Battalion, was born in 1894. He took part in the attempted demolition of the railway bridge at Lusk. He continued with the battalion throughout the campaign. Following release from internment in Frongoch, Weston participated in the reorganization of the volunteers. He served as company and later battalion officer, commanding the company. During the War of Independence, Weston participated in the raid on Collinstown Aerodrome and the burning of a number of RIC barracks. Following independence, Weston served in the Defence Force from December 1922 to December 1923. He died in December 1956.

Thomas Doyle of the Lusk Company of the Fingal Battalion was just nineteen at the time of the Battle of Ashbourne in which he partook. He had been involved in the earlier Howth gunrunning in July 1914. Doyle served throughout the War of Independence and took the pro-Treaty side in the Civil war. He served in the Defence Force up to February 1945. Doyle died in July 1957.

Dr Richard Hayes, medical and administrative officer of the 5th Battalion, was born in 1878. He had been the officer commanding of the 5th but resigned in favour of Ashe. Hayes fought throughout the Easter Rising and was sentenced to twenty years imprisonment. He was released in June 1917, but rearrested during the 'German Plot'. During the general election of 1918, Hayes was elected an MP or TD (*Teachta Dala*) to the Irish Parliament – the Dáil. During the War of Independence, Hayes served as a general medical officer. He took the pro-Treaty side in the Civil War. Dr Hayes died in June 1958.

The year 1959 saw the deaths of Matthew Kelly, Eamon Murphy, John (Jack) Rafferty and Patrick Sherwin. All four took part in the Battle of Ashbourne. Kelly appears to have taken no further part in the fighting after the surrender. Sherwin stood down in 1917. Murphy later joined the National Defence Force in 1922 and was demobilised in 1924. John Rafferty fought at Ashbourne where his brother Thomas was killed. Rafferty later served in the Garda Siochana from 1923.

Edward Joseph Rooney (Ned) was Captain of Lusk Company. He was born in 1885. He took part in the battalion's campaign in 1916. Rooney was wounded at Ashbourne. Thereafter, there is no record of him serving in the War of Independence or the Civil War. He died in 1960.

Peter Kelly, or Peadar O'Ceallaigh as he later became, was a volunteer in Swords Company. He was born in 1886. At the time of the Rising, he was a civil servant with the Irish Land Commission. He joined the volunteers in 1914 and became a clerk to Frank Lawless, helping to organize the Swords Company. Kelly served with the 5th during the Easter Rising. He served in the War of Independence but took no part in the Civil War. Kelly died in January 1961.

Richard Aungier died in March 1962. He joined the volunteers in 1913. He campaigned with Ashe throughout the Easter Rising and later fought in the War of Independence. Aungier did not take part in the Civil War.

Bernard McAllister also died in 1962, as did Bartholomew Weston. McAllister, also known as Bennie McAllister, was born in 1894. He served with the 5th Fingals during the Easter Rising. During the War of Independence, he served as battalion officer commanding. He took part in the raid on Collinstown aerodrome for arms. McAllister joined the National Army and served throughout the Civil War. He resigned in January 1927. Bartholomew (Bartle) Weston of Swords Company was born in 1884. He fought at Swords, Donabate, Garristown and Ashbourne. Weston took part in the War of Independence, including attacks on RIC barracks and the killing of a British spy named Shaw. At the time of the Civil War, he took the pro-Treaty side.

John Eamon Morgan also died in 1962. He served in the Lusk company. Morgan took part in the Howth gunrunning and later in the Fingal Battalion's campaign. Ashe sent him home before the surrender. Morgan worked with Michael Collins in the distribution of money in the Prisoners' Aid Society post-1916. Morgan was arrested during the War of Independence but released at the time of the Treaty. He enlisted in the National Forces and served as a lieutenant. He was medically discharged in March 1924.

Christopher (Christy) Nugent was just nineteen at the time of the Easter Rising. He fought at Rathbeale Cross, Knocksiddane, Donabate and Ashbourne. Following his release from internment in Wales, he rejoined the Irish Volunteers in 1917. During the War of Independence, Nugent took part in the burnings of Rogerstown Coast Guard Station and the burning of Santry and Malahide barracks. He took part in the capture of Rush Barracks and was involved in two ambushes at Lissenhall and Ballough. He did not take part in the Civil War. Christopher Nugent died on 14 June 1964.

Jeremiah (Jerry) Golden, also died in 1964. He fought at both the North Circular Road Bridge and Cabra Bridge before moving north to join with Ashe's column. After Ashe's surrender, Golden and others slipped away and avoided arrest. During the War of Independence, he was involved in a number of small operations. Golden was arrested in January 1921 and sentenced to five years penal detention. He was freed at the time of the Treaty. Golden took the side of the Republicans during the Civil War. He was captured and interned until January 1924. Jerry Golden died in December 1964, aged seventy-eight.

Michael Fleming died in the following year. Like a number of others, Fleming from C Company 2nd Battalion, was prevented from joining his unit, so sought out Ashe and his men. Fleming, from County Wicklow, fought at the RIC barracks at Swords, Donabate, Garristown and Ashbourne. Following his release from internment, he rejoined his battalion. He was involved in the purchase of arms prior to the outbreak of the War of Independence. During the war, he fought in Dublin with the active service units. He was captured for his part in the ill-fated attack upon the Custom House but was released in December 1921. Fleming opposed the Treaty and took part in the fighting against the National Army in O'Connell Street and Parnell Street. He escaped and took no further part in the struggle.

The year 1966 saw the death of Colm Lawless (O'Laosdhlaish) of Swords Company. He was the younger son of Frank Lawless. Colm was just fifteen at the time of the Rising. Nevertheless, he was allowed to fight at Finglas, Lusk, Swords, Donabate, Garristown and Ashbourne. Colm was a student at St Enda's College under Patrick Pearse. At the time of the surrender, Ashe sent him away. Lawless was active during the War of Independence and later as a Captain in the National Army. At the time of his death, he was aged sixty-five.

Patrick Brogan joined the Lusk Company at the formation of the volunteers in 1913. He was appointed a lieutenant. The company numbered about sixty men but disappointedly only half that number turned out on Easter Monday. Brogan took part in the campaign and was with the volunteers at their surrender. Released from internment he rejoined the Lusk Company and fought throughout the War of Independence. He died in December 1967.

John Devine and Paddy Doyle died in the following year. Both men took part in the 5th's campaign under Ashe. Doyle was there at the Howth gunrunning.

Joseph Vincent Lawless, author of the 215-page account of the formation of the volunteers, from which much of his testimony is included in this work, fought in the Fingal Battalion. He died in August 1969. He returned to the National struggle following his release from Frongoch. Joseph Lawless rose to become a colonel in the post-Civil War National Army.

Patrick Birney, who fought at Ashbourne, was a volunteer in the 2nd Battalion of the Dublin Brigade. Like others from his battalion, he found himself cut off and sought out Ashe and his men. Before the surrender, he slipped away and avoided arrest. He went on to serve in the National Army until discharged in 1924. Birney died in October 1970.

Volunteer William Doyle, aged twenty-four at the time of the fight at Ashbourne, later went on to fight during the War of Independence. He took no part in the Civil War that followed.

Francis Ciaran Murphy, from Lusk Company, then just nineteen, fought with Ashe and later during the War of Independence. He died in December 1974.

Volunteer Peadar (Peter) Blanchfield, the grenade thrower who brought about the surrender of the police barracks at Ashbourne, was a cabinet maker by trade and brother to Frank Blanchfield. He was a member of the IRB, and a founding member of the volunteers, having joined at its inception in 1913. He died in February 1976.

Frank Daly also died in 1976 at the age of eighty-nine. Again, cut off by the British as they encircled Dublin from the north, he sought out Ashe. Daly fought at Ashbourne. Earlier in his military career, he took part in the Howth gunrunning. After his Frongoch release, he was involved in training in preparation for the War of Independence. During the war, Daly was involved in intelligence work. Daly joined the anti-Treaty forces in the Four Courts at the outbreak of the Civil War. He was captured but released in 1923.

Paddy Grant of E Company, 2nd Battalion, Dublin Brigade, joined Ashe after being cut off by quick-moving British troops. He fought with the 5th Battalion throughout its campaign. Detained at Knutsford and later Frongoch, he was released at Christmas time 1916. Thereafter, he appears to have dropped out of the volunteers. Paddy Grant died in September 1980.

James Kelly or Seamus O'Ceallaigh as he later was renamed, was the last survivor of the Battle of Ashbourne. He was born in 1897. Kelly fought at the RIC Barracks at Donabate and at the Battle of Ashbourne. Following his release from Frongoch, he became involved in organization and training in counties Offaly, Mayo and Dublin. In March 1921, at the height of the War of Independence he took part in the unsuccessful attempt by the IRA to derail a British troop-carrying train travelling from Athlone to the Curragh. Kelly was arrested in April 1921and interned at the Curragh and later Kilkenny from which he escaped on 21 November 1921. Kelly joined the Irish Defence Force post-Civil War, serving as an acting captain during 'The Emergency', better known to most as the Second World War. Kelly resigned from the army in April 1946. He died on 20 October 1986, at the age of eighty-nine.

Of the women involved, there was Mary (Molly) Adrien. She was born in County Meath in September 1873. She was the daughter of Edward and Mary Adrien of Micknanstown House in Stamullen. The family later moved to Balbriggan, where Molly, as she was more familiarly known, was educated at the Loreto Convent. Her education was completed at Surbiton High School, just outside of London. Molly returned to Ireland and lived at Oldtown, north County Dublin. In 1915, she became a member of Cumann na mBan, later going on to become director of the Lusk branch. Under Cumann, Molly trained in first aid and field signalling. Molly was mobilised on Easter Sunday but instructed to stand down temporarily following instructions from Dublin Central. She was activated late on Monday, and on Tuesday reported to Thomas Ashe. From then until Saturday, she acted as a messenger and nurse. On Friday at Lusk, she heard about the battle at Ashbourne and rushed there to attend the wounded of both sides. At the surrender at Newbarn, Ashe sent her away to safety. Adrien took part in the later anti-conscription campaign. During the War of Independence, she acted as a dispatch rider and scout. Padraig Pearse's mother supported her claim for a state pension when times became hard financially. Molly Adrien died in 1949, aged seventy-six, and was buried in Crickstown Graveyard with full military honours.

Monica 'Dot' Fleming later became Monica Lawless when she married Joseph V. Lawless. She was born in 1897 and died in November 1975. Monica was a member of Cumann na mBan and attached to the 5th (Fingal) Battalion at the outbreak of the Easter Rising. Her sister Kate and her two brothers also served during the Rising, Monica acted as a despatch rider between Fingal and the GPO, and other places. She was briefly arrested after the failure of the Rising but released. During the War of Independence, her home was used as an arms dump by the IRA. Monica took the anti-Treaty stance during the Civil War.

Eveleen Lawless was born in 1900. She became a member of Cumann na mBan sometime prior to 1916. She was attached to the 5th Fingal Battalion and served in a nursing capacity after the Battle of Ashbourne. She carried dispatches and did intelligence work during the War of Independence. In August 1920, she was appointed as a secretary to Michael Collins at 6, and later 76, Harcourt Street. Following the end of the war, she became a nun.

Kathleen Lawless, the daughter of Frank Lawless, was born in 1899. She joined Cumann na mBan, Swords Branch, at the age of sixteen. Kathleen served in various aspects during Easter Week, including carrying despatches and the acquisition and distribution of supplies to the volunteers of the 5th Battalion. She was briefly detained for a day following the surrender but then released. During the internment of the volunteers, she helped to organize assistance for the prisoners. During the War of Independence, Kathleen continued to act as a courier and helped men on the run. Kathleen McAllister, as she became after marriage, died in January 1979.

Chapter 14

An Analysis of the Battle of Ashbourne

The Protagonists

The confrontation at Ashbourne has frequently been described as an ambush. It was not. It has also recently been described as a guerrilla operation. Again, it was evidently not that either. It was an out and out battle, albeit a small-scale battle, with the RIC having the initial advantage, but losing the battle to what may be described as an Irish Volunteer flying column.

The Royal Irish Constabulary

The RIC, founded in 1836, was a para-military force armed with short carbines and .45 revolvers. It was organized along army lines, but in no way trained as such. Constable David Neligan was to write, 'It had neither the strength nor armament for anything bigger that a village riot.'[1]

By 1916, the RIC strength was approximately 10,000 in number. It recruited in Ireland mainly from the rural community. A would-be RIC man had to pass a high physical standard to qualify for entry. He had to be at least five feet ten inches in height and reasonably well educated. The officers, Protestant to a man, and mainly Masons, were for the most part English, or at least Anglo-Irish, and were generally ex-British Army officers. If selected, the young candidate constable would have received his initial training at RIC Headquarters in Dublin. He would have been taught in extended courses, including weapon training, as well as police duties and drill. The successful candidate would then have been posted to another county, to avoid any conflict of loyalty with the local community of his own county. Here in his police barracks, he was instructed to become acquainted with the intimate knowledge of the country and its people. All knowledge acquired, no matter how trivial, was written down and at some stage transferred to RIC Headquarters in Dublin. Irish Volunteer Joseph Lawless wrote of the respect in which the RIC were held by their sheer presence:

> The RIC uniform was imposing, or perhaps I should say, intimidating, as no doubt it was intended to be. The men being invariably fine, sturdy,

well-set-up fellows, were set off to advantage in a tight fitting high-collared tunic and close-fitting trousers of a slightly greenish black cloth. An ordinary round peaked cap and black leather belt with baton completed the attire…A number of these fine looking big fellows were, in such array, a sight calculated to inspire fear in the stoutest heart.[2]

The policemen existed within the community but were not part of it. They were obliged to hold themselves aloof from their fellow citizens. Their disciplinary code was strict and enforced with a Prussian thoroughness that ensured the strictest obedience to orders. A high standard of marksmanship was provided for by weekly miniature practices in each barracks with 'Morris Tubes' fitted to the carbines.[3] This armed police force, spread throughout the towns and villages of Ireland, strove to control the spread of disaffection. The RIC were based in garrisons. In the larger villages and towns, the garrison would consist of a sergeant and five or six constables. In the larger towns, which acted as district centres, the garrison would consist of between ten and twenty constables, at least two sergeants, and the District Inspector.

The Volunteers

The Volunteers were founded at an inaugural meeting held at the Rotunda Rink in Dublin in November 1913. Its aim was to 'secure and maintain the rights and liberties common to all the people of Ireland'. The volunteers were legally established, but there was always a suspicion on the part of the government in Ireland. The RIC were often in attendance at their meetings and marches. Right from the start, the biggest problem facing the volunteer leadership was how to initiate a training policy to bring the men up to a proficiency in drill, discipline, marksmanship and field craft. An instruction was issued by the executive in the spring of 1914 that every effort should be made to recruit volunteers who had served in the British army, who could be utilised as instructors. A drill manual was published by Ponsonby's of Grafton Street, priced at one shilling, an affordable price for senior and most junior officers. It was based upon the British Army's *British Infantry Manual* published in 1911, with some slight amendments. Weeknight training took part, mainly indoors. Each parade began with a roll call, after which the men were instructed for half an hour in the elementary principles of military drill, such as numbering off, forming fours and marching. As rifles were mainly unavailable at this early stage, substitutions for rifles included hurley sticks and spade handles, before the introduction of imitation wooden rifles. If a troop was lucky, it might possess one rifle or handgun. Ammunition was also in short supply.

Instruction was given regarding loading and taking aim. When firing did take place, most Volunteers were only permitted to fire two or three rounds.

As the volunteer organization expanded, particularly with the acquisition of arms, training camps were set up for officer and squad commander training. One such was at Ticknock in the Dublin Mountains. The camp was in the charge of Colonel J.J. 'Ginger' O'Connell assisted by Eimar O'Duffy and Quartermaster J.J. Burke. It was to one of these weekly camps, laden with equipment, that Joseph V. Lawless attended, along with Ned Rooney of Lusk, Dick Coleman of Swords and James Rooney, also of Lusk. Lawless was to write of it:

> We studied British military text books such as Field Craft and Tactical Handling of Troops in the field, Field fortifications, Manual of Military Engineering, and the like, and we listened to lectures and practised these things as best we could. These and weapon training which gave us scope to improve the natural marksmanship of most country men, fitted us, we thought, to make a trial of our strength, even if our armament was miserably inadequate.[4]

For the ordinary men, volunteer summer camps were held. For the Fingal men, it would have been at Wicklow, just south of Dublin. Here 200 men at a time attended. In addition, lectures for officers were organized weekly at Turvey for the men of Fingal. Lectures were given by 'Ginger' O'Connell on tactics, and as Lawless relates, by Thomas McDonagh on supply problems, particularly the feeding of men in the field. Of field craft, Lawless recalled:

> Sometimes we travelled towards the city or even across it to the Rathfarnham side to attack or defend against one of the city battalions, and on at least one Sunday a representative parade of all the city battalions marched out of Swords under Eamon de Valera, and engaged in an exercise at Skerries against the Fingal Battalion, marching back to the city that night.[5]

In order to arm themselves, the volunteers relied upon a variety of sources. The most common in the early days was from soldiers in the British Army in Ireland. These were obtained either by theft or purchase. Sporting rifles and shotguns were purchased legally from gun shops by 'persons of good standing'. Rifles were purchased on a larger scale from Birmingham firms such as Greener & Co. who supplied Lee-Enfield rifles, under licence, to the British Army. These were usually purchased by supposed gun clubs for sport shooting.

The weapon most associated with the volunteers was the 'Howth' rifle, landed from the *Asgard*. This 1870s German Mauser was a single-shot rifle firing an 11mm round propelled by a charge of slow-burning black powder, which gave a terrific recoil. It was a fearsome weapon which led the British to believe that it fired dumdum or exploding cartridges, contrary to the Hague Convention.

The Battle Analysed

At the point of the surrender of Ashbourne police barracks, a sizeable relief column of RIC men approached the hamlet down the road from Slane. There were between fifteen and seventeen cars, holding perhaps up to sixty armed policemen. The convoy was led by County Inspector Alexander Gray. The rear was brought up by District Inspector Harry Smyth; a former British Army officer. As the police convoy approached Ashbourne, they must have heard the shooting down at the barracks on the other side of the Rath crossroads. Gray halted the convoy about 100 yards away from the cross. In the distance, he saw a small group of volunteers. They were Dr Richard Hayes, Bernard McAllister and Christy Nugent. They had been posted to watch the main road, guarding the flank of Charlie Weston's line as he and his men attacked the garrison. Volunteer Paddy Holohan later suggested that Gray had made a tactical error in stopping. He believed that Gray should have gone on to link up with the defenders in the garrison. Gray, however, did what he considered to be right. There were rumours that Ashe had several hundred men under his command. This was based upon the numbers that paraded in Fingal on the previous Sunday. Clearly, there were more than just the three or four volunteers that Gray could see at the crossroads. At this point, seeing the arrival of the police convoy, Hayes ordered Nugent to inform Ashe of the situation, while he and McAllister opened fire upon the policemen. The volunteers had been taken completely by surprise.

Equally surprised were the police who now came under fire. They had not been trained to respond to gunfire directed at them. Diving for shelter alongside and beneath the cars, they returned ragged fire. District Inspector Harry Smyth, who could have made the difference, was at the rear of the RIC column, and in no position to influence what was going on. This was a critical point in the battle. If Smyth had been at the head of the police column, he would undoubtedly, his army training coming into play, have dispersed the men into the fields on either side of the road. Instead, they remained on the road to be enfiladed by the volunteers.

Nugent racing back, found Ashe and informed him of the arrival of police reinforcements. The garrison in the RIC barracks had nominally surrendered but as yet had not emerged. With them in his rear and with an unspecified number of police up ahead, Ashe feared that he might have to fight on two fronts if the garrison joined the fight. The training manuals that he had studied suggested that he should withdraw with his force, either to a new position or to retreat intact to fight another day. Mulcahy, however, was convinced that they could defeat the newly arrived reinforcements. The police reinforcements were unsure of the situation. They lacked accurate information about the volunteers' position and numbers. Mulcahy persuaded Ashe to rescind the order for retreat. Joseph Lawless got the impression that Ashe, though nominally in charge, appeared to 'place himself in Mulcahy's hands'.

To prevent the garrison joining the fight, three or four volunteers were sent to cover the front and rear doors of the barracks, while Ashe and Mulcahy directed the main force to confront the new arrivals. This was the second critical point – advance not retreat. How well Mulcahy heeded the instructions from the British Army training manual:

> The first object of a commander who seeks to gain the initiative in battle is to develop superiority of fire as a preparation for the delivery of a decisive blow. The commander must decide whether the direction of the decisive blow is to be pre-determined or to be left open until the situation has been developed by preparatory action.

Ashe ordered Joseph Lawless to take a unit across the fields to the west of the road and make their way to the rear of the police convoy. This fulfilled two objectives; to prevent the police from escaping, and further, to warn the volunteers of the approach of any additional police reinforcements.

At a very early stage in the battle, Gray was seriously wounded. While he did his best to direct his men, in essence the front of the police column was leaderless. The British Army training manual instructed:

> A decisive attack against some portion of the enemy's front offers a possibility of breaking his army in two and may give great and far reaching results…It is seldom either possible or desirable to attempt to overwhelm an enemy everywhere. The object will usually be to concentrate as large a force as possible against one decisive point, to deliver the decisive attack, while the remainder is employed to prepare the way for this attack, by attracting the enemy's attention, holding him to the ground, and wearing down his power of resistance.

Ashe brought up more men to the Cross to engage the police. Others were dispersed into the field to the east of the road and proceeded stealthily until they were opposite the police positions, where they opened fire. The police were being broken up into separate units. Only the rear, directed by Smyth, was still under some control. Victory was near complete for the volunteers. Ashe now ordered his reserve, back at the camp, to join the fight.

> The general reserve, if not already in position, will accordingly be moved there as secretly as possible. The launching of the general reserve in the attack will be the signal for the application of the greatest possible pressure against the enemy's whole front.

Mulcahy led the reserve up across the fields, past the men firing at the police from the hedges, and beyond to confront Smyth and his section of police.

Now, near tragedy struck. Joseph Lawless and his unit, ordered to prevent a police retreat, disobeyed orders. They moved forward to engage the rear of the police convoy. Mulcahy and the reserve, aware of where Joseph Lawless was supposed to be, were moving towards them on the other side of the road. Lawless saw movement along the hedges on the other side of the road and supposed them to be policemen. He and his men opened fire before clearly identifying the men in the field opposite. Mulcahy and his men believing that the fire directed against them was police fire, returned fire. What prevented the tragedy of death by friendly fire was avoided when Lawless and his men ran out of ammunition and withdrew.

> The climax of the infantry attack is the assault, which is made possible by superiority of fire. The fact that superiority of fire has been obtained will usually be first observed from the firing line; it will be known by the weakening of the enemy's fire, and perhaps by the movements of individuals or groups of men from the enemy's position towards the rear. The impulse for the assault must therefore often come from the firing line.

Mulcahy and his men now confronted Harry Smyth's unit. As they broke through the hedge onto the road, Volunteer Jack Crennigan was killed by Smyth. The police officer was now bravely standing in the open to inspire his men. Frank Lawless shot him dead. The police were now leaderless. One final push would decide the battle. Mulcahy gave the order to fix bayonets. The volunteers charged across the road, yelling like banshees. The police broke and fled before them, running down the road towards the Cross. There they encountered their comrades, hands in the air in surrender. They did likewise. The Battle of Ashbourne was over.

Mick McAllister in later years reflected upon the fight:

They had surprised us; they outnumbered us in the first stages, at least by ten to one, and they had the advantage of ground having caught us in low ground while they were on the high and had observation over us. Had they deployed into the fields from the road they could easily have outflanked us in the early stages.

Appendix I
Volunteers of the Dublin 5th Battalion

Thomas Ashe, Commandant
Richard Mulcahy, Vice Commandant
Dr Richard Hayes, Medical Officer
Frank Lawless, Quarter Master
Jim Lawless, Captain
Edward Rooney, Captain

* * *

Aungier, Richard
Blanchfield, Peadar
Blanchfield, Thomas
Brogan, Paddy
Connor, James
Crennigan John 'Jack'*
Devine, John
Daly, Francis
Doyle, Paddy
Duke, Richard
Duke, Thomas
Farrelly, Walter
Fleming, Michael
Golden, Jerry
Gowan, Jack
Grant, Paddy
Houlihan, Paddy
Kelly, James
Kelly, Matthew
Kent, Edmund
Lawless, Colm
Lawless, Joseph
McAllister, Bennie
McAllister, John
McAllister, Michael

McCann, John
McCardle, James
Maxwell, Tom
Murphy, Eamon
Norton, William
Nugent, Christy
O'Connor, James
O'Reilly, Arthur
Rafferty, Jack
Rafferty, Thomas**
Reilly, Thomas
Rooney, James
Sheehan, Paddy
Stafford, Ned
Taylor, Joseph
Teeling, Nicholas
Thornton, Joseph
Walsh, William
Weston, Bartle
Weston, Charles

* Killed in action.
** Mortally wounded.

Wounded
Kelly, Matt, Corduff Company
Rafferty, Jack, Lusk Company
Rooney, Ned, Lusk Company
Taylor, Joe, Swords Company
Walsh, William, Dublin Company

Women Involved
Molly Adrien, messenger
Monica Fleming and Eveleen Lawless who acted as nurses, attending the wounded.

Volunteers of the 5th Battalion Sent to the GPO on Tuesday, 25 April
Brophy, Dan, Swords Company
Caddell, Patrick, Lusk Company
Clarke, John, Lusk Company

Coleman, Dick, Captain of Swords Company
Crennigan, James, Roganstown Company
Crennigan, John (Jack) Swords Company
Doyle, William, Swords Company
Hynes, Jack, Lusk Company
Keeley, John, unknown company
Kelly, Jack, Swords Company
Kelly, Richard, Corduff Company
Kelly, Patrick, Corduff Company
Lawless, Edward, Rathbeale Company
McNally, John, Swords Company
Marks, James, Swords Company
Meehan, William, Lusk Company
Norton, Joe, Mt. Ambrose Company
Peppard, Thomas, Lusk Company
Wilson, James, Balheary Company
Wilson William (Cooty), Swords Company*

* Killed in action at the Mendicity Institution, Dublin.

Appendix II
RIC Men Killed and Wounded

Name	Rank	Age
Killed		
Gray, Alexander	County Inspector	57
Smyth, Harry	District Inspector	41
Shanagher, John	Sergeant	48
Young, John	Sergeant	42
Hickey, James	Constable	49
Gormley, James	Constable	25
McHale, Richard	Constable	22
Cleary, James	Constable	28
Wounded		
Scully, Patrick J.	Sergeant	48
Glennon, Francis P.	Constable	37
Murtagh, Peter	Constable	41
Leckey, Henry	Constable	36
Johns, William E.	Constable	20
Cunningham, Patrick	Constable	30
Duggan, Michael	Constable	19
Finan, Timothy	Constable	28
Drinan, Patrick	Constable	26
McGann, Henry	Constable	23
Murphy, John	Constable	26
Kenny, Francis	Constable	23
McKeon, Patrick	Constable	24
Mulvihill, Martin	Constable	31
Conneeley, Patrick	Constable	30

Source: *1916 Rebellion Handbook*.

Appendix III
Awards to RIC Men

Name	£.s.d.
Sergeant William O'Connell (Athboy)	5.0.0.
Sergeant John Griffin (Bothermeen)	5.0.0.
Acting Sergeant Patrick Sullivan (Moynalty)	5.0.0.
Constable William Johns (Navan)	15.0.0.
Constable Tim Finan (Bothermeen)	15.0.0.
Constable Patrick Drinan (Nobber)	15.0.0.
Constable Patrick Conneely, (Athboy)	15.0.0.
Constable M.J. Duggan (Crossakiel)	15.0.0.
Constable Patrick McKeon (Slane)	15.0.0.
Constable Eugene Bratton (Navan)	5.0.0.

King's Medal Awarded to Police Officers

Sergeant William O'Connell, RIC, Drumconrath, Co. Meath – Conspicuous gallantry during an attack by a large body of rebels on a party of police, who lost eight killed and fifteen wounded. By his personal example, he encouraged the men under his command to offer a prolonged resistance.

Constable Eugene Bratton, RIC, Navan, Co. Meath – Conspicuous gallantry during the rebellion. As a motorcycle dispatch carrier, he risked his life on several occasions. He volunteered to act as chauffeur in the place of a man who had run away, and, after driving the police to a spot where fighting was taking place, joined in the fighting. He was captured by the rebels but escaped and cycled to the Post Office to telephone for help, afterwards returning to the scene of the fight.

Further Awards to RIC Men Throughout the Country, Issued in 1917

CO. MEATH

HEAD CONSTABLE
Dennis McHugh, Navan

SERGEANTS
Terence McDermott, Ballivor
Hugh Brady, Carnaross
Martin Coyle, Killyon
John Colbert, Navan
Patrick Brady, Kilmoon
Thomas Donoghue, Slane

ACTING-SERGEANT
Daniel Wynne, Kilmainhamwood

CONSTABLES
Peter Murtagh, Slane
Oliver Watson, Kells
Thomas Murphy, Navan
Michael Begley, Kells
John McGearty, Balivor
Thomas Foley, Athboy
John Gronell, Enfield
William Breen, Kells
W.V. Grey, Kells
John Maddock, Drumconra
William Cox, Dunboyne
J.J. Curley, Navan
M.J. McMahon, Duleek
Martin Gara, Killyon
Patrick Neill, Nobber
Thomas A. McCavish, Navan
Roger B. Kelly, Kells
Denis McGillycuddy, Stiruptown
John Shanahan, Collon
Francis Furey, Dillonsbridge
Richard Maycock, Carnacross

W.T. McMillen, Oldcastle
Patrick Gunning, Longwood
J.J. Higgins, George's Cross
Patrick Geoghegan, Kilmoon
Thomas Keighary, Dunshaughlin
John Tierney, Dunshaughlin
Robert McMullan, Kilmoon
Michael Mulvihill, Ashbourne
Martin Syron, Ashbourne
R.M. Tully, Ashbourne
Charles Maguire, Robinstown
Samuel Patterson, Moynalty

Source: *1916 Rebellion Handbook*.

Postscript

In 1959, Fingal Old IRA Society organized the construction of a memorial to the two volunteers killed in the Battle of Ashbourne, John Crennigan and Thomas Rafferty. Meath County Council assisted in securing a site at the Rath crossroads. The memorial was designed by Con O'Reilly and Peter Grant, and it depicts Christ carrying the cross with the inscription, a quote from Thomas Ashe's poem: *Let me Carry Your Cross for Ireland*. In April 1959, the monument was unveiled by President Sean T. Kelly at the site of the battle. In his address, reported in the *Drogheda Independent* for 2 May, he said:

> That monument would help to remind the present generation and the generations to come of the efforts and achievements of the men who helped greatly to make Easter week an effective assertion in arms of Ireland's indefeasible right to national freedom and sovereignty…the aim of Pearse was to end foreign rule in all Ireland; not in twenty or twenty-six counties, but in the whole thirty-two counties which comprised this island. That was still the objective of the vast majority of the people.

The last verse of Ashe's poem is:

> Let me carry your cross for Ireland, Lord!
> For Ireland weak with tears,
> For the aged man of the clouded brow,
> And the child of tender years,
> For the empty homes of her golden plains
> For the hopes of her future too
> Let me carry your cross for Ireland, Lord!
> For the cause of Roisin Dubh

There is a memorial stone in St Mary's Cemetery, Navan, recently renovated, dedicated to the memory of four RIC men killed at Ashbourne, Sergeant John Young, and Constables James Hickey, James Gormley and Richard McHale. County Inspector Alexander Gray and District Inspector Harry Smyth were buried privately.

Notes

Preface
1. The British Army structure for 1914, upon which the Irish Volunteers were based, consisted of a brigade, battalion and company. An infantry brigade consisted of headquarters and four infantry battalions. A battalion consisted of a headquarters, and four companies. A company consisted of four platoons (nominally 260 men), and was commanded by a major, and a captain as second in command. A platoon consisted of four sections and was commanded by a subaltern, with a sergeant as second in command. The Fingal Battalion on the day, consisted of just 65 men.

Introduction
1. Sean O'Luing, *I Die in a Good Cause*, p. 69. Gregory was Gregory Pearl Peck (1886–1962). He and Ashe shared a paternal Irish grandmother, Catherine Ashe. Gregory's son was Eldred Gregory Peck, better known as Gregory Peck, the film actor.
2. Joseph V. Lawless, Witness Statement 1043. At the time of the Easter Rising, he was lieutenant of Swords Company, Dublin Brigade, Irish Volunteers. Lawless was born in 1896, the son of Frank Lawless, who was the brigade's quartermaster. He took part in the partial destruction of Rogerstown Bridge and the assaults upon Swords, Donabate and Ashbourne police barracks. Lawless fought at the later Battle of Ashbourne. Imprisoned at Frongoch, following the failure of the Rising, he returned to Dublin. As Brigade Engineering Officer, he took part in the Collinstown Raid during the early part of the War of Independence. Arrested on 10 December 1920, he was interned at Arbour Hill Prison and the Curragh, from which he escaped in October 1921. Lawless joined the Free State Army and rose to become a Colonel. He died on 3 August 1969.

Chapter 1
1. Peter Whearity, *The Easter Rising of 1916 in North County Dublin: A Skerries Perspective*, p. 14.
2. Doctor Richard Hayes, the medical officer of the 5th Battalion of the Dublin Brigade of Volunteers, was born in 1878. He was appointed commanding officer of the 5th Battalion in June 1915 but relinquished command to Thomas Ashe. Hayes took part in the assaults on Swords, Donabate and Ashbourne RIC barracks. He also fought in the Battle of Ashbourne. Hayes became a TD (Teachta Dála) in the Irish Parliament, the Dáil. For his part in the Easter Rising, he was sentenced to 20 years imprisonment but was released in June 1917. He was imprisoned again between May 1918 and March 1919 as part of the 'German Plot'. He was imprisoned again during the War of Independence between November 1920 and July 1921. During the Civil War that followed, he took the pro-Treaty side. Richard Hayes died on 16 July 1958.
3. Thomas Ashe was born on 12 January 1885 at Lispole, County Kerry, the son of Gregory and Ellen Ashe. He trained at De La Salle Training College, Waterford, and began a teaching career at Corduff National School, Lusk, County Dublin, in

1908. Ashe was a founding member of the Gaelic League and the Irish Volunteers. He raised money for the volunteer movement in America in 1914. Just before the outbreak of the Easter Rising, he was appointed commanding officer of the 5th Battalion of the Dublin Brigade. Ashe led the successful assaults on Swords, Donabate and Ashbourne RIC Barracks, and the Battle of Ashbourne that followed. Ashe's battalion surrendered on the orders of Patrick Pearse. Ashe was court-martialled and sentenced to death, but this was commuted to penal servitude for life. Ashe was imprisoned at HMP Dartmoor and later at Lewes Prison. Ashe and the other leading volunteer officers were released in June 1917 in a general amnesty. Ashe was appointed President of the Irish Republican Brotherhood in late 1916. In August 1917, he was arrested and charged with sedition. Imprisoned in Mountjoy Prison, Dublin, he went on hunger strike. Ashe died after a bungled force feeding on 25 September 1917. His remains were removed to the Pro-Cathedral on Thursday evening. Requiem Mass was celebrated by Fr Michael O'Flanagan on Friday morning before his removal to City Hall where his body lay in state for two days.

4. Frank Lawless was born in Saucerstown, County Dublin, in 1871. He served as quartermaster and captain of the Fingal Battalion during the Easter Rising. Lawless was connected to both to the Gaelic Athletic Association and the Irish language movement. After the failure of the Rising, he was sentenced to death, but this was commuted. In 1919, he was elected a TD and sat in the Dáil. Lawless was re-elected to the Second Dáil and voted in favour of the Anglo-Irish Treaty. In May 1922, he died of injuries received when a pony trap in which he was riding accidentally overturned. Both Éamon de Valera and Michael Collins attended his funeral.

5. Thomas Peppard, Intelligence Officer, Fingal Battalion, Witness Statement 1399.

6. Eimar O'Duffy, in some Witness Statements and other accounts, is credited as being a graduate of Sandhurst, the British Military College. This was not so. O'Duffy was born on 29 September 1893 in Dublin, the son of Kevin O'Duffy, a prominent society dentist. Eimar was educated at the Jesuit public school of Stonyhurst in England. Following in his father's footsteps, he studied dentistry at University College, Dublin but never practised. His father wanted him to study at Sandhurst and become an officer in the British army, but he refused. However, at some time, he did develop an interest in soldiering and warfare. He joined the IRB and the Irish Volunteers and became a serious contributor on military matters in the Volunteers' newspaper, *The Irish Volunteer*. He toured the regions and gave lectures on military matters as Michael McAllister indicates in his Witness Statement. After the War of Independence, O'Duffy became a dramatist and novelist. He died in England in 1935.

7. Michael McAllister, Volunteer, Swords Company, Witness Statement 1494.

8. James O'Connor, Volunteer, Swords Company, Witness Statement 142. James O'Connor (or Connor), a volunteer in St Margaret's Company, 5th Battalion (Fingal) Dublin Brigade, was born in 1895. He fought at Garristown, Newbarn, Kilsallaghan and Ashborne RIC Barracks. O'Connor was at the Battle of Ashborne. Following Pearse's order for them to surrender, Ashe sent him away to avoid capture. He was eventually arrested and is shown in a photograph, being marched away as a prisoner. O'Connor served during the War of Independence but did not take part in the Civil War that followed. James O'Connor died on 7 July 1955.

9. Under the early twentieth-century Haldane Reforms of the British Army, the most dramatic restructuring and redevelopment of the army took place. Included in that restructuring, in 1908, was the introduction of cyclist battalions (eight English, two

Scottish and one Welsh). Though seemingly funny today, the military applications for cyclists were seen as an advance. They became the modern equivalent of the old horse dragoons who rode into battle but fought on foot. The Fingal Battalion, considering the British adoption, followed suit and established their own cyclist unit.
10. Christopher Moran, Swords Company, 5th Battalion, Dublin Brigade, Witness Statement 1438.
11. Jerry Golden, 1st Battalion, Dublin Brigade, Witness Statement 521.
12. County Inspector's Confidential Monthly Report, January 1915, National Archives, Kew, CO904/96.
13. O'Luing, p. 75.

Chapter 2
1. Piaras Beaslai, Witness Statement 261, and Donal O'Hannigan, Witness Statement 161.
2. Tim Pat Coogan, *1916: The Easter Rising*, p. 94.

Chapter 3
1. Joseph V. Lawless, Witness Statement 1043.
2. Christopher 'Kit' Moran, Witness Statement 1438.
3. Michael McAllister, Witness Statement 1494.
4. Joseph V. Lawless, Witness Statement 043.
5. Charles Weston, Witness Statement 149.
6. Bernard McAllister, Captain, 5th Battalion (Fingal) Dublin Brigade, Witness Statement 147.
7. The final total of volunteers and members of Cumann na mBan who eventually rallied to the call throughout north County Dublin were by town and village: Balbriggan, 1; Baldoyle, 3; Blanchardstown, 3; Cloughran, 3; Donabate-Turvey, 10; Drumcondra, 1; Finglas, 4; Garristown, 1; Howth, 4; Lusk, 39; Malahide, 1; Saint Margaret's, 12; Skerries, 23; Sutton, 4; Swords, 36; Dispatchers (Molly Adrien, Mary Lawless, Ita Murray), 3. Giving a total of 148.
8. Commandant Donal O'Hannigan, Witness Statement 161.

Chapter 4
1. Another account has it that the two were Paddy Houlihan and Thomas Blanchfield. The two men did join the 5th, but it was the day after Mulcahy's arrival. They were cut off on the other side of the North Circular Road, and after evading British troops, they eventually joined Ashe and his men
2. Mary Adrien, better known as 'Molly', was born in County Meath in 1873. She was the daughter of Edward and Mary Adrien of Micknanstown House in Stamullen. The family later moved to Balbriggan. Mary was educated at the Loreto Convent and Surbiton High School in England. Back in Ireland, Mary went to live at Oldtown, north County Dublin. She joined Cumann na mBan in November 1915 and later became Director of the Lusk branch. In Cumann, she trained in first aid and field signals. She mobilised on Easter Sunday but was demobilised on the orders of Mrs Touhy of the Central Branch. Then she received a telegram – 'We are having a little party on Monday, and probably you will have a similar one.' On Monday, she heard from a local man, returning from the Fairyhouse races, that the Rising had begun. On Tuesday morning, she met Thomas Ashe and delivered a report by him to Connolly in

Dublin on the position and strength of the Fingal Battalion. Mary made a further trip to Dublin, seeking fresh orders regarding the 5th. On Friday, 28 April, she returned to Lusk. where she discovered that Ashe and his men were fighting at Ashbourne. She rode to Ashbourne to offer what help she could. Mary attended to the wounded on both sides, before returning to Oldtown. On Saturday, she attempted to re-enter Dublin but was thwarted. On Saturday, she was with the 5th at Newbarn, where they surrendered according to orders from Pearse. Mary was not arrested. During the War of Independence, she acted as a courier. Mary opposed the Anglo-Irish Treaty and retired to private life. In 1930, she stood in the Dublin County Council elections. Mary 'Molly' Adrien died in 1949. She was buried in Crickstown Cemetery with full military honours.
3. William Wilson of Swords, known as Cooty, was killed in the defence of the Mendicity Institution in Dublin. Thomas Peppard, Intelligence Officer of the Fingal Brigade, who fought alongside him, recorded that on the Wednesday (26 April) the outpost was overrun by British troops. 'Volunteer W. Wilson was killed while crossing the yard,' as they attempted to withdraw.
4. James O'Connor, Witness Statement 142.
5. Sean O'Luing, *I Die in a Good Cause*, p. 80.
6. Volunteer Jerry Golden, Witness Statement 521.

Chapter 5
1. Charles Weston, Witness Statement 149.
2. Joseph V. Lawless, Witness Statement 1043.
3. Charles Weston, Witness Statement 149.
4. Ibid.
5. Joseph V. Lawless, Witness Statement 1043.
6. Joseph McKenna, *Voices from the Easter Rising*, p. 157.
7. Monica Fleming (1897–1975) who later married J.V. Lawless, was a member of Cumann na mBan. During the Easter Rising, she carried dispatches to Saucerstown, Drumcondra and Wicklow. She attended the wounded after the Battle of Ashbourne. Monica was arrested in Saucerstown on the Monday after the Rising but was released a few days later. Her house was used as an arms dump during the War of Independence. During the Civil war that followed, she took the anti-Treaty side.
8. *Weekly Irish Times, 1916 Rebellion Handbook*, p. 38.

Chapter 6
1. Only Charles Weston, Lieutenant in Lusk Company, names the two ringleaders. The Duke brother mentioned is Richard Duke. His brother Thomas Patrick remained with Ashe and fought at Ashbourne. All the other Witness Statements are more discreet in not holding the two men up to disapprobation. With a sly dig, Weston suggests, 'I think Ashe was glad to be rid of them as they were potential trouble-makers from the start.'
2. Colm Lawless, the youngest son of Frank Lawless, was born in 1901. He was educated at Patrick Pearse's St Enda's College at Rathfarnham. He was with his father and brother at the beginning of the Easter Rising, but Ashe sent him home, not wanting to have his death on his conscious. During the War of Independence, Colm Lawless served as a vice-commandant in the IRA. He was involved in a number of assaults on RIC barracks. Lawless was arrested in January 1921 and interned at Ballykinlar.

During the Civil War, he served in the Free State Army, taking part in operations in the north County Dublin area. Colm Lawless died in October 1966.
3. County Inspector Alexander Gray was born in October 1858 in County Tyrone. His father was a Presbyterian minister, also named Alexander Gray. In 1880, the son was enrolled at the Royal Irish Constabulary Cadet School in Phoenix Park, Dublin. Gray graduated in March 1882 as an officer cadet and would have qualified for the position of sub-inspector as soon as a position became available. In January 1883, he was posted to Dingle, County Kerry, where he served as a 3rd sub-inspector for the district. By 1887, he had become a District Inspector. Gray earned an unenviable reputation for his ruthlessness, overseeing the evictions of small tenant farmers, particularly from the estate of Lord Ventry. This was the period of the Land Wars, where the championing of small farmers by Nationalist Party leader Charles Stewart Parnell was part of the Nationalist struggle for Home Rule. Gray was very much aware of the Nationalist implications of the rent strike by the tenant farmers. In his confidential County Inspector's Report, he wrote, 'the principal office-Bearers [National] League here are bankrupt publicans and needy shopkeepers; it is [in] their interest of course that the landlord should get no rent, and they have used their power effectively for their own advantage.' In June 1889, Gray was transferred to Killarney. Here, he had to deal with a small riot. Leading a detachment of RIC men, he rode on ahead and with lance in hand dispersed the mob single-handedly. Gray went on to hold a number of positions around Ireland, before eventually arriving in Meath as its County Inspector in June 1912. His County Reports note the rise of the various Nationalistic organizations, which he acknowledges to be largely benign. Gray records the formation of the Irish Volunteers, with twelve branches in County Meath by May 1914. From then on, Gray expresses his concern over the gradual increase in Republican activity. By August 1914, there were sixty-one branches of volunteers in Meath and some 5,600 men.
4. Exact numbers of men and vehicles commandeered differ in the various Witness Statements.
5. Harry Smyth was born in 1874 in Baldock, some five miles north of Stevenage, Hertfordshire, England. He served as an officer in the British Army before joining the Royal Irish Constabulary in 1899. Smyth served in various posts throughout Ireland, before being posted to Navan, County Meath, as a District Inspector in 1910.
6. Jerry Golden, Witness Statement 521.

Chapter 7
1. Thomas Devine, E Company, 2nd Battalion, Witness Statement 428.
2. *1916 Rebellion Handbook*, p. 46–47.
3. That evening, Jerry Golden was the subject of some good-natured banter. Joseph V. Lawless retells the story in his Witness Statement, slightly altering the facts to serve a good story. Golden leapt at the sergeant and 'grasped him around the waist before he could reach the carbine. Now, Golden was rather lightly built, and the huge sergeant whirled him around and would soon have put paid to his account but for the intervention of McAllister. The incident provided our funny story that night in camp, Golden being ragged with comments like "who do you think you are, anyway, Hackenschmidt?" or "Have you heard of the fellow who fell in love with the sergeant up at the barracks and threw his arm around him?"' Georg Karl Julius Hackenschmidt, as mentioned above, was an early 20th-century Estonian strongman and professional wrestler. He popularized the 'bear hug'.

4. Bernard 'Bennie' McAllister, Captain, 5th Battalion, Witness Statement 147.
5. Joseph V. Lawless, Witness Statement 1043.
6. Jerry Golden lays claim to have been the grenade thrower: 'I was handed two homemade bombs and given instructions in how to use them. Lieut. Mulcahy was with me and when we got to the wall of the front yard of the barracks I lit the fuse of one of the bombs and then under cover of the Lieuts. fire and the fire of the other 9 men I threw the bomb against one of the two lower windows which were covered with steel shutters it fell down to the ground and went off with a great roar. I looked through an opening in the wall and saw that it had only made a hole about 4 inches in the ground, but apparently all the glass in the front windows was broken in as we all heard the crash of breaking glass.' (Witness Statement 177). Both Joseph Lawless and Michael McAllister confirm that it was Peter Blanchfield that actually threw the bombs. The work of the Bureau of Military History in collecting the statements proved contentious. Tom Barry, a hero of the War of Independence in West Cork, was concerned by the terms of reference and in particular the secrecy clause of 'under seal for whatever period', which noted that the statements could remain unopened until after the 'death of an individual'. This, he believed, would prevent that person from being sued 'for libel or false assertions, calculated to injure other parties'. At Ashbourne, there was enough glory to share around, without Golden stealing another man's fame.

Chapter 8
1. RIC Constable Eugene Bratton, Witness Statement 467.
2. Both the number of cars and the number of policemen involved does vary from account to account. Understandably, from a Republican perspective, the larger the number, the greater the victory. Dr Hayes, however, gives perhaps a more realistic number: 'As regards the numbers engaged on both sides, thirty-five Volunteers were engaged for the first half of the fight, and for the remainder of the time forty-one (35 plus 6) It was a little difficult to estimate precisely the number of police. As far as I can judge about sixty came in the seventeen motor cars, and this with fourteen in the barracks would leave the number at about 75.' This more or less coincides with Eugene Bratton, the RIC Constable. In his Witness Statement, he gives the number of policemen in the convoy as 'about sixty police all told'.
3. In a variation of the narrative of the arrival of the convoy of police cars, Bernard McAllister suggests that it was he who alerted Hayes to the approach: 'I happened to look down the road towards Kilmoon and I saw a car approaching about half a mile away immediately followed by several other cars. I reported to Dr. Hayes that there were cars coming towards us. He put his field glasses on to them and in a moment said: "Those are police. We will have to stop them." He detailed a man to report to Ashe that police reinforcements were coming quickly. He said, "We will try and hold the Cross but tell him to send help immediately."
4. Sergeant William O'Connell, 'The Ashbourne Tragedy by an Eyewitness', *RIC Magazine*, May and June 1916.
5. The Martini Enfield carbine was an adaptation of the older Martini Henry rifle. The Martini Enfield had the same lock mechanism but was modernised by the fitting of a barrel bored for .303 ammunition. This lock mechanism operated by an underneath lever, which ejected the spent case.
6. Charles Weston, Witness Statement 149.

7. *Field Service Regulations*, Part 1: Operations, Chapter VII, The Battle, Section 104, Preliminary measures.
8. Sergeant William O'Connell, 'The Ashbourne Tragedy by an Eyewitness', *RIC Magazine*, May and June 1916.
9. Paddy Doyle differs slightly from Jerry Golden in the names of the section that stopped the police. They were Section Leader Charlie Weston, Michael and John McAllister, Bennie McAllister, Richard Aungier, Mick Fleming and Paddy Doyle himself. He makes no mention of Jerry Golden.
10. Michael McAllister, Witness Statement 1494.
11. Sergeant William O'Connell, 'The Ashbourne Tragedy by an Eyewitness', *RIC Magazine*, May and June 1916.
12. The two innocent civilians were Jeremiah Hogan, driving the car, and his passenger, John Carroll, son of the Chief of the Kingstown (now Dún Laoghaire) fire brigade.
13. O'Luing, *I Die in a Good Cause*, p. 85.
14. Joseph V. Lawless, Witness Statement 1043.
15. The presence of James Quigley at the scene had not gone unnoticed by the authorities. He was subsequently arrested by the police and court-martialled at Richmond Barracks, Dublin, on 7–9 June 1916 on a charge of conveying information by signal to the insurgents as to the whereabouts of the police (which of course he had). The police, and Sergeant Terence MacDermott in particular, testified that they had seen Quigley talking to Ashe at the end of the battle on quite friendly terms. When his house was searched 'a rifle, shotgun, ammunition and seditious literature were found there. Quigley admitted that he had been connected to the local branch of the Navan Volunteers, but so had Lord Fingal, Lord Dunsany the Marquis of Headfort and the Marquis Conyngham. That was back in 1913, but since then he was no longer active. The rifle and other objects were left over from that time. Regarding his presence at Ashbourne, he was on official business and was returning from a meeting in Ardee, he declared, when he stumbled on the battle. With reference to him speaking to Ashe, he had asked if he could continue on his journey and asked if he should fetch a doctor to attend the wounded policemen. His very competent defending counsel was able to secure his acquittal, in that as the county surveyor, his client was in the wrong place, at the wrong time.
16. Curiously, McAllister makes no claim to this in his Witness Statement, which is unusual if he had. Constable Eugene Bratton, who was there, makes the dark claim that Shanagher 'was shot by one of his own men. He was a bad one and had been very tough on the men.' This seems unlikely as Shanagher was shot between the eyes, as one account has it, and this would only have happened if he was facing the volunteers.
17. Constable Bratton, Witness Statement 467.
18. Joseph V. Lawless Witness Statement 1043.
19. Sergeant William O'Connell.
20. Joseph V. Lawless Witness Statement 1043.
21. O'Luing, p. 85.
22. John Austin, Witness Statement 904.
23. O'Luing, p. 87.
24. Report of the State of the Counties 1916, PRO CO904/120.

Chapter 9
1. Jerry Golden, Witness Statement 521.
2. Anthony J. Gaughan (Ed.) *Memoirs of Constable Jeremiah Mee*, Kildare, 1975, p. 48.

3. Sergeant William O'Connell, 'The Ashbourne Tragedy by an Eyewitness', *RIC Magazine*, May and June 1916.
4. Ashe delivered a eulogy on Tommy Rafferty at Casement Fort in the following year:

> On our side there were two men killed; one patriot from Lusk, a fine manly fellow, who ran from his work to take up his rifle when we sent out the call. His body was taken to a house in Ashbourne, and the women of Meath, who had heard the rifles ringing the whole long day, were in the house with the body of young Rafferty. They stepped aside when his mother entered, trembling in fear and sorrow for the young fellow who lost his life, and for his mother, an old woman. She entered and looked at the dead body of her son, and moved the long locks, and looking up towards Heaven, she said – 'Thank God it is for Ireland you died.' (Source: O'Luing, *I Die in a Good Cause*, p. 88)

5. Michael McAllister, Witness Statement 1494.
6. Sergeant O'Connell wrote a letter of condolence to Smyth's brother George, later reproduced in the *Royal Irish Constabulary Magazine*, August 1916:

> Dear Sir,
> Having seen your address in a local paper here, and believing you to be a brother of my late lamented officer, Mr Harry Smyth, I take the liberty of writing you and sending you expressions of the deepest regret on the loss you and your family have sustained. From my pretty varied knowledge of Officers in our Force, I do not think there was one other who had such intimate knowledge of his profession, nor was there another who had endeared himself to his men. The poor man, in a word, the very soul of honour, and outside his own family I do not think his loss will anywhere be so widely felt as among his late subordinates in the RIC. His name among those of us who came in contact with him will live for many a day to come. Words would fail to describe how he was respected. Oh! It's a sin to see such a character and such brains cut off so suddenly under such regrettable and revolting circumstances. I can assure you, sir, as one who was with him, that he fought throughout desperately. There is one thing, he had no fear, I even asked him for God's sake, not to expose himself so much, but he declined. He fought during the six hours the battle was on with a determination characteristic of his race, but the odds were much against him, poor man, and he died about ¼ of an hour after the whole business was over. He was hit during the last five minutes of the conflict by an explosive bullet on the head. He was unconscious from the outset. I was with him when he breathed his last. I never felt so miserable. I must say I never regretted the death of another so much. He will always live in my memory. It would be well if the Empire had such sons. I sincerely trust and hope his soul is enjoying its reward, as I am sure it is, because he was the very embodiment of honesty. Trusting, sir, that in your great grief, you will be some little consoled by the fact that poor Mr. Smyth died a brave death, and in my humble opinion deserves to be classified among the greatest heroes. As one who witness his attitude under fire at the unfortunate battle at Ashbourne, I can testify how bravely he fought. Again expressing to you my personal expression of sympathy in your bereavement, and trusting that perhaps you could see that the band of misguided men who started this unfortunate revolt are but few, and that the bulk of Irishmen deeply regret it. I remain, Sir. Yours very respectively. W. O'Connell (Sergt).
> District Inspector Harry Smyth was 41 years old at the time of his death.

7. Joseph V. Lawless, Witness Statement 1043.
8. Commandant Donal O'Hannigan, Witness Statement 161.
9. Joseph V. Lawless, Witness Statement 1043.
10. Jerry Golden, Witness Statement 521.
11. Piaras F. MacLochlainn, *Last Words*, p. 16. The expression '*Beannacht De agat*' as Mulcahy wished to express it, would probably have been, 'Goodbye, God bless you.'
12. O'Luing, p. 87.
13. James O'Connor, Witness Statement 142.
14. Christopher Moran, Witness Statement 1438.
15. Joseph V. Lawless, Witness Statement 1043.
16. Commandant Donal O'Hannigan, Witness Statement 161.
17. Peter F. Whearity, *The Easter Rising of 1916 in North County Dublin: A Skerries Perspective*, p. 41.

Chapter 10
1. Annie Cooney (O'Brien), Witness Statement 805.
2. Joseph V. Lawless, Witness Statement 1043.
3. Ibid.
4. Christopher Moran, Witness Statement 1438.
5. Dr Richard Hayes, Witness Statement 876.
6. Michael McAllister, Witness Statement 1494.
7. Joseph V. Lawless, Witness Statement 1043.
8. Bernard McAllister, Witness Statement 147.

Chapter 11
1. *1916 Rebellion Handbook*, p. 60.
2. Piaras F. MacLochlainn, *Last Words*, p. 18–19.
3. This was the standard delivery to all repealed prisoners sentenced to death. See Brian Barton, *The Secret Court Martial Records of the Easter Rising*, p. xx.
4. O'Luing, p. 94.
5. *1916 Rebellion Handbook*, p. 62, and Peter Whearity, *The Easter Rising of 1916 in North County Dublin: A Skerries Perspective*, p. 50.
6. Peter Whearity, p. 50.
7. Captain Peter Paul Galligan, C Company, 2nd Battalion, Witness Statement 170.
8. Peadar Doyle, Quartermaster of F. Company, 4th Battalion, Witness Statement 155.
9. Joseph V. Lawless, Witness Statement 1043.
10. Charles Weston, Witness Statement 149.
11. Joseph V. Lawless, Witness Statement 1043.

Chapter 12
1. Captain Bernard McAllister, 5th Battalion (Fingal) Brigade, Witness Statement 147.
2. William Daly, Witness Statement 291.
3. Joseph V. Lawless, Witness Statement 1043.
4. Liam Tannam, Captain, E Company, 3rd Battalion, Witness Statement 242.
5. Hopkinson, Michael, *Frank Henderson's Easter Rising: Recollections of a Dublin Volunteer*, p. 2.
6. J.J. 'Ginger' O'Connell (1887–1944) was born in County Mayo and educated at University College, Dublin. He spent the years 1912–14 in the US army. He returned

to Ireland in 1914 and joined the Irish Volunteers. O'Connell was sent to Cork by Eoin MacNeill to countermand the order for the Easter Rising there. When it began, he returned to Dublin and joined the fight. He was arrested and interned in Wandsworth Prison and Frongoch. During the Irish War of Independence, O'Connell served on the headquarters staff, as assistant to Richard Mulcahy. His abduction and detention within the Four Courts led to the opening shots of the Irish Civil War. O'Connell held various positions within the Irish Defence Force in the Irish Free State.
7. Charles Weston Lieutenant, Lusk Company, 5th (Fingal) Battalion, Witness Statement 149.
8. Margaret Skinnider, *Doing My Bit for Ireland*, p. 25.

Chapter 13

1. Christopher Moran, Witness Statement 1438.
2. Report on the State of the Counties, 1916 PRO CO904/120.
3. Jerry Golden, Witness Statement 522.
4. James Crennigan, Witness Statement 1395.
5. O'Luing, p. 135.
6. Ibid.
7. Alice Stopford Green (1847–1929). Born Alice Stopford in Kells, County Meath, she married John Richard Green and lived in London from 1874 to 1877. He died in 1883, leaving her financially independent. She opposed Britain's involvement in the Boer War and later took an interest in Irish affairs through her association with Sir Roger Casement. As a historian, she wrote a book, *The Making of Ireland and its Undoing*, published in 1908. A firm supporter of Home Rule, Stopford Green partially financed the Howth gunrunning. She moved to Dublin in 1918. Following the ending of the War for Independence, she supported the pro-Treaty side in the Civil War. Stopford Green was appointed a senator in the Irish Free State government in 1922, where she served as an Independent. Alice Stopford Green died in Dublin in 1929, aged 81.
8. Laurence Nugent, Witness Statement 907.
9. O'Luing, p. 197.
10. Benjamin Grob-Fitzgibbon, *Turning Points of the Irish Revolution: The British Government, Intelligence, and the Cost of Indifference, 1912–1921*, p. 132.

Chapter 14

1. David Neligan, *The Spy in the Castle*, p. 31.
2. Joseph V. Lawless, Witness Statement 1043.
3. The Morris tube, named after Richard Morris, its inventor, was a small-bore rifle barrel inserted in a large bore rifle or shotgun for practice shooting. It enabled the participant to fire a smaller calibre round, usually a 0.22.
4. Joseph V. Lawless, Witness Statement 1043.
5. Ibid.

Bibliography

Bureau of Military History: Witness Statements
John Austin, 904
Piaras Beaslai, 261
Constable Eugene Bratton, 467
Annie Cooney (O'Brien), 805
William Daly, 291
Thomas Devine, 428
Peadar Doyle, 155
Captain Paul Galligan, 170
Jerry Golden, 521,522
Dr Richard Hayes, 97
Colonel Joseph V. Lawless, 1043
Captain Bernard McAllister, 147
Michael McAllister, 1494
Christopher Moran, 1438
Henry Murray, 300
Laurence Nugent 907
RIC Sergeant William O'Connell, C.D. 50/1
James O'Connor, 142
Commandant Donal O'Hannigan, 161
Thomas Peppard, 1399
Captain Liam Tannam, 242
Lieutenant Charles Weston, 149

Uk National Archive, Kew
County Inspector's Confidential Monthly Report, C.O. 904/93-101
Intelligence Officers' Reports, 1916–1918, C.O. 904
RIC Inspector General's Monthly Reports, C.O. 904/93

UK Official Reports and Publications
British Infantry Manual, HM Stationery Office, London, 1911
Documents Relative to the Sinn Fein Movement (CMD 1108 of 1921), HM Stationery Office, London
Field Service Regulations, HM Stationery Office, London, 1909
Hansard, House of Commons Parliamentary Debates, Volumes 86 and 87, 1916–17
Lake, B. C., *Knowledge for War: Every Officer's Handbook for the Front*, HM Stationery Office, London, 1916

On the Rebellion in Ireland (CMD 8311 of 1916), Report of the Royal Commission, HM Stationery Office, London

University College, Dublin Archives
Mulcahy Papers
Ernie O'Malley Papers and Notebooks

Books
1916 Rebellion Handbook, Mourne River Press, 1998.
Augusteijn, Joost, *From Public Defiance to Guerrilla Warfare: The Experience of Ordinary Volunteers in the Irish War of Independence 1916–1921*, Irish Academic Press, Dublin 1996.
Barton, Brian, *The Secret Court Martial Records of the Easter Rising*, The History Press, Stroud, 2010.
Brennan-Whitmore, W.J., *With the Irish in Frongoch*, Mercier, Cork, 2013.
Caufield, Max, *The Easter Rebellion*, Four Square Books, London, 1965.
Coffey, Thomas M., *Agony at Easter*, Penguin, Harmondsworth, 1969.
Coogan, Tim Pat, *1916: The Easter Rising*, Phoenix, London, 2005.
Curtis, Edmund, *A History of Ireland*, Methuen & Co., London, 1964.
Foy, Michael T., and Barton, Brian, *The Easter Rising*, The History Press, Stroud, 2011.
Gaughan, Anthony J. (ed.), *Memoirs of Constable Jeremiah Mee*, Kildare, 1975.
Grob-Fitzgibbon, Benjamin, *Turning Points of the Irish Revolution: The British Government, Intelligence, and the Cost of Indifference, 1912–1921*, Palgrave Macmillan, Basingstoke, 2007.
Holman, Hannah (ed.), *The Tommies' Manual 1916*, Amberley, Stroud, 2016.
Hopkinson, Michael (ed.), *Frank Henderson's Easter Rising: Recollections of a Dublin Volunteer*, Cork University Press, 1998.
MacArdle, Dorothy, *The Irish Republic*, Corgi, London, 1968.
McGarry, Fearghal, *The Rising Ireland: Easter 1916*, Oxford University Press, 2016.
McKenna, Joseph, *Voices from the Easter Rising*, McFarland & Co., Jefferson, USA, 2017.
MacLochlainn, Piaras, *Last Words*, Government of Ireland, 1990.
McNally, Michael, *Easter Rising 1916: Birth of the Irish Republic*, Osprey, Oxford, 2007.
Martin, F.X., (ed.) *The Irish Volunteers 1913–1915*, Merrion, Sallins Co. Kildare, 2013.
Moody, T.W., and Martin, F.X. (eds), *The Course of Irish History*, Mercier Press, Cork, 1967.
Mulcahy, R., *My Father the General*, Liberties Press, Dublin, 2011.
Neligan, David, *The Spy in the Castle*, Prendeville Publishing, London, 1999.
O'Brien, Paul, *Field of Fire*, New Island, Dublin, 2012.
Ó Conchubhair, Brian (series editor), *Dublin's Fighting Story 1916–21: Told By The Men Who Made It*, Kerryman Ltd, Tralee, 1949 (print on demand from Mercier Press).

O'Farrell, Padraic, *Who's Who in the Irish War of Independence*, Lilliput Press, Dublin, 1997.
O'Luing, Sean, *I Die in a Good Cause*, Anvil Books, Tralee, 1970.
Rawson, Andrew, *The British Army 1914–1918*, Spellmount, Stroud, 2006.
Skinnider, Margaret, *Doing My Bit for Ireland*, Century, New York, 1917.
Storey, Neil R. (ed.), *The Tommy's Handbook*, The History Press, Stroud, 2014.
Townshend, Charles, *Easter 1916 The Irish Rebellion*, Penguin Books, London, 2006.
Townshend, Charles, *The Republic*, Penguin Books, London 2014.
Whearity, Peter F. *The Easter Rising of 1916 in North County Dublin: A Skerries Perspective*, Four Courts Press, Dublin, 2013.
White, G. and O'Shea, B., *Irish Volunteer Soldier 1913–23*, Osprey, Oxford, 2003.

Newspapers and Periodicals
The Capuchin Annual 1966
The Freeman's Journal
Irish Independent
Irish Times
Manchester Guardian
Sunday Independent

Index

5th Lancers, 84, 89

Abbey Theatre, 13–15
Adrien, Mary 'Molly', 38, 44, 49, 56, 81, 84, 123–4
Allen, Brother, 18
An Barr Buadh, xvi
An Claidheamh Soluis, xvi
Anglo-Irish Treaty, 118
Antrim, County, xv
Arbour Hill, 85–6
Ardee, 35, 50
Armagh, County, xv
Asgard, 7–9, 128
Ashbourne, 35, 52, 57
Ashbourne Barracks 12–16, 18, 59, 128
Ashbourne, Battle of, 62–79
Ashe, Ellen, 56–7, 59–60, 140
Ashe, Gregory, 140
Ashe, Nora, 99
Ashe, Thomas, ix–xi, xiii–xiv, 2–4, 12–16, 18–23, 27–8, 30–8, 40–53, 56–61, 63–5, 67–8, 73, 76–90, 93, 96, 99–102, 114–24, 128–30, 132, 139
Asquith, Herbert, xii, xiv–xv, 98
Athlone, 22–3, 53, 123
Aud, 24–5, 27
Aungier, Richard 'Dick', 65, 70, 121, 132
Austin, John, x, 58–9, 78

Bachelor's Walk, 11, 39, 96
Bala, 105
Balbriggan, 1, 50, 85, 91, 123
Baldwinstown, 50
Ballinalee, 115–16
Ballynlar Internment Camp, 95
Baltic, SS, 95
Bayley, Sir Lewis, 24–5
Beaslai, Piaras, 14–15, 19, 22, 35
Bee, Lieutenant, 25
Belfast, xiii–xiv, 7, 12, 33, 40
Belfast Prison, 95

Belgium, 12
Beneavin Convalescent Home, 43
Berkshire Regiment, 88, 94
Birney, Patrick, 122–3
Birrell, Augustine, xviii
Black and Tans, x, 47
Black Raven Band, 18
Blaenau Ffestiniog, 105
Blanchardstown, 16, 23, 36–7, 90–1
Blanchfield, Peadar/Peter, 43, 56, 60, 68, 70–1, 86, 94, 119, 122–3, 132
Blanchfield, Tom, 42–3, 56, 119–20, 132
Boadicea II, 49
Boland, Harry, 114
Bonar Law, Andrew, xii, xiv, 115
Boot Inn, 31
Borranstown, 52–3, 57, 73, 83
Boylan, Sean, 22–3, 36
Brady, Sergeant, 57–9
Bratton, Eugene, x, 56, 62, 69, 71, 82–3, 136
Brennan, James, 11
Brennan-Whitmore, Captain, 107
British Empire, xvii, 7, 33, 89
British Military Manual, 64
Broadmeadows, 14
Brogan, Patrick 'Paddy', 53, 68, 70, 72–3, 93, 122, 132
Brugha, Cathal, 116
'Buckshot', 106
Bureau of Military History, Irish, x, 5
Byrne, Alfred, 104
Byrne, Miss, 45

Cabra, 36, 42, 121
Caddell, Patrick, 39, 133
Cambridge University, 7
Capuchin Annual, The, xi, 20
Carson, Sir Edward, xii–xiv
Casement, Sir Roger, xvii–xviii, 24–5, 27, 37, 115
Ceannt, Eamon, xvi–xvii, 93, 98

Chance, Sir Arthur, 117
Childers, Erskine, 7–8
Chotah, 8
Churchill, Lord Randolph, xvi
Churchill, Winston, xii, xiv
Clarke, John, 39, 133
Clarke, Tom, xvii, 15, 93, 98
Clontarf, 10, 86
Clyde Valley, SS, 7
Colbert, Con, 17, 93, 98
Cohalan, Judge, 95
Coleman, Richard 'Dick', 1–3, 13, 30–1, 37–9, 102, 116, 118, 127, 133
Collins, Michael, 107–108, 111, 117–18, 121, 124
Collinstown, 113, 120–1
Condron, Thomas, 94
Connaught Rangers, xvii
Connolly, James, ix, 12, 15, 21, 27–9, 36, 38–9, 45, 55, 82, 98, 102
Connolly, Nora, 28
Conscientious objectors, 109
Conyngham, Marquis, 64
Cooney, Annie, 92
Corduff, xiii, 39, 74
Corless, P.J., 42
Cottage by the Lee, 93
Craig, James, xii–xiii
Crawford, Major Frederick, 6–7
Crennigan, James, 13, 38, 113, 134
Crennigan, John (Jack), 13, 76, 82, 130, 132, 134, 139
Cross Guns Bridge, 35, 42
Cumann na mBan, 30, 38, 56, 92, 118, 124
Cunningham, Constable, 67, 135
Curragh Camp, xv, 37, 40, 115–16, 123
Curragh Mutiny, xiv

Daly, Edward (Ned), 15–17, 23, 35, 42, 98
Daly, Frank, 123
Daly, Seamus, 8
Daly, William, 106
Dartmoor Prison, 100–101, 114
Defence of the Realm Act, 94, 99, 115–16
Derham, Matt, 41
Derry, County, xv
de Valera, Éamon, 18–19, 95, 101, 114, 116, 127
Devine, John, 68, 72–3, 115, 122, 132
Devine, Thomas, 55

Devoy, John, 95
Dillon, Father, 82
Donabate, 1, 3, 9, 13, 17, 44–5, 47–8, 91, 115, 121–3
Doran's Ass, 53
Down, County, xv
Doyle, Paddy, x, 53, 122, 132
Doyle, Peadar, 101
Doyle, Thomas, 120, 122
Doyle, William, 39, 123, 134
Doyle's Corner, 42
Drogheda Independent, 139
Drumcondra, 86
Dublin Castle, xviii, 10, 19, 32, 80
Dublin City, ix, 18, 38, 50, 53, 86–7, 111–12, 115
Dublin Fusiliers, 42
Duff, Thomas, 13
Duffy, Mary, 11
Duggan, Charles, 7
Duggan, Eamon, 101
Duke, Thomas, 3, 31–2, 51, 120, 132
Dumdum bullets, 47, 80, 128
Dunboyne, 22–3, 36, 52, 56, 58–9, 63, 94
Dundalk, 20, 35, 55, 66
Dun Leoghaire, *see* Kingstown
Dunne, Mr, 47
Dunsoghly Castle, 3

Early, Patrick, 13
Easter Monday, ix, 5, 13, 20, 27–32, 35, 42, 94, 122

Fairyhouse Races, 32, 40, 48
Fanny, 6–7
Faroes, 24
Fenian Rising, 2, 6
Fenit, 24–5
Fenton, 2
Ferdinand, Archduke Franz, 11
Field Service Regulations, 6
Fianna Éireann, 8–10, 17, 118
Fingal, 1, 5, 9, 12–16, 18–20, 22, 26, 28, 30, 32, 35, 104–105, 113, 115, 124, 128
Fingal Battalion, x, 1–2, 6, 12, 14, 18–20, 22–3, 27, 36, 41–2, 48, 53, 84, 87, 92, 94–5, 114, 116, 118–22, 124, 127
Finglas, 15–16, 18, 33–5, 37–8, 42–3, 91, 122
Fitzgerald, Desmond, 114

Index

Fleming, Mick, 49, 65, 70, 89, 112, 122, 132
Fleming, Monica 'Dot', 49, 124, 133
Four Courts, 35, 123
Franco-Prussian War, 7
Frongoch Internment Camp, 91, 97, 105–12, 114, 118, 120, 122–3

G Men, 93
Gaelic League, xvi
Galligan, Paul, 100–101
Ganley, Peter, 45
Ganley, William, 91
Garristown, 2, 20, 41, 50, 52–3, 63, 70, 73, 84, 121–2
General Post Office, ix, 32, 39, 45, 47, 50, 136
Germany, 6, 8, 12, 23–4, 110
Gifford, Grace, 114
Glasgow, 7
Glasnevin, 16, 38, 42–3, 88, 114, 117–18
Gloucester, HMS, 24
Gola Island, 7
Golden, Jerry, x, 16–17, 42–3, 50, 53, 56–8, 65, 69–70, 77–8, 80, 84–6, 94, 121–2, 132
Gormley, Constable James, 81, 135, 139
Gough, Brigadier-General, xv
Grangegorman, 42
Grant, Paddy, 38, 40, 56, 85, 123, 132
Gray, County Inspector Alexander, 52, 55–6, 63, 66, 70, 77, 79, 81–2, 128–9, 135, 139
Great Northern Railway, 33, 55
Greville Arms Hotel, 115
Griffith, Arthur, xvii
Grogan, Dick, 42
Grogan, Vincent, 42

Haig, Major Alfred, 11
Haldane Army Reforms, 141–2
Hamburg, 6, 8
Harrel, Assistant Commissioner, 10
Hayes, Dr Richard, x, 2, 15, 30–3, 43–4, 50, 56, 58, 60, 63, 67, 70–1, 73–5, 77, 81–3, 88, 93, 100, 115, 120, 128, 132
Heard, County Inspector George B., 79, 113
Henderson, Frank, 107
Heuston, Sean, 8–9, 39, 93, 98

Heygate Lambert, Colonel F.A., 105
Hickey, James, 135, 139
Hickey, Miss, 84
Hobson, Bulmer, xvi, xviii, 4, 15, 17
Holohan, Paddy, 42–3, 56, 59, 128
Holyhead, 97, 110–12
Howth, 7–8, 20, 38, 91, 120–1
Hynes, Jack, 39, 134

I Die in a Good Cause, x–xi, 14
Inishtooskert Island, 24
Irish Citizen Army, 12, 22, 49, 101, 114
Irish Independent, 14–15, 19, 26, 29
Irish Home Rule, xii–xvi, xviii, 4, 7–8, 11–12
Irish Home Rule Bill, xii–xv
Irish National Volunteers, xvii, 12, 48
Irish Parliamentary Party, 4
Irish Republican Brotherhood (IRB), xvi–xviii, 1, 3–4, 7, 12–13, 16–17, 20, 22–4, 26, 28, 38, 53, 107, 113–14, 117, 123
Irish Times, 19, 63, 118
Irish Volunteer, The, 22
Irish Volunteers, ix–x, xviii, 1–4, 7–8, 12–15, 19, 22, 26, 98, 114, 117, 121, 125–7
Irish War News, 49

'Jack Knives', 106
Judge, M.J., 10

Keane, John Joe, 95
Kelly, Dick, 39–40
Kelly, Father, 82
Kelly, Jack, 39, 134
Kelly, James, 45, 89, 115, 123, 132
Kelly, Joe, 87
Kelly, John, 13
Kelly, Luke, 11
Kelly, Matt, 74, 82, 120, 132–3
Kelly, Patrick, 39, 134
Kelly, Peter, 13, 121
Kelly, Richard, 40, 134
Kelly, President Sean T., 139
Kelly, Alderman Tom, xviii
Kelpie, 8
Kennedy's Bakery, 40, 47
Kepp (chauffeur), 64
Kerry, 25, 37

Kettle, Laurence J., 1
Kettle, Tom, xviii, 8
Kevlehan, Father, 51–2
Kiel Canal, 6
Killeek, 39–41, 47–8
Kilmainham, 52
Kilmainham Jail, 94, 97
Kilmoon, 56, 62, 64, 71–2, 137–8
King's Own Scottish Borderers, 10–11
Kingstown, 52, 111–12
Knocksedan, 30–4, 39–40, 43, 49
Knutsford Jail, 97, 102–104, 123
Kynoch Works, 52

Lancashire Yeomanry, 88
Langeland, 6
Larne, 7
Lawless, Colm, 51, 122, 132
Lawless, Edward, 39, 134
Lawless, Eveleen, 124
Lawless, Frank, 2–4, 13, 15, 27, 30–2, 43, 56, 67, 70, 72, 76, 81, 86, 89, 93, 100, 102, 118, 121–2, 124, 130, 132
Lawless, James V., 1–2, 39, 41, 43, 53, 56, 75, 100, 102, 119, 132
Lawless, John, 43
Lawless, Joseph V., x–xi, xvii, 8–10, 13, 16, 18, 20–1, 26, 28, 30–5, 37–8, 45–9, 51, 53, 56–7, 59–60, 65, 67–76, 80–5, 87, 89–90, 92–3, 95–7, 102–104, 106, 108–13, 122, 124–5, 127, 129–30, 132
Lawless, Kathleen, 124
Lawless, Monica, 124, 133
Lee-Enfield rifle, 5–6, 20, 47–8, 62, 80, 81, 86, 127
Let Me Carry Your Cross for Ireland, 117, 139
Lewes Prison, 101, 113–14, 117
Liberty Hall, 28–30, 82
Liverpool, 95
Liverpool Irish, 42–3, 56
Lloyd George, David, 114
London, xiv–xv, 6, 27, 38, 97, 102, 108, 111, 113, 124
Loop Head, 24
Lord Heneage, 25
Lowe, Brigadier General, 39
Lucan Old Cemetery, 77
Lusk, 1–2, 9, 14, 16–17, 26–7, 30, 32–3, 38–40, 49–50, 56, 68, 72, 91, 100, 102, 114, 120–4, 127, 133–4

McAllister, Bernard (Bennie), x, 9, 13, 17, 26, 33, 48, 58, 63–4, 66–7, 87–9, 96–7, 103, 105, 121, 128, 132
McAllister, Dan, 84, 90, 100
McAllister, Kathleen, 124
McAllister, Michael, x, 3, 12–13, 15, 17, 27, 31, 38, 57, 61, 64–9, 77, 80, 82, 94–5, 131–2
McAllister, Richard, 12
McBride, John, 93, 98
McCann, John, 33, 133
McCormack, Inspector, 56, 80
McDermott, Sean, xvii–xviii, 93
McDonagh, Muriel, 114
McDonagh, Thomas, 18, 93, 98, 127
McEntee, Sean, 28, 35
McGinley, Patrick, 7
McGowan, Jack, 45, 51
McGuinness, Joseph, 1
McHale, Richard, 135, 139
McKeon, Constable, 67, 135–6
MacKenna's Fort, 25
McNally, John, 39, 134
MacNeill, Eoin, xvi–xvii, 4, 13, 15, 18, 23, 25–9, 49, 51, 101, 114
Mallin, Michael, 98
Marconi Radio Station, 41
Marks, James, 13, 31, 39, 100, 134
Markievicz, Constance, 116
Marshall, Paul, 9
Martin, Eamon, 10
Masterson, Michael, 3
Mater Hospital, 116
Matthews, Patrick, 1
Mauser rifles, 6–7, 9–10, 20–1, 73, 76, 128
Maxwell, General Sir John, 98–9
Maxwell, Tom, 38, 40, 56, 119, 133
Meath, ix–x, 19, 23, 52–3, 55, 69, 94, 123, 136–7, 139
Mee, Jeremiah, 81
Meehan, William, 39, 134
Mendicity Institution, 13, 39, 134
Meredith, James, 8
Mexico, 8
Midland Great Western Railway, 53, 55, 111
Middleton, Lord, 27
Monteith, Robert, 24–5
Moore, Colonel Maurice, xviii, 11
Moran, Christopher 'Kit', 13–15, 20, 30, 34, 41, 88, 94, 113

Index

Moran, Peter, 119
'Morris Tubes', 126
Mountjoy II, 7
Mountjoy Prison, 114, 117–18
Mulcahy, Richard, 38, 40, 43, 45–7, 51, 53, 56–7, 59, 64–70, 73–4, 76–7, 79, 85–9, 95, 103, 107, 110, 129–30, 132
Mullally, Miss, 36, 45
Murphy, Eamon, 120, 133
Murphy, Francis Ciaran, 123
Murray, Henry, 5
Myles, Sir Thomas, 8, 117

Navan, 52, 56, 59, 64, 72, 77–8, 83, 136–7, 139
Neligan, David, 125
Newbarns, 84, 87–8
New Hudson motorbike, 28
Newsome, Sergeant Major, 106
New York, 12, 95
North Staffordshire Regiment, 49
Norton, Joseph, 39, 134
Norton, William 'Bill', 13, 51, 119, 133
Norway, 24
Nugent, Christopher 'Christy', 13, 63, 121, 128, 133
Nugent, Laurence, 116

O'Brien, Conor, 8
O'Connell Bridge, 11, 75, 78, 81
O'Connell, Colonel J.J. 'Ginger', 18, 107, 127
O'Connell, Sergeant William, x, 56, 62–3, 65, 67, 75, 78, 81, 136
O'Connell, William, 67
O'Connor, James 'Jim/Jimmy', x, 3, 40, 47, 60, 68, 70, 73, 76, 82, 88, 94, 119, 133
O'Donnell, Patrick, 1
O'Duffy, Eimar, 3, 127, 141
O'Duffy, S., 17
O'Hannigan, Donal, 19, 22–3, 28, 35–6, 45, 83–4, 90
O'Hanrahan, Michael, 30, 93, 98
O'Luing, Sean, x–xi, 14, 78
O'Malley, Ernie, 107
O'Rahilly, The, xvi, 25
O'Reilly, Arthur, 43, 56, 86, 133
O'Reilly, Sergeant, 46, 81, 85
Orangemen, xiii, 7
Osgood, Molly, 7

Paget, Sir Arthur, xiv, xv
Parliament, Houses of, xii
Partridge, Thomas, 114
Partridge, William, 101
Pearse, Patrick/Padraig, xvi–xvii, 7, 19, 22–3, 26, 30, 35, 45, 85–8, 98, 117, 122, 124, 139
Pearse, Willie, 93, 98
Peck, Gregory, 140
Pentonville Prison, 102
Peppard, Thomas, x, 2, 27, 38–9, 102, 134
Phibsboro', 19, 23, 42, 44
Plunkett, Joseph, 18, 93, 98, 114
Portland Prison, 101–102, 114
Price, Jack, 42
Pro-Cathedral, Dublin, 114, 117

Queenstown (Cobh), 24–5
Quigley, James, 69, 94
Quinn, Patrick, 11

Rafferty, John 'Jack', 68, 70–1, 82, 120, 133
Rafferty, Tommy, 72, 82, 133, 139
Raheny, 10
Rath Cross Memorial, 139
Rathbeale Cross, 21, 27, 33, 40, 45, 62, 68, 85, 121
Rebellion Handbook, 1916, xi, 41, 52, 82, 135, 138
Redmond, John, xv, 4, 6, 12–13, 15, 114
Richardson, Sir George, xiii
Richmond Barracks, 90, 92, 94–5, 104
Riddle of the Sands, The, 7
Roganstown, 38, 114, 134
Rogerstown, 33–5, 121
Rooney, Edward 'Ned', 1–2, 33, 43, 46, 57, 68, 82, 120, 127, 132–3
Rooney, Jim, 58, 127, 133
Rotunda Rink, xvii, 126
Royal Barracks, Dublin, 39
Royal Horse Artillery, 88
Royal Irish Constabulary, ix, x, 8, 46, 62, 88, 94, 125–6
Royal Navy, xiv, 6, 24–5
Ruytingen buoy, 8

Sackville Street, 11, 39, 84, 111
Saint Enda's School, xvi, 22, 26, 122
Saint Margaret's parish, 1–2, 18, 27, 31–2, 51

Saint Mary's Cemetery, 139
Saint Patrick's Day Rally, 18–19
Sankey, Mr Justice, 108–10
Santry, 2, 16, 88, 94, 119, 121
Saucerstown, 4, 18, 21, 27, 112
Scollan, Lieutenant, 42
Seaver, Tom, 119
Seely, Colonel, xv
Shanagher, RIC Sergeant J., 64, 69–70, 78, 135
Shane, Constable, 67
Shetland Islands, 24
Sinn Fein, 4, 17, 49, 113–15
Skerries, 1–2, 17–18, 26, 41, 49, 51–2, 56, 91, 114, 127
Skinnider, Margaret, 49, 110
Slane Bridge, 52, 56, 72, 78
Slane Castle, 52, 55, 62, 64
Small, Lieutenant, 95
Smith, F.E., xiii
Smyth, District Insp. Harry, x, 52, 56, 62–3, 65, 67, 70–1, 73, 74–8, 82, 128, 130, 135, 139
Spindler, Captain, 24–5
Spiro, Benny, 6
Spring Rice, Mary, 7
Stafford, Edward (Ned), 65, 118–19, 133
Stafford Prison, 106
Staines, Michael, 107
Stopford Green, Alice, 115
Swords, x, xvii, 1–4, 8–10, 12–14, 16–18, 20–1, 23, 26–7, 30–2, 34, 38–9, 44–6, 50, 56, 59, 80, 85, 89–91, 95, 100, 113, 116, 118–19, 121–2, 124, 127, 133–4

Tannam, Liam, 107
Tara, 23
Taylor, Christopher, 13
Taylor, Joe, 13, 26, 30–1, 37, 39, 41, 82, 112, 119, 133
Teeling, Nicholas, 68, 71, 133
Templemore, 42
Third Battle Squadron, xiv
Thornton, Joseph, 1–2, 41, 133
Thorpe, P.C., 48
Ticknock, 18, 127
Times, The, 6
Tolka river, 37, 43

Toomey, Sergeant, 59
Training camps, 127
Tralee Bay, 24–5
Trim, 52
Tully, Sergeant, 56, 58
Turvey Hill, 13, 18, 31, 33, 47–9, 84, 90, 95, 100, 127
Tuskar Rock, 7
Tyrone Restaurant, 19

U-19, 24–5
Ulster Unionists, xiii, xv
Ulster Volunteer Force, xiii–xv, xvii, 6–7, 12
United Irishmen, 2
University College, Dublin, xvi
Usk Prison, 3, 118

V.A.D., 97
Vetterli-Vitali rifles, 6

Wakefield Prison, 97, 106
Walker, Michael, xvii
Walsh, William 'Willie', 42–3, 56, 82, 133
Wandsworth Prison, 97, 108–109
Weekly Irish Times, xi, 41
Weisbach, Lieutenant Commander R., 24–5
Weston, Bartholomew 'Bartle', 13, 48, 58, 66–8, 121, 133
Weston, Charles, x, 13, 16–17, 20–1, 27–8, 32–5, 37, 39–40, 43, 45, 47, 57–60, 63–5, 74–6, 83, 103, 105, 110, 120, 128, 133
Weston, John, 94
Weston, Tom, 89, 94
Whearity, Peter, xi, 140
Wilde, Oscar, xii
Wilson, James, 13, 39, 134
Wilson, Peter, 13, 39
Wilson, William 'Beck', 38
Wilson, William 'Cooty', 39, 134
Wimborne, Lord, 27
Woodenbridge, 12–13
Wormwood Scrubs, 106, 108
Wynn's Hotel, xvi

Young, Sergeant John, 64, 78, 135, 139

Zinnia, 25